BUILDING
ATLANTA

BUILDING ATLANTA

How I Broke Through Segregation
to Launch a Business Empire

HERMAN J. RUSSELL
with Bob Andelman

CHICAGO
REVIEW
PRESS

Published by Chicago Review Press, Incorporated
814 North Franklin Street
Chicago, Illinois 60610
ISBN 978-0-912777-84-9

The Library of Congress has cataloged the hardcover edition as follows:
Russell, Herman J.
  Building Atlanta : how I broke through segregation to launch a business empire /
H.J. Russell, with Bob Andelman. — First edition.
      pages cm
  Includes index.
  ISBN 978-1-61374-694-3 (cloth)
  1. Russell, Herman J. 2. African American businesspeople—Georgia—Atlanta—
Biography. 3. Real estate developers—Georgia—Atlanta—Biography. 4. African
Americans—Georgia—Atlanta—Biography. 5. Community development—
Georgia—Atlanta—History. I. Andelman, Bob. II. Title.

HC102.5.R87A3 2014
333.3092—dc23
[B]

2013037550

Cover design: John Yates at Stealworks
Cover photo: Jennifer Stalcup
Interior design: PerfecType, Nashville, TN

Printed in the United States of America

For my parents, Rogers and Maggie

For Otelia, who lived so much of it

For Sylvia, who helped me tell it

And for Donata, Jerome, and Michael,
as well as grandchildren born and unborn,
who make me prouder and prouder every day

Contents

"If the front door won't open, there's a window open.
If the window's closed, there's a back door. If the back door's closed,
there's a chimney. If the chimney's closed, there's still a way to get in."
—Herman J. Russell

Foreword

Andrew Young

Atlanta is a brave and beautiful city, and Herman Russell has played an essential role in the city's growth and development. It's hard to do justice to Herman Russell. My wife, Carolyn, and I were in his office recently and as far as you could see from his windows were homes and apartments, stadiums, government offices, and corporate headquarters that Herman's company built, but you wouldn't have known it because Herman didn't hold press conferences to announce his accomplishments. He was too busy building Atlanta.

Herman made his first dollar with his shoeshine stand when he was about twelve years old, and when he was sixteen or so he built his first rental house and used the money to go to college.

I came to Atlanta in 1961 with my late wife, Jean, and three young daughters to work with Dr. Martin Luther King Jr. in the Southern Christian Leadership Conference. I couldn't help but be impressed with Herman. The lovely home that he built for his late wife, Otelia, and their three children was a retreat for Dr. King. We were all swimmers and Herman's was the first private home I visited that had an indoor swimming pool!

The strength of Atlanta's black business community meant that I had less trouble purchasing a home for my family in Atlanta than I had when I had moved to Queens, New York, several years before. Herman was an important part of that black business community and a generous financial supporter of the civil rights movement.

Because of his property holdings, Herman was also the movement's bail bondsman, getting student protestors and others out of jail whenever folks were arrested for sit-ins or demonstrations. That wasn't all he did for the movement. When we couldn't get the word out about our concerns in the local newspapers across the South, Herman, Jesse Hill Jr., and Quentin V. Williamson helped finance a black-owned newspaper, the *Atlanta Inquirer* with Carl Holman as the editor, to get out the true story of what we were doing. I don't think it ever made money, but he kept it up and it played a major role in the movement's success.

Just having Herman creating jobs back then was important. You could work for him and be active in the movement and nobody could fire you. He is one of the largest job creators in the city. Those of us in the movement with Martin never thought the answer to poverty was through government. We always thought it was through access to jobs in the private sector and Herman led the way there.

Interestingly enough, my son was fourteen when he got his first job and went to work for Herman. He didn't want to do man's work at first, but Herman put him in a team that was cleaning and renovating apartments; my son would come home so dirty Jean would make him take his clothes off on the back steps and she'd hose him down there. My son came to love it because he was being a man and earning his own way, and he is a businessman today because he liked the way Herman controlled his own destiny as a business owner.

Herman was a part of integrating the politics of Atlanta—I could not have been elected the first black congressman from the Deep South since Reconstruction nor could Maynard Jackson have been elected the first black mayor of a major southern city without Herman's support.

Herman has been such a good friend to so many people. Not that he ever waited for someone to ask for his help. When I became the US ambassador to the United Nations in 1977, we had to move to New York City so we rented out our Atlanta home.

But when it was announced that I would be stepping down as ambassador and coming home, Herman and Jesse Hill checked on my house. They'd heard that it was in disrepair. My wife and I didn't know any of this because we were so busy. Knowing that we would be returning in a couple months, Herman sent his crews in without even asking me. They cleaned it up, fixed everything, painted it, and put down new carpet, renovating the entire house.

Above and beyond all that, Herman was the first black entrepreneur to desegregate the Atlanta economy. Most cities integrated with the children in schools and worked up. In Atlanta, Mayor Ivan Allen and Robert W. Woodruff, for decades the guiding hand and former president of the Coca-Cola Company, decided they needed to desegregate their city from the top down with the Chamber of Commerce leading the way. Herman and Jesse Hill, CEO of the Atlanta Life Insurance Company, were the most prominent black businessmen in the Chamber. They desegregated the Chamber, the Capital City Club, corporate boards, and the entire Atlanta economy.

Herman's personal life has always been desegregated. Even in the years of the civil rights movement, I've never been to a party at his house that was all black people. He has always been integrated at home and at work. He drove himself and he drove those who worked for him.

Herman has an obvious speech impediment yet he could get business when nobody else could. He could talk to anybody, but a lot of people talk themselves right out of business because they say too much. Herman didn't have that problem. He's always said little and made a lot. Some may have underestimated him, but there is nobody sharper with a pencil or better at negotiating than Herman Russell.

When I was mayor I couldn't go to dinner parties at his house because people accused me of favoritism due to our friendship. I was sued three times because of my relationship with Herman. But in each case, I won the lawsuit. In one case, we'd set a $34 million budget for a new city hall. All the other construction bidders came in millions over the ceiling. Herman's company came in $4 million under. That's why

Herman usually got the contracts. It had nothing to do with race or friendships. He always got the job done for a fair price.

He'd worked with architect John Portman on his first building in Atlanta, and they became good friends and did many projects together. Portman built seventeen blocks of downtown Atlanta and Herman was in on at least half of that construction; that sort of business relationship between a black man and a white man was not happening anywhere else in the world at that time.

When other cities started having racial riots, Portman, Herman, and Jesse Hill were part of a group of business and community leaders who formed the Atlanta Action Forum. The idea was to get together ten prominent whites and ten prominent blacks who trusted each other to work out any problems before trouble started. They met in private once a month on a Saturday in their shirtsleeves and they saved Atlanta from itself.

The Atlanta Action Forum organized a committee to put young people to work and keep them out of trouble, and they created 6,500 summer jobs because Herman called all of his contacts, the bank presidents in the group called all of theirs, and the presidents of Coca-Cola and Georgia Power and other corporations who belonged to the forum did the same. There was no press coverage because they did it quietly. For many young people, those jobs created by the Atlanta Action Forum were passports from the streets to the business suite.

The Action Forum didn't stop there. It was a major force in the peaceful desegregation of Atlanta's public schools and the creation of the city's rail transit system. I believe it first met in 1962 and was still meeting when I was re-elected mayor in 1985. I know because when I really wanted to get something done in the city, I went to them first.

When we wanted to create middle-class housing downtown, Herman took the risk and built McGill Place. Others followed his lead and now our intown neighborhoods are thriving. When we needed $30 million to keep the Martin Luther King Jr. papers in Atlanta, Herman was one of the business leaders who signed the note and recruited others to do the same. When our public hospital, Grady, was about to go under, Herman stepped up with a gift of $1 million to save this critical asset in our community.

Looking back on all that he's done for our city and the people in it, I guess the only way to do Herman Russell justice is to say that when it came to building Atlanta over all these years, he's played a role in *everything*.

Andrew Young served as US ambassador to the United Nations under President Jimmy Carter, was a two-term mayor of Atlanta, US congressman, and chair of the Centennial Olympic Games hosted in Atlanta in 1996.

Prologue

There was little a black boy with an entrepreneurial spirit could do to make money in the segregated South except shine shoes.

I could have easily gotten a shoeshine box, stood around on corners, and made a few coins. But that wasn't enough for me. I didn't mind shining shoes, but I wanted a business, not a box.

I decided to start my own enterprise—a shoeshine *stand*. A business with its own location and regular business hours. And it would be mine.

There was a vacant lot in front of my parents' house. It was in the middle of our neighborhood, but no one really paid attention to it. What other folks saw as just an empty lot, however, I saw as an opportunity: it was the perfect place to set up my shoeshine *business*. It was in a well-populated area, easy to find, and large enough for the shoeshine stand and a chair or two for waiting customers. I would collect cast-off wood and build it myself.

When I told my daddy my plan, he smiled a little and said in his quiet way, "All right, son, but that's city-owned land. You got to get permission to use it. You have to go down to the city hall and ask the aldermen."

Atlanta city hall was an unfriendly place for black folks in those days. Not only was it segregated, it was the seat of the unfair treatment we received all across town under the law. Like every other twelve-year-old black boy, the thought of entering city hall or any other government building made me uneasy to say the least. But my mind was already set on that shoeshine stand.

A few days after the talk with my daddy, I set out for the weekly aldermen's meeting at city hall to ask permission to build my shoeshine stand on that vacant lot. It was about an hour's walk from my home, so my older brother Lawrence went with me.

The Atlanta city hall is larger now than it was on that day in 1942, yet it was still an imposing building then. Lawrence decided to wait outside; he didn't want to risk dealing with white folks more than he had to.

I walked into the lobby alone.

Municipal workers, mostly white, were moving about in that slow, southern almost-hurrying way, while a long line of people fanning themselves with newspapers or soiled handkerchiefs snaked through the lobby. I noticed the separate water fountains marked "white" and "colored" and started to wonder if I had made a mistake by going in by myself. But I kept moving forward.

I was one of the few "colored" people there, and the only child, yet no one seemed to notice or care when I joined the line. One by one, citizens stepped to the rail to address the aldermen, all of whom were white.

For the most part, the aldermen's manner was businesslike and courteous.

That is, until it came to us "coloreds."

While everyone in line was asked to give their full names, only the whites were addressed as *Mr.* and *Mrs.*, *Ma'am* and *Sir*. Black people's names seemed to go unheard. The older black folks were simply *Auntie* and *Uncle*. The rest of us were *boy* and *gal*.

I listened and watched it all closely. I saw that those who got the best responses were the ones who stated their business quickly and succinctly. For "colored" folks, that also meant not speaking too boldly and not making too much eye contact, what we called eyeballing.

Over and over I rehearsed in my mind what I would say.

"Please, sir, there is a vacant lot I would like to use . . ."

"Please, sir, there is a vacant lot . . ."

Finally, I was next.

An expressionless white-haired male clerk drawled, "Rus-sell. Her-man Rus-sell."

I stepped to the rail.

The clerk looked over his glasses. When he saw a black boy standing before him, a hard frown set in his face. His lips tightened.

"State your bidness, boy," he snorted.

His sudden curtness caught me off guard. I stood there, flustered.

"What you want, boy?" he barked.

I began to speak as carefully as I could. I tried hard to enunciate, but I just couldn't get the words to sound right. Sweat formed on my forehead.

One of the aldermen looked up from the pile of papers on his desk and asked, "What you trying to say, boy?"

I tried even harder to make myself understood. But by then I was so nervous that I could barely get a word out.

One alderman drawled, "Lord, but this boy do talk funny."

I was really straining to speak now. Finally one alderman made out a few phrases and cut me off.

"Say *what*? You want a permit to use some property? So you can shine shoes on it?"

I blinked and nodded. "Y-yes, s-sir."

He looked to his colleagues and spoke like he was translating a foreign language. "Listen at that. This boy wants us to give him a permit so he can shine shoes."

They burst into laughter.

"Why can't this little nigger just shine shoes on his front porch?" the brown-haired alderman guffawed. He and his colleagues pounded their desks and slapped their thighs, laughing and coughing.

I looked around. Most of the people in the chamber were laughing and pointing at me like I was a joke.

In the midst of the laughter and ridicule, the black folks were still and expressionless. They couldn't tell white people to treat a black child with civility, because that would have been considered "uppity," and to do so was dangerous. They expressed their displeasure the only practical way they could: they stood still, their faces blank, with a sense of dignity and restraint much deeper than the segregated white mind could ever fathom.

As for the whites in attendance, they were having a ball.

"Go home and shine shoes on your porch!" one of the aldermen sneered. He pointed to my own shoes, which had gotten dusty on the way there. "But do a better job than you did with those! Now get!"

I hurried through the broad lobby with the laughter echoing from the marble walls and those hateful words ringing in my ears. Lawrence was waiting on the steps. He could see that something was wrong, but I was too upset to talk. I didn't cry, but inside I was hurting. I had done nothing but expect to be treated fairly. For that, people I didn't even know had made fun of me.

The walk back to Summerhill was the longest of my life. With every step, my ears rang with, "Go home and shine shoes on your porch!"

By the time Lawrence and I reached home, though, I wasn't hurting anymore. I was determined to do as I'd planned. I was focused.

It was then that Herman Russell, the entrepreneur and business-man, was born.

At that moment I made one of the most important decisions of my life: permit or not, I was going to build my shoeshine stand on that lot. In fact, never for a minute did I consider not building it.

I was poor and black in a segregated world, with a speech impedi-ment that was ridiculed by children and adults alike. I'd just been called nigger by the town fathers and laughed out of city hall. Even sympa-thetic souls would have thought that I was in a hopeless situation. But with insults and laughter still fresh in my ears, I decided that I would let nothing stand in the way of my dreams—not poverty, not segregation, not even my speech impediment. I made up my mind, then and there, that Herman Russell would overcome it all.

Nothing would ever keep me from my goals.

▪ ☐ ▪

Thumbing my nose at authority for the first time in my life, I built a shoeshine stand anyway.

I knew those aldermen had no good reason to deny my request. They didn't care about unused vacant lots in black neighborhoods; they didn't even bother to pave our streets. If their ruling had been based on legitimate grounds, I would have respected it. I was raised to be law-abiding. But their actions had nothing to do with justice or due process. Their only concern was to deny yet another black person, and a child at that, an opportunity to better himself—and to enjoy humiliating him in the process.

I acted as if I had never been before the aldermen.

When I shared with my daddy what I'd experienced at city hall, I could see that it hurt him that I had been mistreated and that there was nothing he could do about it. But he wasn't one to dwell on things he couldn't control; he had no use for pity parties and moping around.

"Don't worry about it, son," he said. "You'll be all right."

I told him that I wasn't going to worry about it; I was just going to build the stand anyway. He nodded and smiled.

"If that's what you want to do," Daddy said, "go ahead."

That was all I needed to hear. The next day I got to work. It took me about a week to gather enough discarded wood from the neighborhood, and a day or two to build it. The shoeshine stand was a simple platform that could seat two customers at a time, but I was as proud as if it were the Empire State Building.

My shoeshine stand wasn't just a casual attempt to make a few coins. It was a business. Just like my trip to city hall, I didn't just throw it together; I planned it. And I didn't pick that location just because it was handy. I positioned my business where the market was. There was nowhere else in my neighborhood to get a good shine.

I was right about the market. When I finally opened for business, the neighborhood was ready for it.

■ □ ■

My first day of operation was a Saturday. I arrived at 7:00 AM. Folks immediately started lining up for a shoeshine and I was ready for them. All day long I smiled and popped that shining cloth on every shoe until every customer was satisfied. I didn't let anyone leave until his shine was perfect. Word got around about the excellent shoeshine with the nice manners, and business grew by the week. People started dropping off whole bags of shoes to be shined.

After a month I had so much business that I had to hire help. I brought on an older boy, Joe Moore, to shine shoes with me. I paid him a nickel per shine, which was half the ten cents per shine I charged.

A shoeshine stand might sound a bit quaint today, but in those days there was a lot of demand for well-shined shoes; shoes were a source of pride. There is a well-worn saying that lots of people took to heart back then, especially women: "You can judge a man's character by the condition of his shoes."

For women, if a man's shoes were sharp, that could be an indication that he was a responsible person with strong self-esteem, what we called being on the ball. If his shoes were always dusty and unshined, that was a red flag that he might be less than responsible, lacking in self-pride or discipline.

I started noticing that some of my customers would leave with beautifully shined shoes, but their laces would be broken or unraveling. A truly entrepreneurial mind is always looking for new ways to make money. Within weeks I was selling shoelaces for five cents a pair.

One day a customer wiped his brow and said, "Whew. Sure wish I had a cold drink."

The very next day I started selling ice-cold Coca-Colas out of a cooler.

Of course, most people like something to munch on with a cold Coke, so I added ice cream and other snacks. Pretty soon most folks in the neighborhood were my customers, if not for a shine, then for a snack. If not for a snack, then for a cold drink. Soon I had quite a little enterprise going. All because I saw needs and filled them.

I was able to see what people needed for one reason: I paid attention. In fact, there are always legitimate moneymaking opportunities around.

If you want to recognize them you have to pay attention to people in a way that helps you recognize what they want, what they need, and what would make them more comfortable.

I didn't just make money at that shoeshine stand, though. It enriched me in another way, too: I met a lot of interesting people. Like barbershops and beauty parlors, shoeshine stands were a place of gossip, good conversation, unsolicited advice, and tall tales. Mine was no different. It seemed that every other customer had a life lesson to share with me, or at least a funny story to tell. I listened carefully and said little. It helped that at twelve years old I didn't understand half of what I was told.

One customer stands out in my mind. He was always sharply dressed, except for one thing: his bowtie was always hanging loose. His name was Ed Patterson.

Mr. Patterson was one of the biggest gospel promoters in the South. He was friendly and always told me how impressed he was with my industriousness. But every time I saw him, his bowtie was undone.

One day I said to him, "Mr. Patterson, why is your bowtie always untied? Is that a new style?"

"No, son," he said, laughing. "I just never learned to tie a bowtie, so after I get my shoes shined, I always go looking for one of my buddies to tie it for me."

I told him that my father had taught me to tie a bowtie and that I would be glad to tie his any time he needed. It was just a small gesture, but Mr. Patterson really appreciated it. He began stopping by not only to get his shoes shined but also whenever he needed his bowtie tied. I was always glad to see him because I liked him. And I was glad for another reason, too: he always paid me an extra nickel. A nickel was a big tip, considering that a shoeshine only cost ten cents.

Mr. Patterson and I became friends. Twenty-five or so years later, after I had become well known in Atlanta, Mr. Patterson and I found ourselves doing a Coca-Cola ad together. I was the central character and Mr. Patterson was hired to portray a workman painting my name on an office door. Neither of us knew about the other's involvement, so when we arrived for the shoot, it was like old home week. I was thrilled to see him again, but it was clear he was so proud of me.

I built up quite a clientele at my shoeshine stand. Even at ten cents per shine I usually made eight to ten dollars per day. One day I made fifteen dollars. Not bad, considering that the average daily wage for adult workers in those days was about six and a half dollars.

Part I

Growing, Working, and Learning

1

Life, One Word at a Time

Mrs. Johnson was teaching my fourth-grade class the multiplication tables. I had worked hard at memorizing the times tables, as we called them, so when it was my turn to recite, I went all the way to ten without a mistake. As usual, my classmates snickered when I spoke, but Mrs. Johnson, a plump young woman with a nice smile and an agreeable manner, was all smiles, which made me proud.

The rest of the morning went on as usual. After lunch Mrs. Johnson asked me to step into the hallway. That seemed strange to me; she'd never called me out before. She assured me that nothing was wrong, so I didn't worry about it.

As I was closing the classroom door behind me, I noticed two other teachers standing with Mrs. Johnson. They were smiling. Still, something felt strange.

"Herman," Mrs. Johnson said, "please recite your multiplication tables."

I relaxed. Mrs. Johnson wanted to show off my math skills! I was thrilled, because I wasn't used to being praised at school for anything.

"Go on, Herman," she said. "You can do it."

I took a deep breath.

"One times one equals one," I said softly, then paused. The teachers seemed to have no trouble understanding me, so I continued.

"Two times two equals four . . ."

The teachers were quiet and attentive. Their anticipation seemed to grow by the passing moment. By the time I got to five times five they were really excited.

I paused, savoring a rare success.

"Go on," Mrs. Johnson said with a big grin. "Say six times six."

I heard her whisper to one of the other teachers, "Here it comes."

They both giggled.

Six was a word I had real trouble pronouncing. But I trusted Mrs. Johnson, so I did as I was told.

For a moment there was silence. I waited for the affirmation I was sure was coming. Suddenly the teachers burst into laughter. I don't mean they giggled. They laughed out loud without any restraint.

I couldn't believe my ears. I felt sick; my heart sank. I looked from face to face, but each was the same: they were laughing *at* me. All of them. Doubled over and breathless with laughter.

"Mrs. Johnson," guffawed one of the teachers, "how do you keep a straight face in class? Tell him to say it again!"

"Go on, Herman," said Mrs. Johnson. She was laughing so hard she could hardly talk. "Say it again."

I tried with all my might to enunciate, to pronounce the words correctly, but they came out the same way:

"S-s-shit times s-s-shit equals . . ."

The teachers howled even louder than before.

I hung my head, crushed. These grown-ups whom I had trusted were laughing at me just like my nine-year-old classmates did. Even now it is hard to put words to the pain and betrayal I felt.

That experience could have broken me or made me bitter, but it did neither. Instead, it made me more self-reliant. That is what I learned that day. No matter how hard they tried, my parents couldn't always be there to protect me. When all was said and done, I had to look out for myself.

It was the first of many painful experiences in my life that left marks that will never go away. I can't say that I would choose it again if I had the choice, but I can say that out of that mess I gained something that has played a crucial role in my success: I learned to define myself. I refused to let the teasing and embarrassment make me bow my head. I kept on keeping on.

No one would ever again define me but me.

▪ □ ▪

I was born in Atlanta on December 23, 1930.

At that time, the city was deeply segregated and the nation was wallowing in the Great Depression. The most popular song that year was "Brother, Can You Spare a Dime?" Its title was in the mouths of folks all over the country from coast to coast.

Herbert Hoover was our president then. As the result of Hoover's shortsighted policies, the national economy had crashed. Banks failed and even the most menial jobs became scarce. Camps of desperately poor people sprang up on roadsides and under bridges all over America. Folks showed how much they blamed Hoover for the mess the economy was in by calling the camps Hoovervilles.

The average income that year was $1,650, but my parents' *combined* income came nowhere near that. Even though a gallon of gasoline only cost ten cents and a loaf of bread seven cents, times were still hard for my family.

The average new home then cost $6,500—but not in my neighborhood. Everyone where we lived was poor and lived in shotgun shacks— so called because they were narrowly built, with one room opening into the next in a way that a shot fired from a gun could go cleanly through the houses from front to back if all doors were left open. No one had front yards, just patches of dirt or gravel. My family's home was a shotgun shack and it certainly wasn't worth anywhere near $6,500, maybe because its thin walls let in as much cold winter air as they kept out. Or because it lacked hot water. Oh, and one other thing holding down its resale value: it was in a poor black neighborhood.

My earliest memory is of standing in front of a black, coal-burning stove. It was a strange feeling. The stove was hot, so it warmed my front. But the rest of the house was so cold that my back froze. I didn't know whether to sweat or shiver; I probably did both.

It sounds strange now, but although we lived in the city, we were so poor that not only did we not have hot water, we didn't have electricity, either. We read by candles and kerosene lamps and bathed in a big galvanized tin tub filled with water that we heated on our wood-burning stove. (Toilets were located on the back porch or in the backyard.) My mama washed our clothes in a black kettle in the yard, stirring it with a big wooden ladle until the water boiled, then rubbing her hands raw on the hard ridges of her washboard. She never experienced cooking on a gas range or washing clothes in a washing machine until she was a senior citizen, when I was grown and able to buy appliances for her.

My parents worked hard to provide for their eight children, but I can still remember having to put pasteboard in the bottom of my shoes when the leather wore out to make them last until my parents could see their way clear to have them re-soled. New shoes were something I rarely saw.

We lived at 776 Martin Street in a "colored" neighborhood called Summerhill, located in the southeastern section of the city's downtown business district.* It was typical of black communities of the time. Local businesses consisted mostly of insurance agencies, pool halls, funeral homes, liquor stores, and nightclubs.

You could usually tell where the colored people lived in Atlanta because most of the streets were unpaved. We didn't even have sidewalks. We paid our taxes like everyone else, but it seems that money went to pave the streets and sidewalks in the white neighborhoods. Of course, black people resented it, but mostly we accepted it as the way things were—we lacked political strength and media access to complain or do anything about it.

---

*The name Summerhill was given to the neighborhood by Amistead W. Bailey Sr., one of the original black settlers. It was one of two areas in the city where "freed colored" people could settle.

Some might say there wasn't anything particularly special about Summerhill, but that didn't matter; we still had a genuine sense of community. Everyone knew everyone else and everyone looked out for each other's children. If you did something wrong and a neighbor caught you, you could expect two whippings—one from the neighbor and another when you got home. As a result, we had little serious crime. I don't remember us even locking our doors.

■ □ ■

The difficulty I had pronouncing words and sounds was a trait I picked up from my daddy. But it wasn't clear to my parents that I had a speech problem until I entered school and my teachers and the other students had a hard time understanding me. My father had his own severe challenges making simple conversation, so they may not have been surprised that my problem would be a lifelong one.

My speech impediment made growing up tough. I knew what I wanted to say, but most of the time I just couldn't make it come out right. Children can be cruel to those who are different. That's how it was with me. My elementary schoolmates laughed at me and teased me constantly. It seemed like someone was making fun of me whenever I opened my mouth. It hurt, but because I was loved at home I usually could just ignore it or, at the least, try to laugh it off.

■ □ ■

My mama, Maggie Russell, was a soft-spoken woman, but the lessons I took from her were as powerful in their own way as what my father taught.

Part South Carolina Geechee, she was a pretty woman with flawless skin and straight black hair, always slim and neat in appearance.*

---

*According to the New Georgia Encyclopedia, Geechee and Gullah are the names given to the culture of blacks once found on the islands of Georgia and South Carolina, respectively, likely growing out of West Africans enslaved there beginning around 1750 to build and grow island plantations for rich white slave owners.

She attended Benedict College, a women's school in South Carolina, for several years. That made her better educated than most people she met back then, black or white, man or woman.

In those days, however, there were few jobs open to black women except domestic work, which we called day work. My mama worked as a domestic for a white family on Atlanta Avenue, cooking, cleaning, washing, ironing, and looking after their children. I never heard her complain about her employers, so I guess they treated her right. That said, my mama left home early in the morning to walk the mile or so to work and was gone from her family all day.

Many days, Mama brought home leftovers. That made a difference, because things were hard in the Depression years. And the food was tasty, because my mama had cooked it! She was an excellent cook. What she prepared was not particularly fancy by today's standards, but what she did make couldn't be beat! Her favorite dishes were simple— fried chicken, pork chops, bacon, greens, yams, mashed potatoes, string beans, and banana pudding—but what she did to them was out of this world. My father's favorites were real southern fare: pig tails, pig ears, and lamb chops. The way my mama seasoned those dishes made them almost jump off the plate with flavor. Tastes have changed since then and many people don't eat that type of food today, but my daddy and I loved it.

I have been all over the world, been entertained by diplomats and heads of state, but my mama kept the neatest house I've ever seen anywhere. Our furniture might have been makeshift and homemade, but our home was spotless; you couldn't find a speck of dust in it with a white glove. Our linens were probably the least expensive and lowest quality you could buy, but my mama kept them clean and pretty just like the most expensive grades.

It was Mama who was the disciplinarian of the house. While it is true that my father never whipped his children, that never stopped my mama. She believed in the biblical proverb "Spare the rod and spoil the child." And she was determined not to spoil any of her children. She wasn't mean, mind you, but she never let us get away with a thing. You can be sure that not one of her eight children ever talked back to her or my father or in any way challenged their authority.* She was tough on us because she was determined to raise good, well-mannered, respectful human beings who would one day enter a white-dominated world and had to sometimes go along to get along. In this, she succeeded. None of her children ever saw the inside of a jail or earned bad reports from school or community. All eight of us became good, upstanding, well-respected citizens.

My mama was dedicated to the Allen Temple African Methodist Episcopal (AME) Church on Frazier Street. Folks nowadays make a big deal about tithing, but tithing was just the beginning for my mama; she gave her 10 percent and then some. She didn't give because she was trying to buy God's favor. She sincerely believed it was her duty to serve her church and her community.

Many times in my adult life I have been honored as a philanthropist. If I do have a philanthropic bone in my body, I'm sure it comes from my mama. Even during the Depression when my daddy sometimes only had a few days of Works Progress Administration (WPA) work at a stretch, my mama was always willing to share what little food we had with others.

She was always doing something at the church. She worked hard all week, and still, come Friday and Saturday, you could see her selling hot dogs on our front porch for the church general fund. Or you could find her at the church itself engaged in any number of supportive tasks, anything to serve.

■ □ ■

My mama was forty when I was born.

I was the last of eight children: six boys and two girls. By the time I arrived, most of my siblings had already left home. The oldest was twenty years ahead of me; the youngest, my brother Rogers Junior, was three years older.

---

*Charles was the oldest child, then Ruby, Robert Lee, Viola, Lawrence, Clifford, Rogers, and me.

By the time I came along, my parents were tired from raising the seven that came before me. I don't think either Mama or Daddy had much energy left to give me a lot of personal attention or direction. It's not that they didn't take good care of me—they made sure I was clean, well fed, and safe, and they taught me good manners. There were a few things for which you could really get in trouble in my mother's house: not doing your chores was a big one. You had to do them before you went anyplace. And if you were disrespectful or disobedient, you'd have a big problem under her roof. And I knew my parents loved me. It's just that when I came into the picture, I got the basics and little more.

Between her job and looking after my brothers and sisters and my father and keeping up with me, it's a wonder my mama found time to sleep, much less the time to teach me. She had her hands full making sure everybody was fine and doing what he or she should. My mama obviously had an appreciation for education, but she had so much to do and so many people to take care of that I don't remember her ever reading to me or helping me with my homework. She never taught me my ABCs. When I entered the first grade at E. P. Johnson Elementary School, I was not prepared like the other kids in my class. I couldn't even write my name. I befriended one teacher, Mrs. Ford, who tutored me after school in reading and spelling. The only good news in reports home was that I was pretty good in math.

And Mama certainly had her hands full keeping up with me; I was always into something.

■ □ ■

I may have been Mama's youngest, but I was not the last child Maggie Russell raised in that house. When I was ten, my brother Robert Lee and his wife divorced and their two-year-old son, Calvin, and his older sister, Robbie, age five, came to live with us.

Calvin and I shared a bedroom until I went off to college, and he became more like a little brother to me than a nephew. Before then, I had slept in an old army surplus bunk bed—my daddy tore it down and made it into twin beds.

For the most part, I liked having Calvin around, but there were those moments that any boy with a little brother knows about, such as when he'd get into my prized marble collection. As for Robbie, she helped me learn to read properly, for which I will always be grateful. She was a very smart girl.

Like all the Russell men, whether sons or grandsons or cousins, Calvin became a skilled worker on family plastering jobs. My father put a hawking trowel in his hand when he was nine years old. It wore blisters on his hand and my father told him, "Go over there, boy, and pee in your hand and rub them together. It'll be all right."

When Calvin was old enough, he and our nephew Norris joined me on plastering jobs with my daddy. The younger boys had to get up early in the morning and load the trucks and get to the job, build the scaffolds, and have the mud ready when my father and I and the older crew got to the job.

I taught Calvin not to be afraid of work and how to make a living. As Calvin got older, he trained as a plasterer, eventually moving on to sheetrocking. He became one of my most trusted foremen in the drywall company and a superintendent in the building division.

But our ties go deeper than that. Calvin's daughter, Valerie Callaway, came up through the company to become a vice president of H.J. Russell & Company's property management operation. And his son, Calvin Junior, oversees the maintenance department.

■ □ ■

My father, Rogers Russell, was an enterprising man. Today we would call him an entrepreneur. He had a house full of children to feed, but he rarely worked for anyone else, except for a few days during the Great Depression.

My father only had a third-grade education, but that wasn't particularly rare in those days for black folks. The tightly shut doors of opportunity and the low wages most blacks were paid meant that many had to join the workforce at an early age to help feed their families.

What my father lacked in education, though, he more than made up in smarts. He had a PhD in Common Sense. And he had the self-confidence to make a living for his family with his own hands. My father had his own trade: he was a master plasterer. Not just any plasterer—proud and meticulous, my father was a *master* tradesman.

He worked on many of the grand homes in Atlanta's Buckhead neighborhood as well as commercial properties such as the historic Fox Theatre (originally the Yaarab Temple Shrine Mosque) in downtown Atlanta. Proud and meticulous, my daddy was an artist with plaster.

He rendered walls as smooth as a baby's backside. He also created fancy moldings that are treasured as architectural elements today. White people paid big money for older homes with fine plaster ornamentation and my father's work was considered the best. He was an artisan, though he never used the word himself.

By every account of everyone I ever met who knew him, Rogers Russell was a fine human being, a man of character and quiet strength. But he wasn't a man to do a lot of talking. I think black people in the South in those days generally kept a low profile, maybe because life for black folks then was such a struggle. With the daily insults, indignities, and threats from segregation and the Great Depression, it was a strain just surviving from day to day, and folks didn't want to bring attention to themselves. My father was only a few generations away from the horrors of enslavement, and the stench of lynchings was still in the air. I imagine my father and his generation coped with these stresses by holding in their feelings.

There was still another reason for Daddy's sparse conversation: he had a severe speech impediment. There were many words my father simply couldn't pronounce, and that made him hold his tongue that much more. I inherited my speech impediment from him, but his was far worse than mine.

What he couldn't say with words, he said by quiet example. Simply because of his walk through life, he taught me the fundamentals of how a man should live his life: with kindness, bravery, independence, honesty, and respect for neighbors.

"Herman," he told me, "always treat people right and always give your best in whatever you do." Shining shoes, delivering papers, mixing mortar—whatever I attempted, I was instructed to always do it right.

My daddy was also a snazzy dresser. Nothing extravagant, because with his frugal nature he wouldn't have spent much money on clothes even if he could have afforded it. But he took great pride in dressing up on Sunday after wearing work clothes all week. Like Mama, Daddy was a dedicated member and a longtime steward of Allen Temple AME Church in Atlanta. I don't recall him ever missing Sunday worship. He was lean and trim from working hard, so his clothes always looked good on him.

Daddy favored dark, conservative suits. He didn't have many, but the one or two he had were always sharp and well pressed, even though he'd worn them over and over again for years. He almost always topped his outfits off with a snappy fedora. And his shoes were always shined. He was a proud man and I was proud of him. I guess that's why to this day I am so careful about my own attire. I am by no means a peacock, but I do take pride in looking neat whenever I step out my door.

Daddy never made much money, but he sure knew how to stretch what he earned. He managed to purchase a home and raise all eight of his children in it, and he even bought little parcels of undeveloped land whenever he could. He bought a vacant lot around the corner from our home and built a duplex on it that he rented out to earn extra income.

He was able to do so much more with a dollar than most men. My daddy chose the type of work where he got his hands dirty every day. Whites tended to isolate themselves from those trades, but my daddy was a member of the only plaster and cement finishers union local in the city. Prior to 1960 trade unions were either segregated or completely closed to blacks.

When he died in 1959, my daddy had $12,000 in his bank account—almost $200,000 in today's dollars! All on the meager wages from his manual labor.

How did my daddy do it? He saved. No matter how little he brought home at the end of the day, he saved a part of it. My father got more out of a dollar than anyone else I've ever known. That's one of the biggest lessons he taught me. He always said, "Son, if you don't make but fifty cents, save a portion of it."

His favorite saying? "Pennies make dollars."

My daddy believed it, too, as we discovered after he died of a broken heart following Mama's death from heart disease in 1959. He left behind a will, written in 1920, which made provisions for his wife and children. That might not seem unusual now, but a century ago it was highly unusual for a black man to have a will because most didn't have any money or real property to pass to the next generation.

I wasn't born when he made the will in 1920, but in it he set aside $1,000 for my mama and my older brothers and sisters in the event of his passing.

■ □ ■

The day my daddy installed electricity in our house was truly one of the happiest days of our lives. Three or four years later, we got a multiparty telephone line that you could use to make a call when no one else was using the line.

(Decades later, I would argue with two of my white friends, Charlie Loudermilk and John Portman, about which one of us got indoor plumbing first, the poor black family or the equally impoverished white family. For the record, the Russells won that one.)

And I really thought we were really moving up in society . . . the day my daddy installed a gas heater!

■ □ ■

This may surprise a few people and shock some others:

I started working when I was six years old.

But everyone around me worked hard—from my mama and daddy on down—so it just seemed natural. My father would wake me up at the crack of dawn to cut wood and build a fire after a quick breakfast. Then I fed the handful of chickens my mama kept in the yard. That's right: chickens in the front yard, in the big city. And we weren't the only ones. That's what my neighborhood in Atlanta was like then.

Daily chores would have been enough for most six-year-olds. But not me; I looked for other work, too. The truth is that I always *wanted* to work. Everyone I knew and respected worked, and worked hard. An ugly fiction in the South was that black folks were lazy, that black folks didn't want to work. I can't imagine where that came from, because all we did was work, from can't-see-in-the-morning until can't-see-at-night, as the saying goes. The willingness to work, to be responsible for yourself as long as your body and mind were sound enough, was an important element of self-respect for black people.

I did my chores, performed odd jobs around my neighborhood, helped my father on his construction jobs—anything to make a few coins. When I was eight years old I made my first business decision: to have a paper route. One of my buddies told me that the *Atlanta Constitution*, the largest newspaper in town, was looking for delivery boys. I jumped at the chance to make a little money for myself. I signed up and was assigned a route in my neighborhood.

Every day I rose at 4:30 AM, did my chores, retrieved my newspapers from the drop spot, and carefully stuffed them into a canvas bag slung over my shoulder. I climbed on my bicycle with a stack as big as me and like clockwork made my way through the neighborhood delivering them. When I set out, the sun was just beginning to rise and sometimes it was pretty chilly, but I didn't care. I was working for my future.

■ □ ■

By the time I was eleven, my father started taking me out on his construction jobs during my summer vacations.

I began by hauling water, carrying sand, and mixing mortar. Today, heavy-duty machines mix mortar. But in those primitive days, we used a hoe to mix the sand and cement to make mortar. If you didn't wear gloves, the hoe would blister your palms and rub them raw. And you couldn't just mix mortar and be done with it; you had to keep kneading it and mixing in water to keep the mortar from drying out and becoming too hard to use.

Truth be told, there was almost no equipment of any kind to make our labor easier in those days. A pulley was almost high-tech back then. Sometimes there wasn't even a pulley available, so I had to haul water and mortar up to the workers on a steep ramp. It was hard work for a grown man, so you can imagine how hard it was for a young boy. But it made me physically strong and gave me a growing sense of accomplishment and personal power. More than anything, though, I did it because that's what my daddy expected of me. He expected me to do a man's work like he had done at my age. He never pushed or coddled me.

Daddy told me what to do and I did it.

When I was fourteen years old, he decided it was time for me to begin laying the groundwork for my future. He bought me my own set of tools and began to teach me the trade of plastering. Daddy walked me through the fundamentals: how to measure the ingredients for mixing mortar, the most efficient ways to carry it, and how to use key plastering tools like a hawk and trowel. I learned how to secure the rock layer to the frame, to cover that with a layer of mortar (we called it "mud"), then how to flawlessly spread the white plaster on top of it all. He taught me that certain interior walls, like bathrooms, got an extra layer of plaster. He seldom stopped his work while he explained, and he demonstrated a whole lot more than he explained.

My daddy expected me to pay attention and to learn by watching and doing. After a year of this, I had just about mastered the trade. By sixteen I was making the same wage as the older men, because by then I was as good a plasterer as any of them.

It was in plastering that I made my first big money. And I loved the art of it. I didn't just slap plaster on a wall. Given the opportunity, I could do fancy mold work. If you wanted a pattern on your ceiling, I could do that, too. I did decorative work on archways and around the base of chandeliers as well. As far as I was concerned, I was an artist in my own right and I took an artist's pride in my work.*

Working with my father gave me firsthand exposure to the challenges of organizing and managing a project and the importance of doing a good job.

■ □ ■

Watching my parents consistently find a way out of no way, in the worst of times and without losing faith, without giving up or giving in, gave

---

*Sadly, plastering is no longer a treasured art. It has been replaced by drywall, which is variously known as gypsum board, plasterboard, and sheetrock.

me a bedrock foundation of faith and belief in myself. I'm sure that if I'd had lesser parents I would be much poorer today in every way.

It is a shame that the doors of opportunity in this country were so tightly closed to good people such as my parents. My mama was an educated, congenial, hard-working woman with a sharp mind. There's no telling what she could have been if she had been given half a chance. With such a clear, well-ordered intelligence, I'm sure she could have been a lawyer or a college professor then, or even a corporate executive today.

I have no doubt that with my father's discipline, drive, innate intelligence, and self-confidence he could have succeeded at whatever he chose to do if he had been treated justly by society. That said, my father was successful in his own right and owed his success to no one but himself.

■ □ ■

I remember the unusual day a white insurance agent came to my parents' home in Summerhill. My mama had taught us that it was disrespectful for a man to wear his hat in the house, so when this man didn't take off his hat when he entered, I politely asked him to remove it.

If looks could kill, I'd be dead right now.

The man stood there, in my own home, glaring at me, his face red with righteous anger. My mama ordered me to my room. To my horror, I heard *her* apologize to *him* as I walked away.

And that man still had on his hat. That hurt and confused me, because in essence my mama was admitting that white folks didn't have to show us any respect—not even in the sanctity of our own home.

The man was angry because he had been asked to show the same respect for a black home that he expected in his own. He probably would have been the first one to describe himself as a good Christian in the white world. Because, like so many whites in the segregated South, he only paid attention to the Lord's instruction to love your neighbor as yourself when that neighbor was white.

That was the tragedy of segregation. It diminished everyone.

Despite the pain and sometimes the inhumanity of segregation, the people of Summerhill, and black Atlantans in general, were law-abiding. Oh, we had a few bad apples like everyone else, but even in the face of our unjust treatment at the hands of the police who were supposed to protect us, we were still overwhelmingly people of dignity and honesty and solid moral and ethical values.

Just because people are poor doesn't mean they are uncouth, unintelligent, or criminal. It doesn't mean that they are lazy or have loose morals or lack ambition. My old Summerhill neighbors and especially my own family are proof of that.

■ □ ■

Black folks didn't have much to call our own in my youth. That is why church was so very important to us. For most African Americans, church was the only place we could be somebody. It was there that we did not have to prove our worth or our humanity. It was in church that we could be dignified without being chastised or threatened with harm for "acting uppity."

It was in the black church that we could wear our special finery and be addressed respectfully. There, grown folks were given proper titles. In church we were *Mister*, *Miss*, and *Missus*. I never heard a white man use that term for my father. He was always *Rogers* or *boy*. But at church, he was Mr. Russell.

Even the children were treated special on Sundays in church. As kids, we had our own choirs, and often there were occasions for us to stand before the church and recite verses from the Bible we called pieces, along with cute little stories, speeches, and short historical recitations, often of black history. Even when one of the children forgot his lines and stood in petrified silence, the adult congregants still showered us with hearty applause, proud and affirming amens, and knowing pronouncements of "That child's going to be somebody."

Church was the place all black folks, young and old, felt safe, loved, and affirmed. It was the center of our spiritual lives, our home away from home, and the center of our social world. I loved the church. But it wasn't just church in general that I loved; I also loved our pastor, Reverend W. R. Wilkes.

Pastors were intimately involved in their communities. They were always at community and civic events doing what they could to make a difference. Their dignified presence and their clear sense of conviction meant so much to us. Maybe it was because segregation made our lives so difficult that we needed our ministers to demonstrate faith, strength, and dignity to inspire us to keep going up the rough side of the mountain.

Reverend Wilkes was that kind of minister. He was so popular that, after he left the church, my experience was never the same with any other pastor. Don't get me wrong, I've had some wonderful relationships with my pastors, but none that had the effect on me like the relationship I had with Reverend Wilkes.

He wasn't your ordinary clergyman. He didn't preach fire and brimstone, instead giving us the kind of sermons that motivated and affirmed everybody in earshot. I can hear him now:

> When you have a dream, work hard, stay focused, and you'll be able to do anything you want.

Reverend Wilkes preached that we should start our own businesses so we could keep more of our money to benefit our own community. He said that we had to start relying on each other, that we should pool our money to start businesses, then support each other's businesses.

But he didn't only influence me from the pulpit. What was just as inspiring to me as Reverend Wilkes's sermons was the personal time he took with me. He always had a word of encouragement about my academic progress or just about life in general. And he always took time to give me advice when I needed it. And not just me, either. Reverend Wilkes was dedicated to shaping all us young people into good, self-sufficient citizens. He made sure the church had lots of activities for youths. I was involved in many of them.

But the one church activity that I really liked was the idea of our Cub Scout leader, Frank Hill. His idea was something you'd never expect to see in a church: boxing.

Yes, boxing in the church. Jabs, left hooks, right crosses, and uppercuts in the House of the Lord. I loved God, but I loved boxing, too. I loved it. There was nothing disrespectful about it. We didn't box in the sanctuary, we boxed in the church basement. There was no swearing or anything like that. Just good character-building hard work and clean fun. And it kept a lot of us young guys off the streets.

I was a hell of a boxer, which really helped my self-esteem. I loved to train and I loved to spar. Throwing punches, slipping punches, even taking punches, I loved it all. The weigh-in scale said that I was a lightweight, but there was nothing lightweight about how hard I worked or the skills my hard work produced. I could beat most of the other boxers in our program. I had good footwork and head movement, and my left jab was a sight to behold—unless you were on the receiving end of it, because you'd never see it coming.

The church's boxing program wasn't about violence, though, and it wasn't violence that I craved. It was the competition that thrilled me. Not just competition with my sparring partner, but, more important, competition with myself, to see how fast and sharp and disciplined and exacting I could become. Those of us who took the boxing program seriously gained much from it. It demonstrated to us without a doubt that hard work gets results and without it, you lose. Boxing taught us discipline, focus, and mental toughness. And it taught us to never give up. As a pastor, Reverend Wilkes was much more interested in building character than building muscles. Boxing was just the medium he used to accomplish it.

Except for my parents, Reverend Wilkes's message of self-sufficiency motivated me to seek financial success more than anything else in my life.

2

High School Hero

Ibought my first property when I was sixteen with income I earned working with my daddy and from my unauthorized shoeshine stand.

That land was a vacant lot on South Avenue not far from my parents' home. I'd passed it often walking to work with my dad and never paid much attention to it. One day as I walked in front of it I had a vision that transformed a mundane piece of barren ground into a potential source of income.

This wasn't some hazy dream; I had a clear vision of a duplex. I saw myself quite clearly building it, moving renters in, and collecting twin monthly payments.

I saw no reason to waste time and followed my father to the Department of Revenue and Taxation at city hall, being careful to avoid the chamber where the evil aldermen lurked. There, I looked up the parcel for the vacant lot in a big ledger book. With help from a clerk, who deciphered the legal language and baffling abbreviations, I learned that the city owned the lot because taxes had not been paid on it.

I bought it at public auction for $125. Lucky for me, I was the sole bidder.

The next day I went to the bank, withdrew the funds from my savings account, and paid for the lot in cash, another of my father's best practices.

I was still in high school, and now I was a property owner.

My father had taught me the basics of the building trades and so I began construction on my first house, working Saturdays and whatever vacation days I had from school. The process quickened considerably when four of my friends pitched in. They helped me pour the footings, lay blocks, and haul whatever materials I could buy from brick and lumber yards or scrounge from my father's scrap piles. They even helped me build the wood frame.

The free labor, coupled with thrifty spending on supplies, kept my costs down considerably. The duplex cost about $3,000 to build. Work progressed slowly because of the demands of school and sports and a busy social life, but a few months after high school graduation I was the proud owner of my first rental property.

The duplex stood on a lot that sloped back from the curb. It was wood and stucco painted gleaming white. I rented each side as one apartment to double my rental income. It sort of amazes me that even then I was looking for creative ways to maximize my investments. Because I paid cash for the lot and all of the supplies, the rental income was mine to spend on college expenses.

My parents were proud of me, and I took no little pride in this accomplishment myself. But of course, you know what the Bible says about "pride goeth before a fall . . ."

About a year after I finished building my duplex a stranger approached me. He was middle-aged and of medium complexion. He seemed friendly enough.

"Excuse me, son," he said. "Do you know who the owner of this house is?"

"Yes, sir, I do," I answered proudly. I thought he was a potential buyer or at least a renter. "This is my house. I built it myself."

It felt good saying "This is my house." But it felt better saying "I built it." My smile was so wide he probably could see my tonsils.

He did not return my smile.

"Well," he said, drawing a deep breath. "I'm sorry to have to tell you that it might be *your* house, but you've built it on *my* land."

I thought he was kidding. But it only took a moment to see that he was dead earnest. It didn't matter to me how serious he was, though. Whatever the issue, I was going to set things straight.

"What do you mean?" I said. "I bought this land from the city. For cash! I own it free and clear. I have the deed at home to prove it."

The man looked into my eyes. When his serious expression didn't change, a chill ran through my bones.

"Well, son," he said slowly, "even if you have a deed, it's not for this lot. This is my land. I bought it many years ago. I've got my deed and the surveyor's report right here to prove it."

He handed me the documents. I looked them over. My stomach churned. He was right. I had built my house on the wrong lot! The parcel I'd bought actually was *adjacent* to the lot that I'd built upon.

I felt dizzy from the pounding in my head. All I could think of was losing my house and all the money I'd put into it, not to mention the hours and hours of labor by my friends and me. I labored to calm myself, drawing deep breaths to stay cool and gather my thoughts. I realized there was only one way to handle this huge mistake on my part.

I handed back his documents and humbled myself.

"Looks like you're right, sir. I guess I built my house on the wrong lot."

My response seemed to catch him off guard.

"Do you mean to say that you are agreeing with me, son?"

"Yes, sir, I am," I said, gazing upon the lot I should have built on.

At that moment things looked bleak, but I hoped we could work out a solution that wouldn't cost me all that I'd put into the property. I'd already roughed out a solution but I wasn't sure he would go for it.

"Sir," I said, "these are lots of the same size and the same value. Why don't we just trade? It won't cost you a thing. And it sure would help me."

He sized me up for a minute or two. Then his gaze shifted to the duplex for another minute, before returning to lock onto mine.

"You bought the lot and built this house on your own?"

"Yes, sir, my friends helped. It took us all of two years."

He did another quick appraisal of the duplex.

"Young fella, you are something else."

He smiled and reached for my hand.

"It's a deal. I'll swap lots with you," he said. "Keep up the good work, son."

I realized how lucky I was that he was a good man who did not try to squeeze me or take advantage. Over the years I've often reflected on how things could have gotten ugly had I been dealing with a predator rather than a gentleman. I had not paid attention to important details. I vowed that would never happen again.

From that point forward, I became a stickler for the details of every project and business deal I entered into. I pored over contracts and studied the fine print and always made it a point to step back and think through each step to make certain that everything was in order. We all make mistakes. The important thing is to learn from them, and I certainly learned from *that* one.

My mistake, in retrospect, was that I paid cash for the property. Had it been acquired with a loan, a survey of the parcel would have been required and the surveyors would have steered me to the correct lot!

■ □ ■

I met a new friend at the start of seventh grade when David T. Howard School was only a junior high—William "Bill" Kimbrough. We hit it off that very first day and have been inseparable ever since.

When we reached high school, Bill was my wingman with the young ladies at social gatherings. And if there was a party in the neighborhood, it was likely taking place in my family's basement. My parents knew what a lot of smart parents learn: if your teenagers are going to act like teenagers, better to have them and their friends under your own roof where you can keep an eye on them and help them stay out of bigger trouble.

After graduating from high school, Bill and I often went on double dates to nightclubs. Almost every Friday night you could find us dressed to the nines at the Royal Peacock (previously known as the Top Hat) on Auburn Avenue. The Peacock was the Atlanta gateway for every black entertainer in the South in what was once called the Chitlin' Circuit.

One guy, Pat, worked days for me but spent his nights as a club emcee and comedian, introducing bands and dancing girls. Every show started at 9:00 PM and ran roughly two hours. They had a comedian open the evening, followed by a main attraction such a dance band or orchestra, and the night typically finished with a performance by a "shake" dancer, sort of like a stripper but with more emphasis on talent and less on exposed flesh. And we never had a date walk out on a shake dancer.

Most of the clubs didn't have a liquor license, so we carried our own booze and they would furnish the setup.

Bobby Jones and Felker Ward, whom Bill and I met at David T. Howard High School, also became lifelong friends. Bobby—who went on to become a successful barber in town and once owned a string of Paramount Barber Shops—and I were, like Bill and me, inseparable.

That group would be incomplete without Felker, another one of the guys I hung around with. We later went to Tuskegee together and many years later we were partners—with Jesse Hill—in Concessions International. Felker was another one of my friends who worked for my dad in the summertime. He would push a wheelbarrow full of mud, as we called it, or do some bricklaying or block laying or plastering on small commercial buildings.

I had another high school classmate named Alvin Dobbin. Alvin was a stellar musician. All of us kids went crazy when he played his alto saxophone and clarinet. He had a smooth style like Johnny Hodges, Duke Ellington's saxophone player. He was also a great clarinet player. All the kids loved to hear him blow. One day I was humming a tune I'd heard Alvin play when something clicked in my head and my entrepreneur's instincts kicked in. I thought, Why not start a band that would feature the great Alvin Dobbin?

There was a roadblock—I don't have a lick of musical talent. I can't even carry a tune. That would have daunted most young people contemplating starting a band, I suppose. But I wasn't concerned about music; that would be Alvin's job. The only thing I was concerned about was the money we could make. I would manage and own the band and do the deals. It would be my responsibility to make sure the band had jobs and made money.

I approached Alvin with my idea. At first he was skeptical about a fellow high school sophomore being in charge. But when he realized that I was talking about a serious business venture, not just some kiddie stuff, he was all in.

Alvin recruited a strong lineup of musicians—including future Dizzy Gillespie trombone player Silly Willie Wilson, Duke Pearson on piano, tenor saxophonist Fred Jackson, bass fiddler Willy Jackson, and trumpeter Sam Cook—to round out the group. We kicked around names like the Georgia Pinetops and the Cool Music Makers. But Alvin already had such a following that it would have been foolish not to capitalize on it. So we named our group the Dobbin Rhythm Band.

As manager, it was my responsibility to arrange for rehearsals, which, since everyone lived in Summerhill, we held in my parents' living room. And I called rehearsals quite often. The fellows sometimes grumbled about how often we rehearsed, but I didn't care. I was determined that the Dobbin Band would make such good music that we would be in strong demand. After all, this was business.

After a couple of months of preparation, the Dobbin Rhythm Band played its first gig, a teen dance at the Catholic recreation center in the heart of black Atlanta, right off Auburn Avenue. We tore the place up. Young folks danced and shouted until their voices were hoarse, their clothes were drenched with sweat, and their energy spent. When the crowd cheered us at the evening's end, we knew that the band was on its way.

After that dance, word got out about how good the band was and suddenly we were in high demand all over Georgia. The band became so popular that when Nat King Cole came to town, the promoter B. B. Beamon asked the Dobbin Rhythm Band to perform between Cole's sets.

We couldn't believe it. Old Mr. "Straighten Up and Fly Right" himself! He was so smooth, with his tailored suits and shiny processed hair.

When it was our turn to play we were so excited we almost wet our pants. We weren't Nat, but we gave them some swinging music that night.

Some of the Dobbin musicians went on to successful international musical careers. Our pianist, Columbus "Duke" Pearson (an admiring uncle nicknamed him in honor of Duke Ellington), was an important figure in the jazz world. He became a producer and arranger at Blue Note Records, led his own band, the Duke Pearson Orchestra, and played with such high-flying instrumentalists as Donald Byrd, Art Farmer, and Chick Correa, as well as with stellar vocalists like Nancy Wilson, Carmen McRae, and Joe Williams. Our trombonist, Willie Wilson, better known to us as "Silly Willie," went on to play with Dizzy Gillespie.

After we graduated from high school, the members of the Dobbin Band went their separate ways, but by then I had caught the managing and promoting bug. I had done a pretty good job managing the band, so I was sure I could do the same in other arenas, too.

■ □ ■

In high school, I wanted to be respected and appreciated for what I had to offer—not disrespected for the way I spoke. I had more money in my pocket than most boys my age, but that was not evident to my peers because I have never been the type to try to impress people by flashing cash or talking about my business. There was, however, another area where I excelled: sports.

Physically, I stood about five-foot-eight and weighed about 165 pounds. There were a lot of boys who were bigger, and some who were faster, but no one was more determined to succeed than me.

I stepped onto the football field that first day of tryouts with my mind made up. I would be a star. That's my philosophy: if you decide to do something, decide to excel at it. You might not always excel, but you will have the self-satisfaction of knowing you did your best while trying. Even if you don't reach your goal, trying will always put you ahead of the game.

The football coach was named T. Herman Graves. He was not much older than us boys, maybe in his mid-twenties, but we all looked up to him in life as well as on the football field. He stood six feet tall and had the dignity and bearing of a man much older. He was always neatly dressed and never lost his cool. He had no tolerance for foolishness.

Coach Graves told us that you don't win all the time. The real challenge, he would say, is how a person handles losing. He seemed to know everything there was about football yet he had never played the game himself! His knowledge came from hours of observation and study.

Tryouts for the team were always held in late summer, and about 150 boys showed up. We were told that only forty-four of us would be chosen, so competition was fierce.

In those days there was no specialization between offense and defense; if the coach didn't send a substitute in, you played the whole game. If not for halftime, you'd never get a break. Some of the guys were better at defense and others were better offensive players. I was determined to excel at both. I was an equal opportunity butt-kicker, tackling and blocking with all the grit I could summon.

The coach looked each of us over, then assigned positions. He told me to try out for tight end, which called for toughness. On defense, the tight end must make sure runners don't turn the corner into the open field. He also has to guard against short passes. On offense, the tight end is both a blocker and a pass receiver. In addition to being able to catch short yardage passes, he must make sure that opposing linemen don't get into his own backfield. It is also the tight end's responsibility to clear the way for his team's ball carriers to turn the corner into the open field on sweeps and end-around plays.

I didn't know a thing about playing tight end, but I accepted the challenge.

For the first few practices, I did OK, but I wasn't satisfied with my performance. I paid closer attention to the nuances of the footwork and how to defend against all sorts of plays. By the third practice, I had the hang of it, and there was no stopping me after that. If an opponent came into Herman Russell's assigned area, he'd better watch his butt.

I had natural athletic talent, but so did many of the other boys. What made me excel beyond many of them was my drive and discipline. I was determined to be the best player on the field. I approached every drill at practice like I was in the most important game of my life. I made some hard hits and took some, too, so my head sometimes rang like a church bell. But I'd always get up and do it again. I knew one day all my hard work would pay off.

Early on in junior high school, the equipment that we used for football practice and even during the games was used and handed down from a white junior high or high school. In those days, we never had brand-new jerseys, pants, or shoes.

To understand the importance of athletics to Atlanta's black community back then, you must remember that, outside of church, schools were the only other institutions where our own folks were in charge. Because we didn't have much, we took great pride in the few things we did possess. That was reflected in the names of our two high schools. David T. Howard High was named after an important educator in Atlanta in the early part of the century. The other black school was named after one of my lifelong heroes, Booker T. Washington, the most renowned of all African American authors, orators, political leaders, and educators.

Pride in our schools included avid support of our athletic programs. In those days black teams were only allowed to play other black teams. In terms of the quality of competition, however, that didn't matter, because the black teams were tough and motivated to uphold their school's name.

Booker T. Washington and David T. Howard high schools developed a rivalry that extended beyond athletics. Until David T. Howard High was built, all high school–aged African American children attended Washington. After Howard was built, Washington had to share the spotlight in the black community. For that reason alone a friendly competition between the two was inevitable.

There was also a social class rivalry. Washington was located in a more affluent African American community. Many of its students were children of black professionals—doctors, lawyers, teachers, and the like. Our sports competition was all the keener because of the class distinction that mostly was not mentioned but was there just below the surface.

The annual football game between our two black high schools was always the last of the season and a highlight for parents, teachers, current students, and alumni. Both schools were known for fielding good teams, so the games were usually pretty exciting. But in the fall of my senior year, Washington had steamrolled every team on its schedule. In fact, not one point had been scored against them when we met.

Washington's star was Joe Petty, one of the best schoolboy quarterbacks of any race that Atlanta has seen before or since. Everyone was convinced that Washington was unbeatable.

Everyone, that is, but my teammates and me.

I was a co-captain, so I was expected to provide upbeat, positive leadership. It was the captains' responsibility to make sure that none of our teammates lost heart or focus. That was particularly important against Washington. At every practice session we psyched our guys up with enthusiastic slogans and predictions:

"Howard's got the power!"

"We're going to beat Booker T. Washington like a mangy dog!"

"We're the best, they're the rest!"

We psyched each other up so much with the Washington game approaching that by the time of the big game we were convinced that no one could beat us.

From the first kick-off it was clear why Washington was undefeated. They were big, much bigger than us. Their tight end was about six-foot-three and 250 pounds and a beast on both sides of the ball. He had scored two or three touchdowns in every game that season.

As the opposing tight end it was my job to stop that beast. He towered over me by seven inches and outweighed me by eighty-five pounds! I knew I couldn't overpower him. Every time he touched the ball he was running over my teammates, shaking them off his big shoulders and chest. He hadn't come at me yet, but I knew he would. I had to figure out how to stop him. The question for me was not *if* I would stop him, but *how* I would stop him.

I made up my mind that no matter what, he was not going to run over Herman Russell.

Late in the first quarter, their quarterback dropped a short pass into the big tight end's hands and he came barreling my way. This was the moment of truth. I dug in to hold my ground. When he was almost upon me he lowered his big shoulder to knock me down. He expected me to try to out-muscle him, but since I lacked brawn I used my brain. Instead of aiming my head into his chest, I hit him low, taking his legs out from under him. He hit the ground like an uprooted oak. I swear the ground shook! The best thing about it was that he hadn't gained a yard. And that's how it went for the rest of the night. Every time he came my way, I put him down like a sack of cement.

The game was fierce. We fought like hell to keep them from scoring on us, but we couldn't seem to get into the end zone either. Then in the third quarter we found our first real chance to score. One of their halfbacks fumbled a kick-off. Washington managed to recover the ball, but just barely. When the smoke cleared, Washington had the ball on their two-yard line. It was their worst field position of the entire game and our best.

We had to seize this opportunity, but their quarterback, Petty, was known for working miracles in tight spots like this. As bad as their field position was, Washington was still good enough to pull out a win, and we knew it.

I watched Petty look over our defense. I could see the determination in his eyes. It was clear that he had made up his mind to pull out yet another miracle. But Petty's mind wasn't the only one that was made up. I had made my mind up, too. I didn't care about what the football prophets had predicted. I was determined that this was Howard's time. And I was going to make sure of it.

Petty took the snap. He stepped back, scanned the field for a receiver, then his eyes seemed to lock. Ever see an eagle when it has spotted its prey? Its eyes lock onto its target and the predator goes in for the kill. Well, Petty had that same going-for-the-kill look. He had settled on his receiver.

This quarterback rarely threw a bad pass, so I had to stop him from putting the ball in the air. There were two blockers between Petty and me. I closed my eyes and envisioned running through those lineman like they weren't there.

Petty looked right, then left. He called out the count then barked, "Hike!"

The next thing I remember was the referee shouting "Touchback!"

It took a minute for it to dawn on me that things had happened just as I envisioned. I had run over the defensive line and tackled Petty behind his own goal line for a two-point safety!

We scored on the team that had not allowed an opponent to put points on the board all season! The crowd went wild just like in a movie. Folks cheered so loudly that I could barely hear my teammates congratulating me. Both teams played their hearts out for the rest of that afternoon, but my touchback play ended up being the only score against Washington that entire season. By sheer will, I bulldozed the offensive line and sacked the best athlete in the league.

In the waning minutes of the game, Washington scored a touchdown and won 7–2. Still, Howard students were proud of the fight we put up. Most people in town had expected us to be run out of the stadium by Washington's vaunted stars, but we had come closer to beating them than anyone.

I was the hero of the game for our fans, praised and lauded for weeks. The sports page of every local paper touted how I'd run over the best high school offensive line to clobber the best player in the city and for the only score against them to boot. In fact, I was told that I was the first African American to be featured in a front-page photograph on the sports section of the *Atlanta Constitution*.

At the end of the season, I was chosen as Most Valuable Player of the Atlanta Negro school system.

■ □ ■

I learned some important lessons on the football field that served me well in business. The first was not to let your ego run your game. Be willing to make adjustments. I could have let my pride get in the way and tried to meet that big tight end's brawn with my own. But that was his kind of game, not mine. Even if I had withstood him, as the physically smaller player I would have taken a much bigger battering. I was on the field to win, not to prove a point. It is the same in business. You have to keep in mind that your goal is success, not to prove that you are smarter or slicker or braver or tougher than others.

■ □ ■

I was fortunate to be taught by a group of well-rounded high school teachers. In the fall of 1948, my senior year, our homeroom teacher was John Wesley Miles. Mr. Miles, who was also our English teacher, was a graduate of Morehouse College. He was a dedicated and motivating teacher who cared so much for us that he named our class "the Modernaires." The title had little meaning to me until I attended a banquet that he organized for us in the Graham Jackson Room of the Frazier's Café Society on Hunter Street (known today as Martin Luther King Jr. Boulevard). Class members paid five dollars each for themselves and another five dollars for a parent to attend—a lot of money at that time. The men wore dark suits and ties. The ladies came in dresses. For many of us, this banquet was a first peek into adult-style events.

Mr. Miles was also the scoutmaster of Senior Boy Scout Troop 88 of which I was a member. Years later I was able to repay Mr. Miles's faith in me and my schoolmates in a small way. He had retired from teaching but found he needed a few more years of employment before he could qualify to receive Social Security. I was honored to help him by hiring him for several years in an administrative capacity at H.J. Russell & Company. He worked with us until he met federal retirement requirements.

Our economics instructor, Marcus "Pop" Beasley, challenged us every Monday with provocative questions such as "What would you do if you had a million dollars?" Most of the kids talked about what they could buy. Pop would say that material things are nice to have, but what I actually learned from him was to use common sense in how to invest and how a million dollars itself could generate income for you and your family.

I also remember Clay E. Boyd, who taught mechanical drawing at Howard. He himself was a tradesman, a professional bricklayer and plasterer. He taught us that knowing a trade, we could always go out and make a decent living. When he built his home on Hunter Street, several of his students and I helped out after hours and on weekends.

Mr. Boyd kept us on our toes all the time. He taught us to constantly evaluate priorities and make choices as a person. For instance, if there was a pep rally during school hours, Mr. Boyd would hold class nonetheless.

Mr. Boyd married Frankie Smith, who taught English at David T. Howard High School. I always kept in touch with the Boyds. Long after my school days ended they became godparents of my first child, Donata, and our families traveled together to Mexico and other places.

■ □ ■

When I was seventeen, my father got a call to do a job at the Georgia governor's mansion in downtown Atlanta. Herman Talmadge was the governor at the time; his father, Eugene Talmadge, a staunch and feared segregationist, was himself a former governor of our state. It was Eugene Talmadge who said that the only way that Georgia would be integrated would be over his dead body.

Getting the call to repair the ceiling at the governor's mansion was a surprise. But while we were there, I got an even bigger surprise.

Betty Talmadge, the governor's wife, walked up to us and struck up a conversation with me. We chatted for a few minutes. She must have enjoyed our little talk because she said to me, "Young man, would you like to have lunch with me?"

Mrs. Talmadge was one of the prettiest ladies that you ever wanted to see, and extremely friendly. If ever there was a Georgia peach, she was it. Still, I wasn't sure about having lunch with her. But my father said it would be discourteous to say no.

So there I was, alone with the First Lady of Georgia in the mansion's private eat-in kitchen, enjoying a ham sandwich. Think of that: a poor black boy being served by the wife of the governor. This was first time I'd *ever* shared a meal with a white person—and it was in the governor's mansion . . . with the governor's wife!

I was respectful to Mrs. Talmadge, but I wasn't at all intimidated by her. I found her to be quite pleasant and I hope she found me to be

the same. Knowing my speech could be difficult for strangers to understand, I talked slowly so she could understand me. If there was a word
that wasn't clear, she wasn't uncomfortable asking me to repeat it. As I
munched on my sandwich she asked about my family and my schoolwork, and chatted about her duties as the governor's wife.*

■ □ ■

As a teenager, I was a member of Atlanta's historic Butler Street YMCA
off Auburn Avenue, which was then the civic and social center of the
black community. Many of the civil rights movement's future leaders
and many of Atlanta's future civic and business power brokers grew up
hanging out there. I played pool with other neighborhood kids at the
Butler YMCA, including my schoolmate, A. D. King.

I met A.D.'s older brother Martin there while he was shooting pool
with a rather glum-looking character. Martin had a friendly, teasing
banter going with his opponent. He laughed and joked with him even
as he beat the fellow's socks off. He ran the table, as I recall, so the poor
soul playing him never took a shot.

I spoke just briefly with Martin that first day, telling him that I was a
friend of A.D.'s. He was quite friendly and I liked him right off, though
I made a mental note to never bet against him in a game of pool.

---

*Years later, after Herman Talmadge had left the governor's office and I had
become a successful businessman, well known in Atlanta business, civic, and social
circles, he and Betty divorced. Betty and I found ourselves as colleagues on a Clark
College (now Clark Atlanta University) fund-raising committee and on several civic
boards. At first, she didn't realize that the young businessman in nice suits and
starched shirts was the same teenage boy to whom she'd served lunch at the governor's
mansion years before.

One day, after we had gotten acquainted as colleagues, I decided to surprise her.

"Thanks, Mrs. Talmadge," I said, "for fixing that nice lunch for me."

"What lunch?" she said, confused. "When?"

"When my father and I fixed the ceiling at the governor's mansion."

"You mean that *you're* that young fellow?"

I said, "I sure am."

Martin was two years older than me and already a student at More-house College in Atlanta. I was closer to A.D. in our teen years, but the King brothers were well known around town because their father, Martin Senior—"Daddy King"—was a leading minister in the community as pastor at Ebenezer Baptist Church.

Both Martin and his father would become close friends and important figures in my life, along with another friend made in those high school days, Vernon Jordan. Vernon, who would become a civil rights leader, advisor to presidents, and a national political powerhouse in his own right, was a trumpet player in the Howard High School student band and a few years behind me so I didn't get to know him well until my senior year.

■ □ ■

Because of the ridicule I experienced in my childhood due to my speech impediment, I entered high school shy and socially unsure. After my successes at sports, I started to see myself differently.

I'd always believed in myself, but socially, my self-confidence soared in high school. My peers now looked at me differently. No longer was I tongue-tied Herman Russell; now I was Herman Russell the sports hero. I was suddenly a popular guy.

Especially with the girls.

Being the center of attention was new to me. I enjoyed the newfound respect and camaraderie from fellow classmates and teammates for sure, but it was the attention of the girls that I really appreciated! For the first time I had my pick, because I was the girls' pick. I received a steady stream of love letters and cute little notes. Several girls fixed lunches for me to take with me when we had away games.

The popularity was quite enjoyable, I'll admit. But popularity is fleeting if that's all there is. What was more important for me was that my classmates respected me. They showed it by electing me senior class president of my homeroom. I was also asked to be campaign manager for one of the student council parties, the Progressive Party. Our candidate for president of the student body was a fellow named Ralph Smith. Ralph was smart and such a good speaker that we nicknamed him

"Rabbi." I see our little student council election as kid stuff now, but then it was as important to us as any national election.

I approached the campaign with the same determination to win that had made me a star athlete. I made sure we campaigned at every opportunity. We could be found pushing our candidate during class breaks, when school let out, even in the cafeteria at lunchtime. We were quite serious.

Vernon Jordan later told me that the seeds of what became a life-long friendship between us were planted when he heard me and the smart and beautiful Valencia McClinton campaigning for Ralph Smith. Before that, he knew me as a sports hero, but he'd never heard me speak. He said he thought that it was very courageous for a young man who had a hard time making himself understood to stand and speak to a crowd of his peers without apology or shame.

"The fact that you were willing to stand up and speak in front of all the students despite your speech impediment told me all I needed to know about the strength of your character," he said.

It took courage, I suppose, but I felt accepted by my peers—speech impediment and all. So by then it wasn't as difficult to speak in public as Vernon thought.

After weeks of furious campaigning came the climax of all our efforts: each candidate was to present his platform in the auditorium in front of the entire student body.

Our side had a five-pronged party platform:

- Better food in the cafeteria
- Better prices in the cafeteria
- Better band instruction and instruments
- Better books
- Better academic programs

Ralph the Rabbi gave a great speech that day. That boy could talk! The students cheered him like he was Frederick Douglass, the nineteenth-century former slave turned abolitionist. But it was our platform that pushed him over the top. The students really embraced it. On Election Day, we celebrated an even greater victory than we'd hoped for.

It was no coincidence that my party was the Progressive Party and that our platform was a kind of populist platform that sought changes that would equally benefit all our fellow students. In retrospect, this was an early expression of what decades later fueled my full-fledged political activism during the civil rights era.

When I graduated from David T. Howard High School in 1949, the "Class Prophecies" section of our yearbook predicted my life as it would be ten years hence:

> Herman Russell has become a very successful businessman. He still possesses the confidence to win other people's confidence.

How's *that* for a prophecy?

3

Tuskegee Institute:
An Educated Class

Coming out of high school, I knew more than anything that I wanted to be a builder. The great satisfaction I experienced constructing my duplex had convinced me of that much. The next step was obvious: I was going to Tuskegee Institute in Alabama to study building and construction.

I wanted to go to Tuskegee because that was the only place in those days that a black man could go in the South and study construction. Georgia Tech wasn't an option for African Americans yet.

Tuskegee founder Booker T. Washington believed that it was important that we learn the building trade. In fact, the first kids enrolled had to build their own buildings. I was fascinated that Washington believed that we should use our hands. That's where he and W. E. B. Du Bois ran into some difficulties because Du Bois felt that we should study more liberal arts, not just the trades.

Tuskegee itself can motivate you. In those days, as part of its mission to "uplift the race," Tuskegee had an open admissions policy, so I had no problem being accepted. I hadn't been a particularly successful student, but I didn't let that intimidate me. I needed expert training in construction to reach my goal. Tuskegee offered it, so there I went.

My mama was the only other person in my family who had attended college. In those days only a few black folks did, but I didn't worry about that. Even though my learning disability made it difficult to prosper in my high school classes, I never had any doubts about going to college. I knew what I wanted to do, and advanced training in building and construction was necessary for me to do it.

One day I sat down with my parents to let them know what I wanted to do.

"Mama, Daddy, I want to go to college. And I'd like your blessing."

"College? Where, son?" my father asked.

"Tuskegee Institute. In Alabama." I said it with pride.

My father, always practical, asked, "How much does it cost, son? How are you going to live?"

He knew I was aware that he couldn't afford to pay for it. I was even prouder to tell them that I had saved enough from my businesses to pay for my entire college education myself.

My parents were concerned about their youngest child going so far from home, but they wanted the best for me. There was never any question they would fully support my college aspirations. They were proud that I wanted to make something of myself and that I had saved enough money to pay for it. They knew I was level-headed, that I had never gotten into trouble, and that I handled myself as a good man ought, so they didn't worry about me acting up. My daddy, a man of few words, only asked for one thing—that I do my best. He knew I would.

After high school graduation I didn't leave for college right away. I spent what would have been my first semester helping my father on the job and getting my enterprises in order for my departure. And saving more money, of course.

Finally, the day came for me to leave. Mama was emotional. I remember her voice cracking a bit as she said, "Work hard, son, and take care of yourself. I will keep you in my prayers." My father told me, first and foremost, to "work hard" and to "stay focused." That was his favorite saying. I still hear it in my mind every day and I have often myself reminded others to do the same.

My parents didn't accompany me to the train station; instead, my brother Rogers saw me off with a warm handshake and a hearty "good luck." I picked up my cardboard suitcase and boarded the train. It was the first time I would be away from home for more than a few days. I was eighteen years old.

You have to be willing to step out of your comfort zone sometimes in order to position yourself for success. Because stepping outside yourself often means adjusting and acclimating yourself to a new environment, it means you also have to be willing to take a longer-term view of things.

Only once before had I left the Atlanta area, and that was on a grammar school trip to DC. Going off alone for several years to live with strangers on a college campus—whatever that was like—in another state to boot, was definitely outside of my comfort zone.

Also, the racial climate in rural Alabama was much more threatening than in Atlanta, with its strong and accomplished black middle class. But I had to do it if I was going to accomplish my professional goals.

■ □ ■

The train ride from Atlanta to Tuskegee was a little more than 125 miles, less than three hours from station to station, but it felt like I was going to a foreign country.

I was excited about beginning my college career, but I was anxious, too. My high school friends Bill Kimbrough, Felker Ward, Warren Talley, and Jimmy Haynes were already there. They had enrolled the previous semester, so I wasn't worried about making friends. It was just that I had no idea what college life would be like. Could I do the work? Would I fit in? I was a BMOC—Big Man on Campus—in high school, but that was behind me now. I'd arrive at Tuskegee as a newly minted freshman with the same old speech impediment and no football field upon which to star.

Worry must have shown in my face while I sat alone on the train. I heard a friendly and familiar voice say, "You look a little worried. Where you off to, young fella?"

I looked up into the face of . . . *B. B. Beamon!*

Boy, was I glad to see him.

Beamon, the entertainment promoter, was known all around the South for staging great musical shows and concerts. His shows featured some of the most popular black artists in the business, including Nat King Cole, who had appeared at the Atlanta Municipal Auditorium; the Dobbin Rhythm Band had played during intermission. I'd kept in touch with him since then and had taken him to see my duplex when it was completed. My drive—and my nerve—back then impressed him and he took a liking to me. He'd even introduced me to another B. B.: a then up-and-coming blues artist named B. B. King.

Beamon was a tall man, a sharp dresser, articulate and good-natured. His wingtips were always buffed to a high sheen. He wore the best suits and ties and drove the biggest, fanciest cars. A true entrepreneur, he owned a popular restaurant on Auburn Avenue that bore his name.

And the same man I just described was also a part-time Pullman porter!

Many people think that a Pullman porter was simply a black waiter in a white jacket who fetched and carried on one of the many trains operated by the Pullman Company that crisscrossed the country. This perception of Pullman porters is reflected in both the insulting manner in which they were addressed by passengers and the way they were referred to by their bosses: as "George," which seemed to make the insulting inference that they were owned by the head of the company, Mr. George Pullman. No matter what their real names, no matter their dignity and intelligence, their ingenuity, hopes, or talents, every Pullman porter was called "George," as in "Oh, George, get me some coffee" or "Get one of the Georges to help you."

But Beamon was a prime example of the caliber of Pullman porters. And he was thrilled that I was going to college. Whenever he could take a moment from his duties that day on the train ride to Tuskegee, he stopped by my seat to offer a few words of praise and encouragement.

It was brief though, because he had to give most of his attention to the "whites only" section of the train.

Like all the black passengers, I was seated in a segregated Jim Crow car. The "colored" section offered second-class accommodations at best. They had the least desirable location on each train—directly behind the noisy, smoke-spewing locomotive—and tended to be older and more decrepit than the "white" cars. The much better appointed observation and lounge cars in the more comfortable rear section were off-limits to blacks. Even after the Pullman Company bought new steel-bodied coach cars in the early twentieth century, with electric lights and steam heat, black passengers were still relegated to the older, less safe wooden cars with coal stoves and gas lamps. The restrooms in the white cars had every luxury available for rail use, while our restrooms lacked nearly every amenity. There was no soap, water, or washbasin; there were no towels or flushing toilets.

The discomfort and humiliation I experienced in the Jim Crow car lifted each time Beamon walked up and called me "college boy" before hurrying off to serve some passenger calling out, "Oh, George!"

Beamon will never know how much good his encouragement did me on my train ride to the unknown.

■ □ ■

The only place I'd visited outside Atlanta was Washington, DC, so I expected Tuskegee to be a similar city. In Atlanta we had many black colleges—Clark, Spelman, Morris Brown, and Morehouse, as well as Atlanta University—so I expected a real metropolis and campus like the ones with which I'd grown up; I'd never even imagined anything else. But instead of entering a city, our bus wound past farm after farm.

My God, I thought nervously, this place looks like it's out in the middle of nowhere. When we pulled onto Tuskegee's main street my heart sank. It wasn't a city or even a college town. It was just a country village.

The train arrived at the Tuskegee, Alabama, station at about one o'clock in the afternoon. It was tiny, nothing like I was accustomed to in Atlanta. Outside, a yellow bus with the words TUSKEGEE INSTITUTE in black letters was waiting to transport students to the campus. The dozen or so other young people I'd seen on the train turned out to be incoming students like me. We all scrambled onto the bus, happily chatting, full of anticipation for the exciting college life that awaited us.

Today it is Tuskegee *University* with handsome buildings and facilities, modern research centers and laboratories, a state-of-the-art conference center, and a full service, one-hundred-plus-room, AAA-rated hotel, great athletic facilities, and a host of other structures and buildings, some of which I had a hand in developing and supporting years later. But on that day in 1949, all I saw were a few buildings and a lot of wide-open spaces. No hustle and bustle like you'd see today. Just a pace as slow as pouring a glass of molasses in cold weather.

I shook my head and thought, What have I gotten myself into?

But for better or worse, I was there. I have never been a quitter and I don't discourage easily, so I decided to make the best of it. Besides, as soon as my feet hit the campus grounds I was a college student! I'd decided to get there and there I was. There was nothing to complain about in that equation so I opened my eyes and ears and shut my mouth so I could get into the college routine as quickly as possible.

The first day was all orientation, then dinner in the cafeteria. When I finally made it to my assigned dorm room it was just before dusk. Hunched over his desk deep in study—despite the fact that classes had not started yet—was my roommate, an upperclassman from Mississippi named Walter Moore.

Walter was in his late twenties. He had served in the army and was at Tuskegee on the G.I. Bill. Walter was bookish and studious in manner, but he wasn't stiff. He was, however, so serious that he seldom wasted good study time by talking. I didn't mind though, because I was serious about my studies as well.

College life was different from anything I had ever experienced, but I never got the chance to get homesick because my first day on campus I fell in with my buddies Bill, Felker, Warren, and Jimmy. When I arrived they were already firmly involved in college life. Oh, boy, were they! They had mastered all of the school's procedures and requirements, and they knew which professors and classes to take and which to avoid.

Felker already had history in Tuskegee when we went there to school. His dad had been an aircraft mechanic for the army's all-black Tuskegee Airmen corps when Felker was thirteen. Felker had some kind of little old car that we used to ride back and forth from Atlanta to Tuskegee when all of us went home on holidays. And, of course, we shared a house in our sophomore year.

We rented a three-bedroom house off campus at 111 Church Street—owned by a local pastor—and took the money that we would have otherwise separately paid for room and board on campus, put it all in a fund together, and paid our rent and bought our food with Bill doing most of the cooking.

We were together, literally, every day and every night.

By the time I joined them at Tuskegee, my friends had already mastered what, in some ways, was most important for an entering freshman: they knew all the girls by name.

Don't get me wrong. My buddies and I were serious about our schoolwork. We knew a college education was a rare privilege for a black person in those days, especially coming from our backgrounds, and an even greater privilege at a great institution such as Tuskegee. Still, we were young and full of bluster and energy, so we were also serious about having fun. And we did have fun! Translation: We were popular with the girls.

Our house just happened to be near John A. Andrew Memorial Hospital in Tuskegee, a Veterans Administration facility that employed dozens of black nurses to serve black soldiers. The nurses trained there and lived in a dormitory just a block away from the on-campus hospital. When we rented the house, we honestly didn't know about that particular fringe benefit, but when we figured it out we felt like we had died and gone to heaven. Beautiful nurses around all the time—and we didn't even have to be sick to get their attention.

We worked hard during the week, but seldom did a weekend go by when we didn't have a party at our place. Bill was the cook, and he was quite good at it; nobody ever went hungry in that house. Our little place off-campus was a popular destination for many Tuskegee students. Nothing scandalous, mind you. A little beer and wine, nothing much harder than that.

There was always a lot of good music and a whole lot of dancing: the St. Louis shag, the swing, the Lindy hop, the jive, and the slop were popular then. My favorite was the jitterbug, which was sort of like the Lindy hop but with steps and moves from all the fast, acrobatic dances of the time. Because I was so athletic, I could dance the pants off anyone when it came to the jitterbug. My feet were fast, my legs were strong, and I was limber. I couldn't wait for the music to start. Cab Calloway, Louis Jordan, Count Basie, Benny Goodman, Louis Armstrong, Earl "Fatha" Hines, Duke Ellington, Sarah Vaughn, Ella Fitzgerald—we swung with the music of them all.

One of my roommates had one of those little Symphonic record players that you could carry around like a suitcase. It played the 78 rpm vinyl records that were state of the art then. The sound that came out of those suitcase record players wasn't the greatest, but that was before any of us had ever seen a stereo so we didn't mind. It was all we needed to kick up our heels.

I had my share of girlfriends and then some. I sometimes had trouble making myself understood, but I was trim and athletic, and I've always been polite and a gentleman, so girls liked me just fine. But come Monday morning, my mind was always back on the books.

▪ □ ▪

Tuskegee's curriculum was much more challenging than anything I'd ever encountered in high school. No matter how hard or long I studied, I struggled in each course—except my primary course of interest, building construction. I had been interested in and participating in the construction trades since I started working with my daddy. It was the main reason I was at Tuskegee and I did well with it.

For the rest of my time at college, I focused my academic energies on building construction. I took drafting, masonry, and carpentry—every construction-related course that Tuskegee offered—and excelled in each one.

I caught the attention of my professors in one area in particular: plastering. I was already a master plasterer when I arrived at school, so in this, I was way ahead of other students. Not surprisingly then, one of my professors asked me to do some work at his home. That went well, and soon not only was I getting requests from other faculty members to work on their homes, but also from folks in the outside community.

I found myself doing schoolwork during the day and plastering around town in the evenings and on weekends. I hardly had a minute to breathe, but I didn't mind: the more I work, the better I feel. I've always been like that. And I was starting to feel better and better in Tuskegee, because the demand for my services in town grew so fast that I needed help to keep up.

I wrote home to my brother Rogers and told him that I had more work than I could handle. He knew that meant there was money to be made. A week later Rogers arrived by bus in Tuskegee.

With Rogers, I assembled a crew, mostly fellow students. The demand for our services was growing every week because we did quality work and we did it on time. Even then I wouldn't accept any less than the best from my workers. I made sure every member of my crew knew how to do the work, even if that meant teaching them myself. I also made sure they understood that we would cut no corners. *None.*

All things being equal, your success and profitability is related to the quality of your work, and the quality of your work determines the kind of reputation you will carry. A bad reputation can kill a business and a career. In business your good name is your most important asset. I've never been a jealous person—until it comes to my reputation. I don't want anyone to be able to say a bad thing about me or the quality of my work. Even back in college, I made sure my employees understood that. Friend or not, I'd drop any or all of them fast before I'd let them hurt my reputation because of shoddy workmanship.

My insistence on delivering quality work paid off immediately. Before long we were doing three or four different jobs simultaneously. We were young and making money and we were thrilled. Business grew to the point that we were grossing $300 to $400 per week, which in today's dollars is about $3,000 a week. As the requests for our crafts-manship rolled in, we thought the sky was the limit.

As it turned out, it was our very success that did us in.

In a small town like Tuskegee there was only so much work to go around. For years the demand for any kind of construction work was pretty well balanced across a couple of local contractors. That was the way it was and it seemed to work for everyone involved. But when my crew and I came on the scene and word got out about the quality of our work, we totally upset the balance.

Instead of calling the local contractors they had used for years, folks starting calling us. And they kept calling. Eventually, so many folks called on us that the local contractors experienced a big drop in their business. Tuskegee was a close-knit town; all the contractors knew each other, so it was inevitable that they started talking about us. When they compared notes they realized that we were the reason their fortunes had changed. They decided to "do something about them college boys."

When I started working in the faculty members' homes I had no idea that it would turn into a business, so I never thought about legal matters like a business license. When the local contractors identified us as their common enemy, it didn't take long for them to learn that we were operating without the required paperwork.

One day the local sheriff visited a Russell job site. He was the stereotypical small-time white southern sheriff with his dusty boots and sunshades, slow southern drawl, and that peculiar mix of civility and arrogance.

I was in class at the time. Most of my fellow student workers were as well, so my brother Rogers was in charge of the crew.

"Who's the boy that's running things around here?" the sheriff drawled. When he said "boy" it had nothing to do with age.

Rogers stepped forward.

"I am, sheriff, sir," he said politely. He knew he had better be polite. This was a *southern* sheriff. "Is there a problem, sir?"

The sheriff spat a brown glob of tobacco juice no more than an inch from my brother's boot.

"Yeah, boy. There's a problem awright. You boys are operating in this town without a *bidness la-cense*. We got laws around here. Don't you boys know that you need a *la-cense* to do *bidness* in this town?"

Rogers could feel there was more coming, so he quickly tried to placate the sheriff. "No, sir, sheriff, we didn't know. But we'll be glad to get a license just as soon as we can, sir. I'll go down to the city hall building right now."

The sheriff spat again.

"It's too late for that now, boy. You done broke the law."

"But we didn't know, sir. We—"

The sheriff cut him off.

"I don't care. You done broke the law, I said. By this time tomorrow I want y'all to be gone."

Rogers knew better than to protest.

"OK. Yes, sir, we're closing this job down right now."

The sheriff took off his sunglasses and looked Rogers right in the eye.

"I don't mean gone from this job. I mean gone from this town. You understand me *now*?"

Rogers nodded.

"Yes, sir. I understand."

"*Awwwright* then. I don't care where you go, but you got to get on away from here. Tomorrow this time, you'd best be gone. You don't want to find out what's going to happen if you ain't."

When a white Alabama sheriff told you to get out of town . . . *or else* in the Jim Crow South, there was nothing to do but get out of town. There was no asking for another chance and there was no one to appeal to. Rogers knew it. He just said yes, sir, packed up our tools and supplies as fast as he could, and caught the next bus home to Atlanta.

It meant that we wouldn't get paid for our time or our materials. But that sure beat the alternative, whatever it was. Luckily, I wasn't there or I might have had to leave school and go back home with Rogers. But by the time I heard what happened, Rogers was already on his way out of town.

Looking back now, I don't think that sheriff would have physically harmed us over a simple business dispute. He probably was just trying to scare us. But it worked. The prospect of spending even one night in a southern jail was almost as frightening as the grave for a young black man.

■ □ ■

In my youth, Walter A. Aiken was the largest African American builder in Atlanta. Everyone called him Chief because of his commanding manner. He was a large man with a serious demeanor. He didn't have to say a thing for folks to know that he was a man worthy of respect.

During the 1930s and '40s, Mr. Aiken built a successful construction company from the ground up. Mr. Aiken's firm developed a large housing subdivision on the west side of Atlanta called Hunter Hills. It was built on one hundred acres and encompassed fifty-two houses. That was a major achievement for any builder, but for a black builder to do it at a time when black folks were by law second-class citizens was extraordinary. Mr. Aiken was also a pioneer in FHA housing. And if that wasn't enough to recommend him, Mr. Aiken also coached the Clark College football team.

I admired him greatly for his ingenuity and drive because it took courage and vision to develop real estate projects on a scale that had never before been undertaken in the Atlanta real estate market. I looked at Mr. Aiken and knew he was the kind of businessman I someday wanted to be.

That's why one of those memorable days at Tuskegee for me was when Mr. Aiken came to campus and talked to students. I arrived early and sat in the first row soaking up every word. His presentation was absolutely inspiring, and after the speech I had the opportunity to talk to him. It must have seemed to him like I had a hundred questions about building and construction, but he answered every one. What I learned from him that day about the nuts and bolts of the construction business was priceless. By the time he left campus, I was convinced that the sky was the limit for me.

■ □ ■

When my plastering business was in full swing I learned to schedule my time and schoolwork to free me up to do the plastering jobs. When the sheriff shut us down, I suddenly found myself with a lot of free time. I couldn't study every minute, and although I really liked the girls I wasn't the type to waste much more time chasing them.

Instead, I decided to focus my energy on Army Reserve Officers Training Corps (ROTC), which Tuskegee required all male students to enlist in whether they planned to go on to formal military service or not.

ROTC took up much of my free time. We had drills every morning and every evening, rain or shine. Every Sunday we marched to chapel, we boys in our military uniforms and the girls in white nurse uniforms with little white caps. Chapel services were mandatory then for every Tuskegee student. From my high school football days I had learned to enjoy this feeling of being part of a team.

The ROTC program was well thought of because of the discipline it taught. What impressed me most about it, though, was that cadets got to wear those snazzy military uniforms. I liked the fellowship and discipline of ROTC training, but I truly loved parading around campus in my olive green uniform—dark green jacket, beige shirt, dark beige trousers, and our heads crowned with a green beret.

No other black college in the Deep South had a ROTC program. That was another point of pride at Tuskegee. But there was an additional benefit as well: no other young men from black colleges had access to the handsome uniforms we wore. My buddy Bill and I thought our uniforms looked extra handsome . . . because we were wearing them! Good-looking guys in good-looking uniforms—that was a double whammy as far as we were concerned. We were legends in our own minds.

One semester break we decided to show off our ROTC uniforms to college students—that is, the female student bodies—back home in Atlanta. Bill and I were so tight—we were what in those days were called "cut buddies"—that we decided to take the young female population of Atlanta by storm, together.

We rode home in Felker's car, and by the time we arrived in Atlanta we had thoroughly convinced ourselves that we had been anointed to conquer the female world. We were sure that our uniforms would make us even more desirable to young black women than we already were, because we weren't just Herman and Bill; we were Herman and Bill *in uniform*. We didn't take them off the whole time we were home except to sleep and bathe. We strutted around Atlanta like we were real soldiers.

We convinced ourselves that we looked so sharp that no girl would be able to resist us. After all, while there were four black colleges in Atlanta, there was not one military uniform among them.

After we dropped our bags at home in Summerhill, Bill asked, "Where do you want to go first?"

I knew *exactly* where I wanted to go.

"Let's go to Clark." We both laughed.

Today it is Clark Atlanta University, a well-respected, co-ed liberal arts school. But back then it was Clark College, and all Kimbrough and I cared about was that it was full of smart, cultured, ambitious, curvy young women, what the guys called "built from the ground up."

We'd gotten a little rumpled on the ride home so we pressed our uniforms, shined our shoes, creased our pants to a sharp knife's edge, cocked our caps at just the right angle, and set off to make the Clark College girls swoon.

There was another reason I wanted to go to Clark: a young lady named Evelyn. We'd met and talked a few times before I left for Tuskegee. I told her I'd look her up when I was home. I knew Evelyn liked me and would be glad to see me, but I was feeling pretty cocky, so I decided to really cement things by impressing her girlfriends and maybe making her a little jealous in the process. And it worked. The girls were smiling at Bill and me and whispering and giggling among themselves. What we didn't realize was that not all of them were whispering because they thought we were handsome. Some were talking about "the two fools" parading around trying to look cute.

At the time, Evelyn wasn't any more aware of what those girls were thinking than we were. As far as she knew, all the girls wanted us. It didn't take long for her to get tired of the attention her classmates were giving us. She turned to one of them and said loudly enough for all the girls to hear, "You better stop looking at my boyfriend."

I found out later that the classmate to whom Evelyn said that was a young woman named Otelia Hackney. Otelia chuckled and said, "I don't want that fool, strutting around like a peacock," and walked away laughing.

But Bill and I knew nothing about that then. As far as we were concerned, we were a big hit. We met enough young ladies who were impressed by our exaggerated military demeanor and the little salutes we gave each other to convince us that *all* the girls felt that way.

We had a ball that whole semester break. By the time we had to leave for school we had gotten so much attention that we thought we were twin Billy Eckstines.* Lord knows we hated to leave all that feminine admiration behind, but it was time for us big-time soldiers to become civilians again. So we packed our bags, returned to school, hung up our uniforms, and went back to cracking our schoolbooks.

A couple months later, a friend of my older brother Robert's wife, Ruth, complained that she had lost her watch at a basketball game. The young woman was a student, so it was a major loss for her because she didn't have the money to replace it. Ruth commiserated with her for a little while, then suddenly brightened up.

"I'm going to introduce you to my brother-in-law, Herman," Ruth said. "He's a student, too, but Herman always has money. He gave his last girlfriend a sewing machine."

For any single girl in those days that was a big deal.

"A sewing machine? Really?"

"Oh, yes. Herman always has money. If you two hit it off, maybe he'll give you a watch for Christmas."

Even though my Tuskegee business was gone, I was still receiving rental income from my duplex, and I did plastering work with my father during the summers and on breaks from school when I wasn't playing Casanova alongside Bill. Plus, I had been saving money since I was a child, so Ruth was right—I always had cash in my pocket.

The next time I saw Ruth, she told me about this pretty college girl she knew and how nice it would be for me to meet her. A few weeks later she tried to act casual when she told me her girlfriend would also

---

*Billy Eckstine was, for all intents and purposes, the black Frank Sinatra, his smooth voice, good looks, and excellent taste making him popular with black and white audiences beginning in the 1940s and continuing for decades after.

be there on a night she knew I was coming over for dinner, but we all knew this was really a blind date. A setup was fine by me, though. I was excited from the moment Ruth told me that she had an attractive young lady for me to meet, because Ruth knew the kind of young lady I liked: smart and pretty and fun-loving, but serious about life, too.

I'm sure her friend was excited as well, at least at the prospect of a new watch. Of course, I knew nothing about that then.

I got there first. I have always believed in being on time, which, for me, usually means arriving early. You can't miss anything by being early. Sometimes you'll learn something while you're waiting that will give you a better sense of who you're meeting with, particularly in business settings. What is really important, though, is that being on time says that you are in control of yourself and your situation. That's an important statement to make in any setting.

Ruth and I chatted for a while. Ruth was a lovely person and I always enjoyed talking to her, but I have to admit that on that evening she didn't have my full attention. My mind was on who was soon to appear through Ruth's front door. My sense of anticipation was just starting to turn to impatience when the doorbell rang. I took a deep breath to relax and to appear cool, but *man*! My heart was jumping like a grasshopper on a skillet. The mystery young lady and my sister-in-law didn't make it any easier for me. They took their time whispering and giggling in the hallway. It seemed like they were going to talk out there *forever*. I cleared my throat and made a little noise hoping that might hurry them along. It didn't.

Finally, my sister-in-law ushered her friend into the living room. I stood like the gentleman my mama had raised me to be.

Ruth said, "Otelia Hackney, this is my brother-in-law, Herman Russell."

I flashed my most charming smile. What I saw was a beautiful and poised young woman.

But what Otelia Hackney saw was the cocky young guy she'd laughed at on the campus of Clark College as he strutted around in his ROTC uniform, the one she called "a peacock" and "a fool." Her eyes opened wide—I thought it was because she was surprised at how good-looking I was. Suddenly she frowned, threw up her hands, said, "Oh Lord, what am I doing here?" and started for the door.

Ruth looked at me as if to ask, *Herman, what have you done now?*

I wondered the same thing.

Ruth rushed out and caught Otelia at the front door. In the meantime, I looked myself up and down, made sure my zipper wasn't opened and my breath wasn't tart, but I didn't have a clue what went wrong. In the hallway Ruth was furiously whispering something. Otelia, however, wasn't concerned about being subtle. That's how I found out what was wrong. Otelia said it out loud.

"Ruth, *that's* the fool I told you about, strutting around campus like Groucho Marx in a military suit. I don't want *anything* to do with a *fool* like that."

"Oh, he's not so bad, Otelia," Ruth said, defending me—sort of. "And don't forget the watch."

Otelia didn't care. "I'll go without a watch from now until doomsday before I'd have a date with *that* fool."

Ruth started whispering again. I had no idea what watches had to do with anything. Ruth was whispering real low now, but I could hear enough to know that she was pleading. Finally Otelia said, "Oh, *all right!*" and marched back into the living room. She plopped down on the sofa with her arms folded. I sat in the armchair opposite her feeling like a hang-tongued dog.

At dinner, Otelia was cordial, which only meant that she'd been raised with manners, because it was clear that she was none too pleased to still be in my company. However she felt, I immediately liked her very much. I wasn't just intrigued because she was a challenge. I could sense that she was someone special.

On the other hand, Otelia had made it clear that she wanted nothing to do with me. But like I said, I have never been a quitter. I don't care how much the odds are against me if I believe a goal is worthy of my efforts. And if anyone was worthy, it was the beautiful young lady before me. Her spunk, her self-assurance, and her clarity about the kind of people she wanted in her life told me that.

I spent the rest of the evening trying to demonstrate to Otelia that I was different from that guy she'd found so obnoxious. It wasn't easy, but I must have made some headway, because by the end of the night she had given me her address and telephone number.

That was in August. By Christmas, Otelia had her watch.

■ □ ■

One of Otelia's sisters, Marva Hackney, remembered my future wife not being in any big hurry to find a husband. Their daddy was trying to nudge Otelia along to set a date with me but she could be as stubborn with him as with anyone else.

"I've got time enough," she said.

"You may not have as much time as you *think* you do," Mr. Hackney said.

She said, "Well, I'm not in no big hurry. I don't need to hook him necessarily. He'll be around."

She was *real* confident.

II

H.J. Russell & Company: Atlanta's Do-It-All Contractor

4

Black Entrepreneurship
Takes Hold, Part 1

E ven as I received my Certificate of Masonry from Tuskegee in
1953, events back home in Atlanta took precedence in my life and
decisions.*

My daddy's health was getting worse, and I had little choice but
to step up. It was, after all, what I'd spent my life training to do, but
instead of being an option upon graduation it became a necessity.

Even though he tried to do a full day's work, he just couldn't do it
any longer. When it was clear that he wouldn't get any better, he made
the hard decision to retire and to turn his entire operation over to me—
his tools, his truck, his customers, everything.

---

*Years later I also received a number of other degrees, including an honorary
doctorate from my alma mater, now known as Tuskegee University.

Even though I was the youngest of eight siblings, I was the one uniquely positioned and trained to take over my daddy's enterprise. My brothers had pursued other interests while I remained active in his plastering business. I was saddened that he and I would not be working together. My parents relied on the income that the plastering business produced. And other families whose husbands and fathers worked for my daddy were also at risk of losing their livelihoods.

I took charge of my father's operation and named it the H.J. Russell Plastering Co., Inc. I bought a used pickup truck and we operated out of my parents' basement, where I stored my wheelbarrows and tools. The biggest difference between the business run by my daddy and the one I put into action was that I was determined to take it to the next level.

From day one, I offered plastering services to general contractors all over the city of Atlanta. I'd either visit them at their offices or on-site at their building projects. And, thanks to my daddy's existing reputation and my own experience in business and as a Tuskegee graduate, the new business was a quick success. The crew began with myself and two others, Billy Mitchell and Charles Wynn; by the end of the first year there were seven of us on the payroll.

■ □ ■

Even as I sought plastering jobs, I pursued an expansion of my real estate holdings, buying land and building on it as soon as possible, creating a stream of rental income.

My projects were mostly residential homes and medium-sized apartment buildings ranging in size from eight to twenty-four units. As the size of the projects continued to grow, so did my personnel. Soon I hired a bookkeeper and a full-time secretary.

I bought a parcel in Summerhill that particularly excited me: it was adjacent to the land where I used to have my shoeshine parlor. I built a large tool house and stored my growing inventory of supplies and equipment in it. By 1956 things were going so well it seemed H.J. Russell & Company needed to lease more office and warehouse space every month.

I've never minded spending money for necessary things; after all, you have to be willing to spend money in order to make money. But after a certain point, spending money to rent space in other people's buildings made no sense when one of H.J. Russell's lines of work was constructing commercial buildings.

Around this time, I took what was a huge step for a young man: I constructed the H.J. Russell Building to consolidate all of our operations into one headquarters, a sturdy brick building on the corner of Northside and Fair Streets in Atlanta with four offices and a warehouse for our equipment and materials. Outside the warehouse we even installed our own gas pump. Black folks owned very little commercial property in those days, so a black man constructing his own office building was a big event in Atlanta's African American community.

When the building was completed we held a big gala open house. In those days we didn't believe in hors d'oeuvres and little finger foods. For folks used to hearty eating, that stuff was just enough to make you mad. Instead, we served fried chicken, potato salad, macaroni and cheese, and homemade cakes and pies.

I invited my family and the firm's clients, most of whom were white, and several city officials to the opening. No one said much about business, except when I made a little speech to mark the occasion. We—Otelia and I, our family and guests—just talked and laughed and enjoyed ourselves. In many ways, it felt like a reunion.

Consolidating all of our operations was a huge step forward. It announced to the business community that H.J. Russell & Company was a serious player and that we were here to stay.

■ □ ■

Two years later, the company really took off.

By then, we had already built four four-unit and four eight-unit rental properties. Those were nice, profitable properties, but they were only the beginning—test runs, if you will. I was confident that I could successfully build and manage properties of that size, so there was no reason I couldn't develop larger ones.

I found the perfect parcel on Verbena Street in the Dixie Hill section of northwest Atlanta. I built a twenty-four-unit luxury apartment complex there.

Because this would be the first signature property of H.J. Russell & Company, I wanted a classy look, settling on a New Orleans red brick exterior with handrails around the terrace. I'd always admired that style and it was rare in Atlanta at the time, which added to its appeal.

The Verbena Street development got a lot of attention. It was one of the nicer rental properties open to black people in Atlanta. What caused even more interest was that the developer—*me*—was still in his twenties. With all the excitement it generated, Verbena Street became the chic place for black folks to live in Atlanta. Applications flooded in. Every apartment was rented long before construction was completed, with a long waiting list of hopefuls. By any measure, Verbena Street was a major success.

Among the first tenants was my old high school friend Vernon Jordan, just starting his career as a thirty-five-dollar-a-week lawyer back home in Atlanta, and his new bride, Shirley. Vernon always reminds me of that, too! As a young couple starting a family, he and Shirley had economic challenges, but he always paid his rent on time. To this day he still kids about it.

"Herman was my first landlord," he said. "Sometimes my check to the diaper service bounced, but I made sure Herman's rent checks never did!"

After our Verbena Street success it was clear that we had the infrastructure in place to go on to bigger things. We took another big step in 1961, building a one-hundred-unit luxury apartment complex called Paradise.

Paradise Apartments didn't have the classy New Orleans design of Verbena Street, but it was still a nice luxury development. It was also the largest built to date by an African American in Atlanta, and it was fully rented soon after completion.

I consider myself a builder, so I didn't want H.J. Russell & Company to spend its time and resources managing our properties and collecting rents when we should be out building. For several years we engaged a real estate management firm to do that for us. But with the completion of Paradise, we now owned so many rental units that we paid a small fortune in management fees. I decided that H.J. Russell & Company would manage our own properties and pay ourselves the fee. To make sure that the real estate management business didn't get in the way of our construction business, we formed a subsidiary, Paradise Management.

By 1962 we added a couple of four-hundred-unit complexes to our holdings. H.J. Russell & Company's real estate holdings swelled to more than fifteen hundred units throughout Atlanta. Paradise Management alone had more than forty employees.

I was all of thirty-two years old.

Forming my own management company was a great business decision. It saved a huge amount of money and significantly widened our profit margins. But we were now paying almost $250,000 a year for insurance on our various properties, which, while a fair amount of money now, was an especially huge number in the 1960s.

I made another leap of faith and decided that we would eliminate the middleman and become an insurance agency for our own properties. I rented space in the Citizens Trust Bank building, and our next company, Interstate Insurance, was born.

At first we only handled H.J. Russell & Company properties. But soon we realized that Interstate could do more than save money for us; it could also *make* money by serving others without any significant additional capital outlay for us. Interstate became a significant profit center.

■ □ ■

In 1967, H.J. Russell & Company was a plastering and fireproofing subcontractor on the Equitable Insurance Company Building, one of the first large buildings to be built in downtown Atlanta. It was the largest subcontracting opportunity to date for any African American firm, and we won in an open bid process.

We competed for that job against one of my white friends, E. L. Thompson, who owned the largest plastering and fireproofing company in the Southeast. He called me and suggested that I had made a mistake in the bid.

"Herman," he said, "this isn't sour grapes, but I think you should look at your bid again. The margins on our bids are razor-thin as it is. If your bid is less than ours you must be losing money. If I were you I'd call the general contractor and tell him that you made a mistake in your figures." I stayed up all that night reviewing our bid but I could not find any mistakes that I, nor my staff, had made.

There was a problem, however, once work was in progress. Fire erupted on the twenty-fourth floor during construction. Fortunately, we were ahead of schedule and had already fireproofed several floors above it, which kept the fire from spreading.

The Equitable Building project ended up being one of the most successful jobs that we had ever done as a subcontractor. We made a good margin off that job thanks to lower overhead costs, and we received recognition for being ahead of schedule and thereby saving much of the building from the fire. It became a springboard for us to enter the big time and be recognized for our capabilities.

■ □ ■

I'm often asked how I could have owned a portfolio of almost two thousand rental units, a property management company, and an insurance agency before the age of forty. The answer is easy: I didn't spend money on showy, expensive offices. I didn't do a lot of unnecessary travel. I didn't spend my money on expensive clothes and jewelry. I didn't eat in expensive restaurants and I didn't drive expensive cars. I didn't even buy a car or move out of my parents' home until I was twenty-six. I held onto my earnings and reinvested in my company—and myself. That increased my return on investment (ROI) manyfold.

5

Otelia Hackney: A Black Woman Emerges

I was about twenty-five when I decided it was time.

Otelia and I dated for more than three years before I asked for her hand. By then she had graduated from Clark and was teaching school in Atlanta and living there with her sister Nell. That's what people did then. She was one of eight siblings—she had two brothers and five sisters—and the married older sisters looked after the younger ones until they got married. And before a young lady could marry, her prospective husband had to visit her parents to seek their permission. Few young ladies in black communities in the South would marry if their parents denied them permission. Otelia accepted my proposal, but it wasn't final until her parents said so.

On a Sunday in June 1955, Otelia took me to her parents' home so I could ask for their blessing. They lived in a little place called Union Point, in Georgia's Taliaferro County, which was way out in the country. But they weren't country hicks. Although he never went to college, Otelia's father, Miles Hackney Sr., was the county agricultural agent—he was the only African American in the position. It was his job to instruct black farmers on how to get the highest crop yields from their land. This included teaching them the latest agricultural techniques and making them familiar with the best ways to protect their crops against pests and plant diseases. As you might imagine, Mr. Hackney was a popular man in those parts.

When we arrived at her parents' home, Otelia led me into the sitting room where the Hackneys were waiting. Otelia's family home was quite impressive; it was nothing like the little house in Summerhill that I grew up in. It was located on a farm of more than 130 acres. The house featured a living room, dining room, four bedrooms, and a full kitchen. There was beautiful wall paneling throughout the house. It had sizable front and back porches. And it was the only house in the area with its own paved road.

The Hackneys were pleasant and talkative people, but they rarely responded when I made a point or asked a question. They just looked at me and smiled. I was happy that they were so pleasant because it made it easier at the end of the evening to ask if I could marry their daughter. Of course they were expecting it, but I still had to ask *twice* before they gave their permission.

When we left that night, Mrs. Hackney gave me a big hug and Mr. Hackney shook my hand and called me son. On our way out, however, Otelia's father called her back for a moment. She told me later that he looked at her with confusion written all over his face.

"What's wrong, Daddy?"

He shook his head.

"Otelia, he seems like a nice young man, but I could hardly understand a word he said. What language was he speaking, French or German?"

▪ ☐ ▪

I was a hard worker, a gentleman, and always generous with Otelia. But our courtship wasn't always easy for her.

Years later, I learned from an old neighborhood friend, Ella Yates, that several young ladies tried to talk Otelia out of marrying me. They didn't think I was good enough for her because of my speech impediment. But Otelia Hackney always had her own mind.

"As long as *I* can understand him," she told them, "don't you worry about it."

And that was that.

▪ ☐ ▪

One day, my wife made the typical Otelia-like observation that "if the company can build beautiful homes for others, it should do the same for us."

So before our wedding took place, we hired architect J. W. Robinson to design our dream house. Then I built it on South Avenue. I gave more than my best work to our new home; I built it with love. It was a stucco residence with a finished basement that housed my office, a recreation room, and a full kitchen. Upstairs there were two bedrooms, living room, dinette, and the main kitchen. This was not only my first house, it was also our pride and joy. We finished building and furnishing it a week before the wedding. So much of us went into it.

Otelia Hackney and I were married on August 19, 1956, at Allen Temple AME Church. Both sets of our parents were there. Otelia was beautiful in her formal white wedding gown. And you couldn't tell me I wasn't the sharpest dressed man in town in my white dinner jacket and formal black satin-trimmed slacks.

Otelia's sister Nell and her husband hosted a reception at their home. We were not extravagant people. Instead of being luxurious, our wedding reflected what we valued and how we planned to live: with warmth, laughter, and great love in the midst of our family and friends. Other than the births of my children, that was the happiest occasion of my life.

▪ □ ▪

After the wedding reception, Otelia and I flew to Montreal for our honeymoon. It was my first trip out of the country. My wife and I were very excited. We boarded an Eastern Airlines flight full of anticipation. After a five-hour trip, we stepped off the plane holding hands with faces full of smiles. We hailed a taxi to take us from the airport to our hotel in downtown Montreal. As we wound our way through the streets, we marveled at the beautiful Old World architecture. There was no mistaking that we were tourists. We pointed and gawked the whole way.

With all the grandeur we were seeing we couldn't wait to bask in the luxury and charm of our honeymoon hotel. We thanked our lucky stars that our travel agent had had the foresight to book us into a grand hotel in downtown Montreal like these. At least that's what we thought.

As we continued to admire the beautiful facades of brick and stone through the open car windows, our taxi suddenly stopped in front of a dinky little building. We didn't hurry him, though. His little detour would give us more time to admire the city. We just sat there chatting happily.

Finally, the driver turned us.

"Monsieur."

I answered, "Yes, sir?"

"Monsieur, we are here."

I looked at the tired-looking little building we were sitting in front of.

"*Here?* Where?"

"This is your hotel, monsieur."

I shook my head.

"No, sir. There must be a mistake. Our travel agent said we were staying in a quaint, charming hotel." I pulled our itinerary from the travel agent out of my pocket. That's exactly what it said: "a quaint, charming hotel." Then I looked at the address listed for our quaint, charming hotel and felt sick. This little rundown, nondescript, decrepit-looking place *was* our hotel, the place where we would be spending our honeymoon.

I couldn't believe it. We had dreamed of our honeymoon trip for months and months. I wanted to make sure we had wonderful surroundings to spend together as husband and wife. Instead, the travel agent had booked us into a little place so dreary that even a blind man would have been disappointed. But he was in Atlanta with our money and we were stuck in low-rent Montreal motel hell.

Otelia and I commiserated for a while, assigning the travel agent a few choice nicknames, but we knew none of that would change things, so after we got over our initial shock, we decided to make the best of it. We were relieved that at least there was no problem with our reservation. Our room was not the presidential suite, but it would have to do. We unpacked and decided to unwind with our first honeymoon meal delivered to us by room service. We looked for a menu, but we couldn't find one, so we called the front desk. That's when we got the next bad news.

"Room service? Monsieur, we have no room service."

"No room service? How can you be a hotel and not have room service? My bride and I are hungry, man. What are we supposed to do?"

All he could say was "Sorry, monsieur." But sorry wasn't going to quiet our growling stomachs. I asked where we could go to get some dinner. And there he was again with his "Sorry, monsieur."

But he wasn't as sorry as we were, because by that time all the restaurants in the area had closed. We hadn't eaten since breakfast so we weren't just a little hungry—we were starving. Our stomachs were competing to see which could growl the loudest.

I went from floor to floor looking for a vending machine so we could at least have a snack, but the hotel didn't have one. I had all but given up finding anything for my new bride and me to eat when one of the hotel employees saw me roaming around and felt sorry for me.

"Wait here, monsieur, I will see what I can find for you."

I was praying that he could find a couple of nice steaks. He was gone for a good little while. When returned he was smiling like he *had* found a couple of steaks for us.

"Here, monsieur," he said proudly.

My mouth was just beginning to water when he handed me two cheese sandwiches. That was our first honeymoon meal. And they weren't even *good* cheese sandwiches. In fact, those were the worst cheese sandwiches we had ever tasted.

But things did get better. Not even those nasty cheese sandwiches could put a damper on our honeymoon night. The next morning we had a nice breakfast at a café across the street, then spent the rest of the day enjoying the sights of Montreal.

The next few evenings were even more enjoyable. One night we saw a fantastic show by singer Della Reese. She sang every love song like she was singing only to us. Another night we took a romantic boat ride down the Saint Lawrence River. All the other passengers spoke only French and we spoke only English, but that didn't matter. We all laughed and carried on together.

Our honeymoon had a rough start, but all and all it turned out to be wonderful. But to this day I still don't have much use for cheese sandwiches.

■ □ ■

Otelia didn't care about petty things. But what did really, really bother her?

When we started courting I didn't have a car to drive her around in, just an old pickup truck. I could have traded the truck in for a car, but I was more concerned with business than appearances. Even after I made my first million, I would not part with my old pickup truck. I wasn't just being cheap. I was following my father's advice.

"You can't make money with a car," he said. "But with a truck you can."

Like every other piece of advice that he gave me, I took this line to heart.

The whole time I courted Otelia, we rode in that pickup truck. It ran well, but it did look pretty beat up. It was embarrassing for Otelia to pull up to a party in a pretty dress in that old truck. Over and over she said, "Herman, why don't you get a car so we can ride like normal people?"

But I wouldn't budge. My unwillingness to buy a car didn't sit well with Otelia. She was tired of being embarrassed. She retaliated by making me park the truck a block from our destination, out of sight. Then she would fuss all the way to the door. Even so, it was still a long time before I bought a car. Otelia didn't like being embarrassed like that, but she knew I was building for the future, so she hung in there and she began to focus on that future, too.

The business was really growing and Otelia had become a firm source of support—she was now keeping my books and helping me with the payroll. I finally decided that we could commit some of our resources to a decent car. Otelia was thrilled.

"We're finally going to go out in a car like normal people," she said. I laughed, but she was only half joking.

We went from car dealer to car dealer and looked at every make and model of automobile in our price bracket. I looked under every hood and asked about every feature. The car salesmen weren't used to so many questions. And the fact that it was a young black man who was asking the questions didn't make them feel any better about it. They would have rather I just got carried away and made a snap judgment, but I never make decisions based on appearances.

Otelia was getting a little impatient, too, but I wasn't going to spend my money until I was sure I was spending it on the car that suited me best, inside and out.

Finally, Otelia and I talked about it and made our decision. The Buick dealer's eyes glazed over when we walked into his showroom—yet again. He probably thought, Here's this worrisome couple again, come to take up my time. He was shocked that we were ready to make a purchase. He almost fainted when I paid for the car in cash. I'll bet he was never impatient with a customer again.

It was a beautiful car. Everywhere we went, people stopped to admire it. You see, there weren't a lot of black folks with new cars in the Deep South in those days. But not only did my new car get a lot of attention from admirers, it caught the attention of the police, too.

It wasn't just the *car* that caught the eye of the police. To them its most glaring feature probably was not that it was a gleaming new Buick; it was a gleaming new Buick driven by a young black man.

Otelia and I were on our way to visit my parents. I'd always been a careful driver, but I'd become even more careful after I bought a new car with my own hard-earned money. I made sure I drove within the speed limit, observed every traffic sign, stopped—not paused, *stopped*—at every intersection, and looked both ways twice before proceeding. I was determined not to get a scratch on that car. I didn't even want a gnat to land on it.

But no matter how careful you are, you can't control the behavior of other people. I was reminded of that fact when some no-driving joker rear-ended my new car just as I turned into my parents' yard. I made sure that Otelia was all right, then I jumped out to see if there was any damage to my new car. Well, it certainly didn't look new any more. My right rear fender was crumpled. I couldn't believe it. I was mad and sad at the same time, but there was nothing I could do but call the police to take the accident report. It wasn't too long before two young white police officers drove up. The officers eased through the crowd of neighbors that had gathered to gawk and gossip. That was when they saw the new Buick. They couldn't hide their surprise at seeing an expensive new automobile in Summerhill.

One of the officers barked, "Whose car is this?"

I raised my hand. "It's mine."

"*Your* car?" one of them asked. New automobile and young black man: that was an impossibility for them. They just couldn't imagine those two together, especially in Summerhill. He looked at his partner, they both looked me up and down, then the officer asked in a menacing tone, loudly enough for everybody in the crowd to hear, "Boy, are you in the numbers business or the liquor business?"

I was livid. I had called the police for assistance, but instead of offering to help, this one was questioning me like I was some kind of criminal. And I sure didn't like his insinuation that a young black man couldn't acquire nice possessions with smarts, hard work, and discipline. Apparently it was their opinion that if anyone who looked like me accomplished anything it had to be by theft or deceit. It was all I could do to keep my cool, but I wasn't about to hold my tongue. I took a breath and looked that policeman dead in the eye.

"Both," I said. I made no effort to hide my displeasure. "Both. I run numbers *and* sell liquor."

The officer turned red as a beet. The crowd burst into laughter. Folks in Summerhill didn't get much chance to poke fun at white folks, so they laughed until they cried. The more they laughed, the redder that policeman got. I'm sure he would have loved to teach someone a hard lesson for laughing at a white cop, but so many people were laughing that he probably didn't know where to start. After a while he just turned and got back into his car without a word. He left his partner to fill out the accident report. With that officer I was cordial and cooperative because that's the way he treated me.

That's how I've always handled racism. I didn't argue or call names. I stood tall, kept my dignity, and showed no fear because I knew I hadn't done a thing wrong.

■ □ ■

Otelia and I had a number of run-ins with the authorities while we were courting. After all, it was the segregated South. You couldn't escape the effects of racism. Another of these experiences stands out in my mind because it was so insulting.

One night Otelia and I decided to go to the Fox Theatre in downtown Atlanta to see a movie. I bought our tickets, then started the humiliating walk across the lobby to climb the stairs to the balcony, the crow's nest as whites called it, which was the only place black folks were allowed to sit in the Fox and in every other movie theater in the segregated South.

But for the Fox management, it was apparently not humiliating enough to force black folks to be hidden away in the crow's nest. An usher put up his hand and pointed to an alley.

"Y'all got to go *that* way."

We turned around and headed toward the alley thinking there we'd find a separate entrance to the lobby. When we reached the alley what we saw was black folks trudging up a three-story, open wrought iron staircase to the balcony. It was raining that night, so black folks had to stand in the rain with no shelter from the weather whatsoever waiting to climb that open staircase to enter the movie house.

By the time Otelia and I finally reached our seats, wet from the rain and sweaty from climbing the outdoor stairs, we were seething. I was angry all the way through the movie. I couldn't tell you what that movie was about if my life depended on it. I did know this, though: I would never submit anyone in my care to such humiliation again.

From that day until this, no member of our family has ever set foot in any place that refused to treat black folks with respect. There were a lot of great movies we missed, but one thing that was never missing was our sense of dignity and self-respect.

■ □ ■

We lived in our home on South Avenue for six years, until we built our next dream house at the corner of Waterford Road and Shorter Terrace in the Collier Heights area of Atlanta. It was the first community in Atlanta that African Americans built from the bottom up. I came in late and nobody wanted this sad corner lot. It was on a hill, but where other buyers saw inconvenience, I saw opportunity.

The house I built will fool you to look at it from outside. Once they get inside, visitors are always surprised how much else we built into that hill. Our new home was ten thousand square feet on two and a half acres of land and included five bedrooms and six bathrooms, an indoor swimming pool, and tennis and basketball courts. The dining and living rooms were spacious because Otelia and I were outgoing, socially minded people and we expected to do a lot of entertaining. For example, when Vernon Jordan left Atlanta to take over the United Negro College Fund in Washington, DC, I gave a big going-away party for him in that house.

That house was so beautifully designed and Otelia decorated it so tastefully that, years later, *Ebony* magazine showcased it in a feature story. Our house on Shorter Terrace was the most special because Otelia and I put so much of ourselves into it. We raised all three of our children in it—our youngest, Michael, was born there—and hosted many prominent figures there.

One day Vernon called me and said, "Herman, there's a young, dynamic general that's taken over Fort McPherson. I know him. I like him. I want you to call him and take him out for lunch."

I did just that, and General Colin Powell, the commander of the US Army Forces Command at Fort McPherson, and I went to lunch. We got to know each other and I told Colin whatever I could do, I'm just as near to him as the telephone. A month later, he invited Otelia and me to have dinner with him and his wife, Alma. I didn't know a general lived so well, you know? He had this nice home with servers and we really loved it.

From time to time after that we would take him and Alma out or go back to his place for official functions there. And when Colin was promoted to serve in the first Bush White House as chairman of the Joint Chiefs of Staff, we threw a memorable going-away bash for him at the Collier Heights house.

During the days of segregation in Atlanta and the Deep South, we hosted both blacks and whites in that home, formally and informally; it was one of the few integrated places to socialize in the city. In fact, it was the *only* place we could entertain guests because the hotels in downtown Atlanta would not open their doors to African Americans.

■ □ ■

Once our first child, Donata, was born in 1959, Otelia gave up her teaching job in Conyers, Georgia, and assumed full-time responsibility for raising the children.

Like most fathers of that era, I left early in the morning and worked long days away from home. I was always at PTA meetings when the children were little and, when they got involved in sports, I was always at their games. I was a hard-working father, but my children always knew I was there for them. I don't think I ever gave them reason to doubt my commitment to the family as primary in my life. Otelia was the one who nurtured the kids and drove them here and there. If there was a situation, I would intervene, but Donata, Jerome, and Michael knew that I would always support their mother.

There were certain family rituals that I never missed, including Friday night steak dinners during which Otelia and I and Donata, Jerome, and Michael would turn off the television and have extended rap sessions in which we'd all talk about whatever was going on in our lives—business, school, and play.

It would give them time to tell us whatever was on their minds. We learned from them; they learned from us. I taught them to be independent and work hard. I encouraged my children to equip themselves with the best education that they could receive because that knowledge would be with them for the rest of their lives. I told them that their education would be something that nobody could take away from them. People can take material things away, but never what you have learned. That's what really makes a difference in anyone's life.

■ □ ■

Of our three children, Donata—the firstborn—was always a motherly spirit. Jerome—the middle child—was more in the box. He tended to be kind of careful and take fewer chances on the unknown. Donata and Jerome are probably 70 percent like their mother, with Donata inheriting her mother's earthier persona and Jerome the nurturing components. Michael—the youngest—was more rambunctious, a little more free-spirited than the others. He was a risk-taker, always willing to try different things. Of the kids, he is probably the one who reflects both his parents' characteristics most evenly.

I am not afraid to admit that if the children got in serious trouble over the years, Otelia and I gave them a traditional whuppin'. Just knowing that was the start of punishment probably saved us from doing it too often, but there were times when we felt we had no choice. We were strict parents who maintained tight controls.

There was no doubt of the love found in our household, but we weren't a family of huggers, although we were certainly affectionate. We laughed a lot together; still do. The kids knew that there were certain things that were expected of them, that they were always expected to give their best effort and respect. They knew the importance of integrity, honesty, and respecting others.

III

Dr. King and the Civil Rights Movement

6

Swimming at the Deep End of Social Change

I decided at an early age to get active in Atlanta's civil rights struggle. I went to Wheat Street Baptist Church in November 1955 to hear the great civil rights lawyer (and future Supreme Court justice) Thurgood Marshall talk about the long struggle to victory in the *Brown vs. Board of Education of Topeka* case. I was so impressed with his commitment and that of his colleagues at the NAACP Legal Defense Fund to our people that the next day I bought a lifetime NAACP membership.*

---

*I didn't know it then, but I was the youngest person at that time to buy a lifetime membership. (While my children were still in grade school I bought lifetime memberships for each of them, too. Ironically, I was also the youngest person to buy lifetime memberships for children at that time.)

In those days, there were four major civil rights challenges:

(1) Protecting our gains in voting rights from segregationist state and local officials seeking to roll them back;

(2) Continuing to fight for desegregation of Atlanta's schools;

(3) Providing decent housing for Atlanta's growing black community; and

(4) Desegregating the city's public transportation.

We hadn't yet entered the protest and confrontation phase of the struggle with which most folks are more familiar. Our leaders still thought it was possible to accomplish the black community's goals through negotiated compromises and federal lawsuits. In retrospect, I think it was the right path for the times. If we had started out with protests and confrontations, the white community would not have gotten the opportunity to see the dignity and quiet determination of our leaders.

Without that familiarity, public protests appeared threatening to whites, which fueled a sometimes deadly backlash. Instead, our leadership's measured approach to social change left room for dialogue and, I like to think, gained the respect of some members of the white power structure. Not respect for respect's sake, but respect led to dialogue. And dialogue opened the door to change.

I chose to focus my own efforts on voter registration and pushing for better accommodations. I've never let outside activities distract me from my business; still, I gave a lot of time to movement activities.

As my business grew, so did my dedication within the movement. Its leaders knew I was committed to the struggle. Also, my mother's lessons about service and giving were so deeply a part of me that I let Reverend Martin Luther King Sr.—"Daddy King"—and other leaders of the movement know that I was committed to being a source of financial support for the movement whenever I was needed. This involvement moved me into the inner circle of the Atlanta civil rights movement.

■ □ ■

While much of black Atlanta was staging lunch counter sit-ins and protests in the 1960s, I was involved in a different, less visible way.

My commitment to the civil rights movement, coupled with my growing business empire, put me in a unique position to lead from behind. I knew Dr. Martin Luther King Jr. and his family all the way back to junior high school. Vernon Jordan, as I explained previously, was a few years behind me in the same school. Reverend Ralph Abernathy was someone I got to know as well. I met Andrew Young when he moved to Atlanta from New York in 1961 and began working with Dr. King and the Southern Christian Leadership Council. And through them, I came to know Reverend Jesse Jackson.

Atlanta had an established civil rights movement, led in part by Reverend Martin Luther King Sr., when his son Martin Luther King Jr. returned to the city. Together, this formidable group pursued nonviolent policies devoted to changing laws, hearts, and minds. These leaders specifically asked people such as fellow black businessman Quentin V. Williamson and myself *not* to march or participate in sit-ins. That wasn't *our* role in the 1960s. There were hundreds—often thousands—of students and other folks who did that, putting their lives on the line for the cause. We used our financial resources to bail the protestors out of jail when they were arrested.

Instead of our bodies, Williamson—who in 1965 became the first black man elected to the Atlanta Board of Aldermen—and I put our business careers and real estate holdings at risk for the movement. Other than parents bailing out their own kids when they could afford to do it, Williamson and I were the key ones working with the movement to bail out complete strangers.

▪ □ ▪

Lunch counter sit-ins staged by college students in Greensboro, North Carolina, inspired young people—black and white alike in many cases—across the country. In Atlanta, a group of students that included Lonnie King, Julian Bond, Herschelle Sullivan, Marian Wright (Edelman), Carolyn Long, and others organized the nonviolent Committee on Appeal for Human Rights (COAHR) to conduct similar lunch counter sit-ins.

In secret meetings at a Yates and Milton Drugstore, a popular local mainstay, they put together a document that outlined a civil rights strategy that was quite different from the approach of the old guard leadership.*

"An Appeal for Human Rights" was published on March 9, 1960, and called for direct action through sit-ins and demonstrations. Most significantly, the Appeal advocated making demands rather than holding negotiations. It read in part:

> We, the students of the six affiliated institutions forming the Atlanta University Center—Clark, Morehouse, Morris Brown, and Spelman Colleges, Atlanta University, and the Interdenominational Theological Center—have joined our hearts, minds, and bodies in the cause of gaining those rights which are inherently ours as members of the human race and as citizens of these United States.
>
> We pledge our unqualified support to those students in this nation who have recently been engaged in the significant movement to secure certain long-awaited rights and privileges. This protest, like the bus boycott in Montgomery, has shocked many people throughout the world. Why? Because they had not quite realized the unanimity of spirit and purpose which motivates the thinking and action of the great majority of the Negro people. The students who instigate and participate in these sit-down protests are dissatisfied, not only with the existing conditions, but with the snail-like speed at which they are being ameliorated. Every normal human being wants to walk the earth with dignity and abhors any and all proscriptions placed upon him because of race or color. In essence, this is the meaning of the sit-down protests that are sweeping this nation today.
>
> We do not intend to wait placidly for those rights which are already legally and morally ours to be meted out to us one at a time. Today's youth will not sit by submissively, while being denied all of the rights, privileges, and joys of life. We want to state clearly and unequivocally that we cannot tolerate, in a nation professing democracy and among people professing Christianity, the discriminatory

---

*A collection of the records from the Yates and Milton Drugstore can be found at the Auburn Avenue Research Library.

conditions under which the Negro is living today in Atlanta, Georgia—supposedly one the most progressive cities in the South.*

The *Atlanta Daily World*, the *Atlanta Constitution*, and the *Atlanta Journal* all published "An Appeal for Human Rights" in its entirety. Eventually it was published in the *New York Times* as well.

The appeal created quite an uproar. Students were energized by it, while the old guard black leaders thought it was too confrontational. Georgia governor Ernest Vandiver claimed that it was a "Communist-inspired document and that students couldn't have written it."

On March 15, 1960, students demonstrated their commitment to the appeal. COAHR led a series of extraordinary sit-ins at lunch counters and major retail establishments in downtown Atlanta to protest the businesses' unwillingness to serve black customers. One of their main targets was the A&P supermarket on Georgia Avenue, located in my old neighborhood. Most of the market's customers were black, including my family and me. Management enjoyed the fruits of their business but not enough to hire even one black supermarket employee. And lunch counters and cafeterias throughout the city were still segregated.

About two hundred students from Morehouse, Spelman, Clark, and Morris Brown Colleges took part in the public protests. Seventy-seven students were arrested. Later a judge added the names of the eight initial students who signed the appeal to the seventy-seven already in custody. He charged them all with breaching the peace, intimidating restaurant owners, refusing to leave private premises, and conspiracy.

As soon as I heard about the arrests I hurried to the police station.

So many civil rights marchers had been arrested for demonstrating in Atlanta on that single day that the court system couldn't handle the strain of providing due process. Attorney Donald L. Hollowell single-handedly represented everyone who participated in the sit-ins and the backlog of cases to be heard was enormous.

My old friend Vernon Jordan graduated from Howard University School of Law on a Friday during the first week of June 1960 and went

---

*Read the entire "An Appeal for Human Rights" online at http://www.atlanta studentmovement.org/An_Appeal_for_Human_Rights.html.

to work for Hollowell the following Monday. That very day, he was in Atlanta Municipal Courts with Hollowell getting student demonstrators out of jail.

The arrested young people had to appear in Fulton County Superior Court before Judge Durwood T. Pye, a known segregationist. Pye repeated the charges facing each defendant and ask them all the same three questions: "Are you in a position to post bond? Are you employed? Do you have enough money for the bond?"

Many of those arrested were unable to post bond. That's where Q. V. Williamson and I came in. The judge allowed each defendant to meet with Williamson or me prior to his or her case being called. As the defendants appeared before him, I posted their bond. We bailed out mostly poor, young, educated blacks who didn't have any fear of the white supremacists. But I bailed out anyone regardless of race if they were out on the front lines doing the right thing.

I asked the desk sergeant how much it would cost to post bail for *all* of the students. He told me the amount, probably expecting me to have to leave to raise the money.

"This should cover everyone," I said as I placed the completed form neatly on the counter. I signed a bond secured by several of my properties, then turned back to the desk sergeant. I have never seen surprise make a man's mouth open so wide. You could have put an apple in that desk sergeant's mouth and still had room for an orange. It was all I could do to keep a straight face.

The desk sergeant's surprise didn't last long, though. Soon he was seething, both because a black man had that kind of money and he didn't and because I didn't bow my head when I spoke to him. I'm sure he thought I was "uppity," and he would have loved to try to teach me a lesson, but there were too many witnesses. There was nothing he could do but write me a receipt and release the students.*

---

*The student protest was dramatized in the 2001 HBO movie *Boycott*, starring Jeffrey Wright as Dr. Martin Luther King Jr. and Terence Howard as Reverend Ralph Abernathy.

Meanwhile, Pye, a senior judge, decided that all of their cases would be heard before him a few weeks later and we would all return to court at the appointed time.

When that day arrived, the students—as well as their bondsmen, Williamson and me—appeared again before the judge. Pye became particularly frustrated with me because of the ease with which I was able to provide bail using my property holdings around the city as collateral. He didn't know me, didn't like what I was doing, and didn't like that I had the resources to do it. *Not one bit.*

"Looks like you got a lot of property here," he said. "How many pieces do you have?"

"I really don't know, Judge," I said. "But I'm going to use these for legitimate purposes here."

"Just tell me how much they're worth!" he demanded.

"'Bout a million, your honor," I said.

That stopped Judge Pye cold.

"I guess that'll do."

Pye could not believe that I had such substantial real estate holdings with such a high value. He even "invited" me to the stand to testify under oath, which I did. Pye was visibly torn that a man of color was able to shortcut his process of dishing out punishment to blacks and whites alike who dared challenge the segregation status quo.

The charges against the students eventually were dropped altogether. Not one student was ever tried. The property that Q. V. Williamson and I put up to secure the bond was safe. The students' protest demonstrations were successful as seventy-five individual and chain stores officially opened 177 lunch counters to black folks.

I'll never forget that day and I'll always remember that Hollowell and the others well knew what they were doing when they asked Williamson and me in advance to hang back and be prepared to open our wallets.

My friend Vernon Jordan said of those days:

During the civil rights movement, Herman was always there. He was never out front, though. He understood the difference between leadership and followship. He supported the leaders. He gave financial, moral, and material support. They knew he was one guy they could depend on.

There was no strategic move contemplated or executed that Herman did not know about. If there was an issue to be dealt with, whether it was by ACCA or the local branch of the NAACP or by Dr. King and his group, Herman knew about it.

There were assigned roles and functions. You didn't see Benjamin Mays* out in the street marching, either, but everybody knew what was going on and everybody understood their role and function. Much of the older conservative community thought the students were crazy until it was their grandchild in jail, or their nephew or niece, and then they had no choice.

The average person did not know of Herman's role behind the scenes because he was not the frontline leader. It was Martin and it was the student leaders, but the students knew where Herman was and how to find him. On the national scene, Martin was in the streets, Hollowell was in the courtroom with Thurgood [Marshall], and Whitney Young was in the boardroom, and they all coalesced to make something happen.

Herman was not in the publicity-seeking business. He was in the helping and support business. That was his role. People understood that he had to do his work to make his money so that he could be financially supportive of the movement.

▪ ☐ ▪

The civil rights movement in Atlanta was one of the most dynamic in the nation, although the Atlanta-based, black owned and operated newspaper, the *Atlanta Daily World*, which was founded in 1928 by William Alexander Scott, took a cautious and conservative approach to its reporting of racial politics.

---

*Benjamin Mays was best known for his tenure as president of Morehouse College. While there, his most famous student was Martin Luther King Jr., to whom he served as a mentor for the rest of his life. Mays also held leaderships posts with the NAACP, the Urban League, the YMCA, and other prominent groups.

The owners of the *Daily World* believed they had to be extra careful of what the paper published because it could lose valuable advertising by offending some people. The greatest way to intimidate most people was to take their meal ticket. Our generation of black leadership disagreed with such conservatism and published our own paper.

Times had changed. The caution and conservatism that had served us well in the past was no longer productive in the present. And the message certainly wasn't getting out through the mainstream dailies, the *Atlanta Journal* and the *Atlanta Constitution*. A younger generation of rights activists needed a new forum that was as politically bold as they were.

Jesse Hill and I were a decade older than the student activists who fueled the new civil rights offensive, but we shared their frustration and discontent with the black establishment's elders. When a group of students, including Julian Bond and Lonnie King, floated the idea of starting a weekly newspaper that would take a more aggressive stance on political issues, Dr. Clinton Warner Jr., Q. V. Jones, Jesse, and I put up the seed money to start the *Atlanta Inquirer*. We believed in the *Inquirer* so deeply that even though we were very busy executives, Dr. Warner, Jesse, and I each went door to door in the city's black neighborhoods selling subscriptions.

True to its mission, the *Atlanta Inquirer* became the voice of the civil rights movement in Atlanta. It kept the people informed of significant developments and inspired them to keep up the fight. We knew we had tapped into a need in the black community as the paper reached a circulation of fifteen thousand almost overnight.

John B. Smith joined the *Atlanta Inquirer* as a part-time ad salesman. The paper was six months old when we hired him in February 1961. He was a mathematics teacher in the Atlanta public school system, but many of his Morehouse College friends, including Julian Bond, were all students participating in the civil rights movement. He wanted to be a part of the paper simply to make a contribution to the movement, never seeing it as a lifetime career. But in less than a year, John demonstrated a passion for the paper itself. Jesse and I taught him the business and made him vice president of the operation.

When Jesse, Clinton, and I—or Martin, Andy, or Ralph—needed information to support decisions that were being made with regard to the movement, John would be the one who would do that research for us. It gave him an eagle's eye view of what was happening behind the scenes, an insight to which few others had access.

Our editorial meetings were usually held at night, often at the original Paschal's Restaurant but sometimes at my house, in other homes, or even in churches. Sometimes we'd meet all night. Whatever else was going on, we never once missed publishing the newspaper.

Obviously, I had my own business to run full-time so I didn't get too involved in daily editorial decisions at the *Inquirer*, especially in the years after Martin's assassination. Sometimes I might suggest we approach a topic differently in order to have more impact in the community, but even that was rare.*

■ □ ■

During my youth, the police in Atlanta—who down to the last man were all white—treated our people badly—*very badly*. In fact, the police and the Ku Klux Klan (KKK) often were the same persons. Imagine the tension of living with the knowledge that many of those who wore the police uniform by day wore white sheets and hoods by night. And everybody knew it. Atlanta's all-white police department presented the black community with two faces: indifference and brutality.

So it should come as no surprise that most policemen refused to address us respectfully or treat us with civility. No matter how old we were, we were often referred to as *boy* or *gal*. Some of the policemen were unwilling to even acknowledge our humanity. When they saw black skin, they saw animals, not people. Most refused to even patrol black

---

*In 1985 the major shareholders of the newspaper sold our interests to John B. Smith, who started at the *Inquirer* as a part-time advertising sales representative and rose to publisher. Smith had worked solely on commissions based on his sales production. But he was so true blue to the newspaper's mission that even though it meant lost income for him he refused to sell advertising space to firms that engaged in racially discriminatory practices.

neighborhoods. When our kind did encounter police, we were routinely arrested, searched, beaten, sometimes even killed, for no reason except the color of our skin. In one horrific case a sixteen-year-old black youth arrested in Atlanta and accused of burglary was tortured with a hot iron.

An especially dangerous charge—although it wasn't on the books—was what they called reckless eyeballing. It meant that a black person had looked a white person in the eye or, more specifically and far worse, a black man was spotted looking at a white woman like he admired her sexually. If you were charged with reckless eyeballing—especially for allegedly looking at a white woman—you could expect a horrific beating, if not death, whether or not it was true—and the crime never fit the punishment.

Between 1889 and the year of my birth, 1930, there were 465 recorded lynchings in Georgia, more than any one state, including Mississippi. By the time of my youth the number of lynchings in Georgia had come way down, yet the residue of the horror remained. Well into my teenaged years I still heard people speak with horror about the 1922 lynching in Davisboro, Georgia, of fifteen-year-old Charles Atkins, who was slow-roasted to death.*

In Atlanta itself, in the very year I was born—1930—a white mob tried unsuccessfully to storm the "Negro clinic" at Grady Hospital to remove a black man, Robert Glaze, suspected in the shooting death of a white.†

What made things worse still was that lynching was often carried out with the complicity of the authorities. The October 26, 1934, edition of the *Macon (GA) Telegraph* announced that there would be a public castration and lynching of twenty-three-year-old Claude Neal in Greenwood, Florida—just about fourteen miles from the Georgia border. The newspaper's headline read: BIG PREPARATION MADE FOR

New York Times, "Negro Boy Tortured and Burned at Stake In Georgia After Killing White Woman," May 19, 1922.

†Donald Lee Grant and Jonathan Grant, *The Way It Was in the South: The Black Experience in Georgia* (Athens: University of Georgia Press, 1993).

LYNCHING TONIGHT. It matter-of-factly announced the timetable for the teen's suffering:

> Local citizens have been preparing all day for the lynching. . . . At sundown the negro will be taken to the farm. . . . There he will be mutilated.

Despite the boldness of the announcement, not one law enforcement official intervened.

It was not just bad memories that haunted black people in my youth. Some of the terror was current for them. In July 1946, when I was sixteen years old, two young black married couples, including a recently discharged army veteran, were dragged from their car by a white mob in Monroe, Georgia, beaten, and so riddled with bullets—sixty in all— that their bodies were barely recognizable. No one was ever brought to justice.* An eighteen-year-old Morehouse College student named Martin Luther King Jr. wrote to the *Atlanta Constitution* to declare that his people, too, "are entitled to the basic wants and opportunities of American citizenship."

It was a bad, bad time. Segregation was everywhere and in every walk of life: housing, transportation, healthcare, restaurants, hotels, and every type of recreation and social space. There was no form of public accommodation that was not segregated. Still, compared to places such as Montgomery, Alabama, or Memphis, Tennessee, Atlanta was considered a racially progressive city!

Beginning in the 1940s the white city fathers of Atlanta coined the slogan: "The city too busy to hate." Atlanta was not as bad as other areas of the South, but it certainly wasn't too busy to hate. The specter of lynching haunted the lives of the community's black citizens and kept us from feeling fully secure, as it did all blacks in the Deep South.

▪ ☐ ▪

---

*Source: Harry S. Truman Library & Museum (online), "Desegregation of the Armed Forces," www.trumanlibrary.org/whistlestop/study_collections/desegregation/large/index.php.

Segregation had a crippling effect on many black people. It was designed to squeeze all of the hope out of us and make us feel like lesser human beings, to fill our lives with insecurity and fear. Everything about segregation was calculated to beat us down and make us feel less than fully human.

It is not always understood that when Reverend Martin Luther King Jr. accepted the leadership of the Montgomery bus boycott in 1955 he was carrying on the tradition of the civil rights activism he had grown up with in Atlanta. It was a dangerous time to challenge white supremacy in the segregated South. There were well-known groups that were dedicated to racial terrorism, such as the KKK. More dangerous were the institutionally legalized racists who wore badges and carried positions of authority, because there was no one to control them.

Despite the constant threats of racial violence, courageous black community leaders pushed on. In the early 1920s leaders such as Reverend A. D. Williams, head of the local NAACP (and Martin Luther King Jr.'s grandfather), community organizer and educator Lugenia Burns Hope, and *Atlanta Independent* newspaper editor Benjamin Davis successfully rallied blacks around a number of issues, including the building of Atlanta's first black public secondary school, Booker T. Washington High.

The political activity of blacks in Atlanta was civil and law-abiding. Leaders stressed negotiation and voting power to bring change, not confrontation or disobedience. Organizations such as the NAACP, the Atlanta Urban League, Atlanta University, and a number of women's clubs and fraternal organizations like the Prince Hall Masonic Lodge engaged in voter education and registration to give the black community more political clout. However, a poll tax, all-white primary elections, and other exclusionary machinations limited the number of black voters, thereby limiting the power of the black vote.

Between 1944 and 1946 three things happened that helped black folks politically: the US Supreme Court outlawed Georgia's white primary (in which only whites could vote), the poll tax (in which all voters were charged money to vote on the assumption by white officials that blacks couldn't afford it) was abolished, and Georgia's voting age was lowered from twenty-one to eighteen. This brought new energy to black political circles.

Groups such as the Fulton County Citizens Democratic Club, the All Citizens Registration Committee (ACRC), and long-standing organizations like the Atlanta Civic and Political League each placed increased emphasis on registering black voters. The Hungry Club at the Butler Street YMCA, the black YMCA in town, was established to provide a forum for discussion of black folks' political issues and interests. Various other organizations engaged in voter education and registration as well.

The desegregation of Atlanta's schools was a different issue. That was a much harder nut to crack. The three Georgia governors who served during the 1950s all solemnly vowed to keep Georgia's public school system strictly segregated. Of the three governors—Herman Talmadge (1948–55), whose wife had quietly befriended me, Marvin Griffin (1955–58), and Ernest Vandiver (1959–63)—it was the avowed white supremacist Talmadge who set the tone for the others.

Under the leadership of the "schoolmaster of the civil rights movement"—Dr. Benjamin Elijah Mays, the president of Morehouse College—the NAACP filed a federal lawsuit in 1950 to force the Atlanta Board of Education to desegregate Atlanta's public schools. Talmadge lobbied against it like his life depended on it.

To no one's surprise, the lawsuit was defeated.

When the US Supreme Court's 1954 *Brown vs. Board of Education of Topeka* outlawed segregation in all public schools in the United States, Herman Talmadge still did not give up. He persuaded the Georgia state legislature to pass a bill that required all public schools to be closed, then immediately reopened as segregated *private* schools.

■ □ ■

It was dangerous for any black man in segregated Atlanta to insist on being treated with respect, but Martin's father, Daddy King, was no ordinary man. He had no fear of white folks. In fact, it was his fearlessness that is my most vivid memory of him.

I was in my early teens, hanging out at the Butler Street YMCA shooting pool. I noticed that, one by one, some of the most distinguished leaders of the black community came through the front door and briskly took the stairs to the meeting hall on the second floor. It was clearly no social gathering they were attending; there were no smiles or friendly banter.

I wondered what was going on, but it was grown folks' business, and I usually knew enough to stay out of that. I kept on shooting pool, but I still wondered what had brought the top leaders of our community together. Were they planning a new civil rights strategy? Was there a sudden crisis that had to be addressed?

After about forty-five minutes, curiosity got the best of me and I quietly climbed the stairs. The meeting hall door was slightly ajar and I could hear loud, angry voices coming from inside.

I peeped in.

I was most surprised to see the segregationist governor of Georgia, Herman Talmadge. He must have come in a back door because no one downstairs seemed to know he was there. Talmadge was seated, and clearly agitated. Someone was talking loudly. I looked in, a little more anxiously than before. I couldn't believe my eyes.

A black man was standing over the governor, pointing his finger at him and fuming. It was my friends A.D. and Martin's father, Daddy King.

"You *know* what you're doing is wrong!" he said. "We're children of God just like you! We pay our full share of taxes but only get a half share of our rights! You claim to be a Christian man. Then act like it and treat Negroes right!"

I'd never seen anything like it—a black man dressing down a white man, and the *governor* no less! Daddy King was short in stature—built like a fireplug, as the saying goes—but he had the courage of a giant.

Years later, Martin told a story that captured his father's special courage. He and his father were out driving when they were stopped by a police officer. The officer approached their car and addressed Daddy King as boy. Daddy King looked the officer in the eye, then pointed to little Martin.

"*This* is a boy," he said. "I'm a man. Until you address me as a man, I don't want to hear a thing you have to say."

At times he faced opposition from black clergy as well as whites because of his uncompromising activism. To some he was just a trouble-maker and a rabble-rouser. They wanted him to keep his ministry within the four walls of the church. But Daddy King felt he had no choice.

He received many death threats, but soldiered on in his fight for the freedom and equality of blacks and all people in need of justice. He believed that it was a divine calling. He said that when he felt his resolve beginning to weaken, God would speak to him.

"Don't stop now," God would say. "Too late to quit now, King."

■ □ ■

When Dr. Martin Luther King Jr. was called to lead the 1955 bus boycott in Montgomery, Alabama, he invited a number of leaders in Atlanta's black community to the original Paschal's Motor Hotel and Restaurant at 830 West Hunter Street to ask for our support. Those present included Vernon Jordan, Jesse Hill Jr., Carl Holman, me, and several others.

At twenty-five, Martin was only a few years older than me, yet by the time the meeting was over we all knew that Martin Luther King Jr. was someone to be reckoned with. He was aware of the dangers to which his leadership of the boycott would expose him and his family, but he believed so deeply in the necessity to act that he pressed on without hesitation.

Martin moved back home to Atlanta a few years after the success of the Montgomery bus boycott. By this time he was a national civil rights icon. He found here a civil rights movement that was already unified, organized, and strategized. In fact, when Martin arrived in town, the old guard leadership of the city, including King's father, Daddy King, told Martin that he should focus on regional and national civil rights initiatives and leave leadership of Atlanta's civil rights movement to them, which he did.

In the 1960s, Martin would often drop by our home on Shorter Terrace in Collier Heights to visit and swim, often with Andy Young and Ralph Abernathy in tow. They were always welcome.

Our home became a place for him to get away and relax from all the pressures of his work. He loved that pool; he could swim like a fish. It was his getaway. In fact, he used it more than I did! Many days I came home to find him contentedly swimming and lounging. Sometimes while I was at the office, Martin and his staff would drop by for casual afternoon gatherings.

▪ ☐ ▪

Andrew Young was a minister in the United Church of Christ, first in South Georgia from 1954 to 1957 and then in New York at the National Council of Churches from 1957 to 1961. He and his wife, Jean, bought a home in Queens and settled in. One night they saw a report on the evening news about the Nashville sit-in. Andy looked at Jean and said, "It's time for us to go back home."

Still working for the United Church of Christ, he was assigned to work for the Southern Christian Leadership Conference in Atlanta developing adult literacy programs to teach people to read and write, to register to vote, and to organize voter registration drives.

He moved south ahead of Jean, who was pregnant with their third child, and took up residence at the Butler Street Y. His new job put him in an office on Auburn Avenue, upstairs from the T. M. Alexander real estate office, and right across the hall from Dr. Martin Luther King Jr., who asked him to start by helping his staff answer its mail.

Martin and Andy had met several years earlier at a weeklong religious program at Talladega College. They happened to belong to the same fraternity and they happened to have married wives from the same high school in Marion, Alabama. And both of their wives, ironically, had gone to northern schools where they had studied nonviolence as part of their college curriculum.

"We had a lot in common and we worked together well and I just kind of blended in," Andy recalled.

Martin had moved back to Atlanta from Montgomery and he was kind of in a crisis.

He was, by that time, just thirty-one years old and his house had been bombed, he'd been stabbed, he'd been jailed, and in 1960 when he came back here, he had been arrested with the students, but they sent him to the DeKalb County jail and, in the middle of the night, they put him in chains and drove him down to Reidsville. And when a black man is taken out of jail in the middle of the night, it usually means they're going to find a way to kill him.

They drove him, in chains, in the back of a paddy wagon from Atlanta to Reidsville, which is at least a four-hour drive. And there were no expressways back then, so they drove these winding, curving country roads, and he was in the back with a German shepherd.

It was an attempt to intimidate him out of the leadership role and I think it was really catastrophic for Martin, emotionally. His parents had brought him back to Atlanta because they wanted him to be safer than he had been in Montgomery.

John Kennedy called Coretta and helped arrange his getting out of jail and it got Kennedy elected. But no one ever realized what had happened to Dr. King. He always said that was the worst night.

He said there are some things worse than death: "I've never been afraid to die. But if you're going to die, you need to hope that it's quick." He spent I don't know how long thinking that his death was imminent, and not knowing where he was or what was happening to him, and he was alone.

I came into his life just as he was in a kind of recovery period.

I met Andy at the Butler Street Y, where my friend Jesse Hill and I were heavily involved in voter registration drives and get out the vote efforts.

"Herman had built a house with an indoor swimming pool and he had invited Dr. King and Reverend Abernathy and I to come over and bring our families," Andy recalled. "He has a picture of that day that makes me look like a little boy." He explains:

I was coming to swim; I don't know what Martin and Ralph were coming for. We all ended up going swimming, but they came in their preacher clothes and I came ready to go swimming.

It was an interesting evening because all of Herman's kids and Martin's kids and my kids and all of our wives were pretty good swimmers. Ralph saw everybody else jumping in the pool and he jumped in, too, even though he couldn't swim. He just figured that it was easy to do, so he just jumped in the deep end.

Fortunately, I saw him floundering and I had been a lifeguard in college. But he was 260 pounds or so, and I went down to the bottom and pushed him up and sort of walked him to the side of the pool with me being under water keeping his head above the water.

Otelia knew the pressures these men faced every day, so she was attentive to making them comfortable in our home. We would throw hot dogs and hamburgers on the grill and eat and drink and laugh like there was no tomorrow. It was always touching to see the three of them together. Andy and Ralph were devoted to Martin, and he to them.

There were a lot of conversations about strategy in my home, but whatever was planned, there was one basic rule: no violence on our parts. We had to literally turn the other cheek over and over again because we knew we couldn't win by being violent. Martin insisted it had to be a nonviolent movement. We didn't want guns—that wasn't the answer. The answer was a peaceful movement to win the hearts of those people that could be convinced to make a difference.

Sometimes it was just Martin and me, talking about any number of things. Money was always a big issue—who else could we tap for more support? In several of those conversations, we discussed my growing success in business. He encouraged me because he knew that the movement would need much more financial support in the coming months. He needed me and others who had resources to be ready to lend financial support as it was required.

"Herman," he said, "it's important that you stay focused, that you keep building your business, because it's one thing to have opportunity; it's another thing to be able to cash in on it."

■ □ ■

The mailman delivered an unexpected gift to the office of H.J. Russell & Company in November 1962.

It was an invitation to join the Atlanta Chamber of Commerce. It was a mistake, of course. The Atlanta chamber only accepted white members. Everybody knew that; blacks need not apply.

On paper, in the world of sheer numbers where black and white were replaced by green, my company was big enough to attract the attention of the chamber's membership committee. My name was as American and standard as anyone else's; it didn't scream out "Black man!"

There are local and regional chambers of commerce throughout America. All of them seek to bring together persons in the business sectors of their local communities to network with other businesspeople there and, most important, to bring them together to engage in constructive civic activities. Besides word of mouth, one of the ways local chambers of commerce identify new member prospects is by going through Dun & Bradstreet Reports of local businesses. If the report shows a certain level of revenues, the president, CEO, or owner of the business is invited to join.

I guess that is how the Atlanta Chamber of Commerce found me.

The chamber did not know H.J. Russell & Company was owned and operated by a black man deeply involved in a local and national civil rights movement that had become the bane of the whites-only standard. Despite the odds against it, I held in my hands a key to a door no Atlantan of African descent had ever unlocked before me.

I completed the application.

They probably didn't know that H.J. Russell was a black-owned enterprise because while my business had grown quickly, I kept a low personal profile. I did not toot my own horn or seek public recognition. Another reason could be that I came from poor folks and hadn't yet become fully a part of even the inner circle of successful black businessmen with whom the white business community was already familiar. The chamber officials had never heard of me. And I'm sure it never occurred to them that a black man could be as successful in the construction field as I was. If they were going to intentionally seek out a black member, they would have asked one of the already prominent black businessmen—there were plenty around who would not rock the boat. If nothing else, my support of the civil rights movement surely would have excluded me from consideration.

I knew they had made a mistake, but they had issued the invitation, so I took them up on it. Within the hour I dropped the completed application and a check for the membership fee in the mail. Just as promptly, I forgot about it.

About a week later, a second letter with the chamber of commerce logo arrived in the mail. I expected that they had asked around and found out who I was and were sending me a pro forma letter of rejection. Imagine my surprise when I opened it and realized that I held in my hands a letter of acceptance as a member of the Atlanta Chamber of Commerce! My membership was approved sight unseen. There was no interview, no in-person screening. I was making money and someone at the Atlanta Chamber of Commerce wanted Herman J. Russell on its membership roster.

It didn't matter if it was a mix-up or not. It was a major step for the civil rights movement in Atlanta to have a black man in a business organization that was as influential as the chamber of commerce. I reported my acceptance only to my wife and a few close confidantes. I didn't want word of it to get out and prematurely alert chamber officials to throw out my membership on some technicality before I even got there.

The day came that I was to attend my first meeting of the Atlanta Chamber of Commerce to be sworn into membership. By then the general membership of the chamber had finally learned that I was African American so my arrival was not a complete surprise.

Except to one man—Lester Maddox.

Lester Maddox was a rabid racist. I mean it: he *hated* black folks. Maddox was known to hand out ax handles to patrons at his Pickrick Restaurant to keep black folks from entering it. When he found out I was at that meeting to stay he pitched a pure fit. He couldn't hand out ax handles at a chamber of commerce meeting, so he hollered and bellowed that he wasn't going to be in any organization that had a "nigger" as a member.

But before you get the impression that most white Georgians thought Maddox was a nut, or that they disagreed with his antics or the baldness of his racism, consider this: four years later, in 1966, Lester Maddox was elected governor of the state of Georgia.

I cannot say how the general membership felt about accepting a Negro into its ranks, but I can say how those that were there acted. They were *not* overly enthusiastic about my presence, but they were respectful and civil to me, if not cordial. If anyone else found my presence problematic, they did not let it show.

When the front page of the *Atlanta Constitution* reported that the chamber of commerce had accepted its first Negro member, it caused quite an uproar. Some in the white community were up in arms, calling it another encroachment on privileged territory and yet another victory for the integration they so hated. The black community, however, was ecstatic. It might seem like a small thing today, but as far as black people were concerned, it was celebrated as another blow against segregation.

Years later, my friend Ella Yates shared a story that seems to capture the general response of black folks to my integration of the chamber of commerce. She said that one evening she was helping her father-in-law, the prominent Atlanta businessman Clayton Yates, with his cufflinks as she, her husband, and her parents-in-law dressed to attend an evening event.

"Ella," Yates said, "guess who got into the chamber of commerce? That little Herman Russell." She threw up her hands with such joyful surprise that Mr. Yates's cufflinks hit the ceiling.

Despite the euphoria in the black community, the going for me at chamber of commerce meetings was a little rough at first. But I did not return evil for evil. My fellow members gradually got to know me and little by little they came to respect me. They saw that I was as competent at business as they were, and that I had the same goals for Atlanta and the chamber of commerce as they did. And to their eternal surprise, I had no chip on my shoulder that would cloud my judgment or detract from the business at hand.

They also discovered that I was secure, confident, and totally comfortable in their company, even if they were not comfortable in mine. As a businessman and as a person, I fit right in with them without having to change who I was, how I acted, or what I thought. Within two years I was elected to the board of directors, a position I held for eighteen years. For one of those years I served as president.

In the end, nothing Lester Maddox had said or done mattered at all.

■ □ ■

I encountered Daddy King often in the movement, but despite my admiration for him we never had a personal conversation until I was in my early thirties. In the mid 1960s I joined the board of directors of Citizens Trust Bank, Atlanta's most prominent black owned and operated banking institution. Daddy King was a longtime member of the board and took me under his wing there.

Otelia and I often invited Daddy King, Dr. Benjamin Mays, and other directors of the bank to dinner at our home. Daddy King had high blood pressure, so he was supposed to be on a special diet. But he grew up a poor child out in the country, so he was used to eating all kinds of rich, fatty, relatively unhealthy foods. His daughter, Christine, on the other hand, couldn't stand to have certain foods that Daddy King liked anywhere around her, such as squirrel, rabbit, and oxtail.*

Between the foods he wasn't supposed to eat and the foods she couldn't stand, Christina kept watch over Daddy King's diet like a hawk. But whenever he was determined to get his hands on some of the childhood delicacies he loved, he called Otelia and asked *her* to cook one of his favorites. Christina knew his tricks, though. She called Otelia and said, "What did King ask for this time?"

Otelia would reluctantly confess and Christina always raised a fuss. "Otelia, don't cook him that mess!"

They always found it hard not to laugh at the disappointment on Daddy King's face when he realized that the forbidden dish he'd secretly requested was not going to be on the night's menu.

■ □ ■

When the Milwaukee Braves relocated south and became the Atlanta Braves, black ballplayers such as Henry "Hank" Aaron had the opportunity to interact firsthand with leaders of the civil rights movement,

---

*Daddy King's wife, Alberta, died in June 1974 in a tragic church shooting at Ebenezer Baptist Church as she sat at the organ. After Alberta's death, Christine looked after her father.

sometimes at the ballpark, sometimes at Paschal's Restaurant, and just as often in the seclusion of my home.

A mutual acquaintance of mine and Hank's, real estate agent Brady Barnett, brought him out to Collier Heights many times. We began a friendship then that continues to this day.

Here's how Hank remembered that period:

I had been in Milwaukee for all those many years and it was a place that I always considered home—even though I was born in Mobile, Alabama. I knew that outside of Atlanta you might run into the nest of the Ku Klux Klan and things like that. Whether a black ballplayer lived in Milwaukee or Atlanta, he still had the problem of white people not wanting you to be their next-door neighbor or not being able to go to a theater. When I learned that the ball club was moving to Atlanta, one of the things that I always wanted to do was to meet Mr. Russell. He had such a tremendous track record of doing so many great things and being involved in so many wonderful things in this city.

I learned an awful lot from Herman. I'm a very good listener and a very good observer. I look and I listen and I do know that all the success that Mr. Russell has had in life was certainly not just because he happened to be smart. He *did* happen to be smart, but it was because he, too, was able to observe.

I think the two of us hit it off because I observed and I listened to him, you know, seeing him as a father figure. He had done so much in his life that it would certainly behoove me to pay attention. The two of us hit it off quite a bit because he was somebody that I admired tremendously.

■ □ ■

I'll never forget the day I heard that Martin was dead.

It was April 4, 1968. I was called out of a meeting near the airport with my business partners Jerry Blonder, Dave Berkman, and Irwin Parnes to take a phone call. It was Otelia. She was weeping.

"What's wrong?" I asked. She said that Martin had been assassinated at a motel in Memphis. I stood still, not speaking, the telephone receiver still in my hand. I was in a state of shock. Then I broke down. I excused myself from the meeting and tried to call the King house, but I wasn't able to get through so I just went home.

■ □ ■

My daughter, Donata, was just eight years old when Martin was killed. "Martin III and I are still friends," she says.

He is about a year and a half older than I am, and Yolanda is probably at least three years older than me. I remember playing with them, and Dexter and Bernice, who were very little at the time. Dr. King would get in the pool and play with us. I remember playing ball and all kinds of things in the pool with him and the kids.

I remember very clearly the day that he was assassinated. My mom had gone to the store and she had left me to sweep the family room. The TV was on and there was an emergency news report. I remember hearing that he had been shot and maybe an hour later, at most, they came back and said he was deceased.

I ran to the garage door trying to figure out when my mom was going to come home, and when she did, I told her what happened. She had a bag of groceries in her hands and she dropped it on the garage floor.

Some of my fondest memories are to know that, as a child, I actually knew a man who had that kind of impact on the world.

■ □ ■

The next day I went to Martin's house to be with his family. Everyone was in a state of shock. The grief was as thick as fog. I remember Motown Records founder Berry Gordy coming in, but little else. For the next few days, like most everyone else, I alternated between grief and numbness.

We lost a man who can never be replaced, but I think it sort of motivated lots of people, white and black, to face reality and be concerned even more about how people were being treated in this country. I don't think he was taken away in vain. It didn't kill the movement. I think it gave the movement more depth, more determination that we must make sure that one day his dream, what he saw for this country, would be a reality. We've got to just keep working on it.

My friend Martin was a human being, a man of love and compassion. It wasn't an act. His entire life was dedicated to the welfare of others.

▪ ☐ ▪

One of Atlanta's finest white politicians was Mayor Ivan Allen Jr., who took so many positive steps in the advancement of our great city. Allen provided leadership to all Atlantans during the civil rights movement. He made some mistakes in his political life, but I have never seen anyone before or since who made corrections like he did. He was my hero and still is. Allen was the right person at the time he served as mayor.

When Dr. King was assassinated in Memphis, Ivan Allen was one of the first at his home to comfort Coretta. Fearlessly, he also paid a visit to my old neighborhood, Summerhill. People were gathered in large numbers protesting in the streets upon hearing the news of Dr. King's assassination, and he came to express his sorrow and ask them not to do anything they would later regret.

The mayor climbed on top of a car to address the crowd. He begged the men and women around him, many of them furious young people to whom Martin was a familiar neighborhood face, to calm down. Instead, those closest to him shook the car, rocking it back and forth, trying to force him from it. Allen never wavered from his position. He was the only white face, other than policemen, on the scene. That took guts.

The next day, he personally escorted Coretta to Memphis to bring Martin home.

After Martin's death, I was supportive of his widow, Coretta, in every way that I could be. She was a queen of a lady and bore a substantial burden being the widow of Dr. Martin Luther King Jr. and a single parent of four children. She carried all of it with grace but it was really hard on her, even if the public couldn't see it.

▪ ☐ ▪

One hundred percent of H.J. Russell & Company employees participated in some way with the civil rights movement, whether marching, helping behind the scenes, or contributing financially. Ours was one of the first companies in Atlanta to declare Dr. King's birthday a holiday. We wouldn't work on Dr. King Day. Many of our people went to Ebenezer Baptist Church for services.

At the fiftieth anniversary celebration of H.J. Russell & Company's founding, Coretta told the story of how I was one of the first to give funds for the building of the King Center. The center was just an idea then, but I gave her a modest amount and said, "I'm giving you this check today just to let you know that I'm serious, but this is only a small portion of what I'm going to do."

When the actual plans for the King Center were in place, I served as its cochair with Maynard Jackson, who was the mayor of Atlanta at the time. I was also one of the first to make a substantial contribution to the fund-raising campaign.

7

Black Entrepreneurship Takes Hold, Part 2

Pace Setter was an upscale apartment complex that we started in 1972 in a predominantly black area of southwest Atlanta, although my vision was that it would be integrated. Its 450 units—plus two large swimming pools, a tennis court, luxury clubhouse, and first-class child-care facilities—were constructed under the US Department of Housing and Urban Development (HUD) 221 program in which all of the units were leased at market rent, meaning they were priced at whatever the market would bear.*

---

*The federal HUD 221 program insures mortgage loans to facilitate the new construction or substantial rehabilitation of multifamily rental or cooperative housing for moderate-income families, the elderly, and the handicapped.

Unfortunately, the first two years of operation at Pace Setter were marred by a couple of murders at the complex that had an adverse impact on attracting tenants. My dream of building and owning the first predominantly black upscale apartment complex was shattered as the project subsequently fell on hard times. I was determined to make it work, which took its toll on me. I visited the property frequently at varying hours looking for positive signs. We hired a public relations firm to respond to the negative publicity caused by the murders, and our team worked tirelessly to make Pace Setter residents feel more comfortable. We even renamed the complex Dogwood. Eventually management of the complex was turned over to HUD.

That was a real difficult time—but like all other difficult moments in my business life, I got through it.

▪ ☐ ▪

The Atlanta Mortgage Brokerage Company was organized in 1961 by a group of African American business people that included Quentin V. Williamson, J. T. Bickers, Johnny Johnson, Gladys Powell, and me with the intention of issuing Federal Housing Authority (FHA) mortgages. It was the first black-owned mortgage company in the Southeast; there were no others because of the initial capital outlay required: $100,000 just to be licensed. The business enjoyed a fifteen-year run. We made loans to African Americans that allowed many families to purchase and/or build their own homes for the first time.

▪ ☐ ▪

One of the disappointing things that I observed as a black business-man was that we did not have a first-class social club that we could call our own. I tried to change that as part of a group that pooled its resources and purchased fifty acres of land located in southwest Georgia. We called ourselves the Pine Acres Country Club group and used an old cabin as our clubhouse. Members of the group socialized with their families for picnics and other gatherings. Some thought it was a little too far from Atlanta to build a country club, however, so we searched for a location closer to the city.

A 235-acre parcel near Bakers Ferry Road satisfied the general membership and we bought it. Soon, a professional club developer was hired. The initial meeting to discuss construction was held over a scrumptious five-course dinner at my home in Collier Heights. In attendance were some of Atlanta's most successful black doctors, lawyers, and businessmen. Our recreation room was arranged to create the effect of a nice supper club. Guests arrived in cocktail attire for an evening to be remembered.

The developer presented the idea to those who weren't already on board. He discussed the capital needed to finance the project and we raised enough money to get started on the design. In a sign of faith, my company started construction without all of the necessary funds in hand: the foundation was poured and all of the main walls were erected. But we had to stop building because the money was not coming in fast enough to keep up with costs. Then it dried up altogether as a result of internal squabbles.

Eventually, we voided the developer's contract because he was not able to raise the money that we needed. A group of us started but were unsuccessful in our efforts to see the club through to completion. Frustrated, we eventually sold the land and building to someone else. A big lesson learned: You can't let your heart get ahead of your mind. I was eager to make the country club a reality—*too* eager.

It was a big disappointment to me personally. I felt we needed that social component for our community, for our race. The concept, if completed, would have been a great networking venue within our community. I also think it would have been ideal for future generations.

It did teach me an important lesson about why some people cannot work together successfully and fail to develop confidence in one another—jealousy and ego. Jealousy is a disease that eventually kills the source and paralyzes the mind to the point that a person cannot stay focused and give his best to be successful. Ego, when it is deep down in the soul, gets in the way of individuals devoting 100 percent to being a team player. It poisons the mind. It blindfolds an individual from seeing beyond himself. Egos keep people from bringing out the best in themselves.

■ □ ■

For a large apartment complex and nightclub project I built in 1970 called the Birdcage, I hired two young white Georgia Tech instructors, Gordon Davis and Gary Draper, to help guide me through the most complicated phases of construction. Gordon and Gary worked with building contractors to help them efficiently plan and schedule what had to be done on a project. They would check in on construction on a biweekly basis to see how we were proceeding against their models and what needed to change accordingly. They used the critical path method of organization as well as some proprietary methods they developed themselves.

And when the new Atlanta International Airport was being conceived, I went back to Gordon and Gary and said, "I can get the work and you guys know how to do it. Let's team up and form a company," so we did. We called it DDR, using our initials, which at the time we didn't realize had some meaning in Europe. I owned 50 percent of the company and Gordon and Gary split the other half. Our fee-based services encompassed the five phases of any project—concept, design, contracting, construction, and operations.

Within the first two years of operation, the staff grew to twenty-five employees; over the next decade, we employed as many as sixty people and worked on everything from Lemoyne Garden Apartments in Memphis, Tennessee, to the New York City police headquarters and Staten Island Community College.

"Gary and I had our own perceptions—misconceptions maybe— about what the black business community was like," said Gordon Davis.

> We couldn't help but like Herman, and through him we met a lot of other black business people, some of whom looked at us with very jaundiced eyes, you know, "What's this honky doing down here messing with our business?" We met a lot of fine people; we met some others that never lost their animosity, but that was to be expected, I think, in the situation. Most important, we developed a lot of admiration for Herman's style of doing business. He was never offensive or never acted as if you owed him anything, and when you got through

dealing with him, you always felt good and you realized, "Hey, Herman just carved out a piece of work for himself!"

DDR even established an international office in Cairo, Egypt, from 1981 to 1983. "The Egyptian cities that were involved were Cairo, Alexandria, Sadat City, and several small cities up and down the Nile River," Davis recalled. "The program was heavily funded by the United States Agency for International Development (USAID). Our task was to help Egyptian contractors familiarize themselves with project management approaches used in the U.S. And of course, the Egyptians loved Herman!"

It was a remarkable experience, a broad but logical expansion in my general contracting resume.

■ □ ■

When you build as many apartments as I did over the years, you start seeing related opportunities in all kinds of housing, including condominiums, HUD housing, and even retirement facilities. My friends Dr. Irwin Parnes and Lester Colodny and I saw a growing need for extended medical care for elderly citizens in metropolitan Atlanta. We formed a partnership called CPR Engineering and Development Co. and built our first one-hundred-bed nursing home near the Atlanta airport on Springdale Road. It was state-of-the-art in its day, offering private, semi-private, and four-bed rooms.

Specialized retirement housing was a booming industry and we caught the wave at the right time. A few years later, we built our second nursing home, 175 rooms, this time in Cartersville, Georgia. We sold both facilities at a solid profit for all the investors.

More important, as our personal relationship grew, Irwin—whose day job was as a dentist—and I bought a vacation condo together in Aspen, Colorado, in the mid-1970s. My first trip to that western city really blew my mind. To be in winter temperatures at ten degrees below zero and see people taking a dip in an outdoor swimming pool in that same weather was a real eye-opener!

Over the years, we enjoyed many happy days together, including the birthdays of all of our kids, bar mitzvahs for his, and weddings for them all. One time, Irwin and I took our young kids with us to Aspen. Irwin, unlike me, had champagne tastes. He traveled first class; everything that he did with his family was first class. My family and I, on the other hand, were back in coach—by choice.

At one point on our flight, Irwin's son Gary invited Michael to keep him company in first class. Gary was about two years older than Michael—and white. It must've been strange to the stewardess to see my African American child in first class.

She actually asked Gary, "Who is this kid?"

"This is my cousin," he said.

Not true, but the possibility that it was blew her mind!

▪ ☐ ▪

In the late 1980s, I acquired land from Central Atlanta Progress at the corner of Bedford Place (now Central Park Place) and Ralph McGill Boulevard. It was intended as the first new 180-unit condo building in the downtown area. It was a dandy location, less than a block away from the Civic Center and a couple of blocks from Georgia Power's new headquarters building. No one was certain how well it would perform. East of this tract was an African American community, north of it was a commercial area, and to the south was vacant land.

The time was right, however; before the project was completed, it was almost 100 percent sold out. Ralph McGill Place, as we named it, honored the publisher and editor of the *Atlanta Constitution*, who as a newspaper columnist in the 1940s, '50s, and '60s was an advocate of racial justice and equality. I knew Ralph from serving with him for many years on the Butler Street YMCA board.

A year later, I acquired another nearby tract of land and began construction of two hundred more condos. McGill Park was located on the southeast corner of Ralph McGill Boulevard, right in front of Georgia Power's headquarters. It, too, sold out quickly. That was the beginning of development of the downtown area on the east side of Atlanta.

▪ ☐ ▪

In 1980, I built a nine-story, mid-rise senior citizens home and named it Maggie Russell Towers to honor my mother. Leon Allain, one of Atlanta's greatest architects, designed the building. It is located across from Atlanta Medical Center (formerly Georgia Baptist Hospital), and there is always a long waiting list for vacancies. My mother's portrait hangs in the lobby of the building as a reminder to all of why the towers exist.

8

My Big Greek Brother (From Another Mother)

I bought land all over the South, particularly in Georgia. But there was only so much real property that a black man alone could buy from white sellers, even as late as the 1970s, no matter how much money I offered. Staunch, committed racists simply would not sell to me at any price.

In 1970 the US Department of Housing and Urban Development created a program called Section 236 in which the federal government made periodic interest-reduction payments to mortgagers on behalf of owners of low-income projects. The program appealed to me as a developer because it gave us the opportunity to build decent housing for low-income families.

I saw several parcels of land that I thought would make good sites for HUD housing, but at the time attractive properties like those were seldom sold to black people, especially if they were located in or near a white neighborhood. In fact, some landowners actually stipulated in deeds that their land was never to be sold to a "Negro." They went so far as to record that information in every pertinent state and local courthouse to make sure blacks could never buy their land.

When I found out that parcels of land that I was interested in had those restrictions attached, the thought of dismantling those racist arrangements made them even more attractive to me. As hard as I worked, I wasn't going to let some long-dead—or still living—mean-spirited strangers stand in the way of progress.

I made up my mind to buy those properties. The question was, how?

■ □ ■

The story of my business and personal relationship with Greek real estate broker Jim Coclin is unlike any you've probably ever heard before or will ever hear again. And on top of everything else, he is one of my best friends in life; he's like my brother from another mother.

White property owners would happily sell to Jim—and at a much fairer price than they ever would me. Jim looked, acted, and sounded just like them—with one little exception. He couldn't hate anyone. Despite his own southern upbringing in Waynesboro, Georgia, Jim Coclin, a second-class navy quartermaster during World War II, loved everybody, a genuine man of hospitality and sweetness who didn't know the meaning of prejudice.

Meeting Jim was another twist of fate stemming from my relationship with the family of former Georgia governor Herman Talmadge. Jim's brother-in-law, Al Lamas, was an architect and knew the governor's son, Gene Talmadge, who was in real estate. One day in 1970, Al introduced Jim to Gene.

"You acquire land for apartments?" Gene asked.

"Yes," Jim said.

"Well, I know a gentleman who's a large apartment developer and he's looking for somebody like you."

A Saturday afternoon meeting was arranged in the southern Atlanta neighborhood of Jonesboro, near the airport, and we looked at a site together. It wasn't what we wanted, and I didn't see Jim again for about three months.

My friend Bill Orkin, possibly America's most famous exterminator and whose father founded Orkin Pest Control, had built a new home (my company put up all the interior drywall) and was throwing a big party to celebrate. With the event in full swing, Jim was walking outside in the yard when he met Atlanta mayor Maynard Jackson for the first time.

"Look here," Jackson said. "I haven't seen you before. Who are you? Where are you from?"

Jim, who can make conversation with anyone, amiably answered Jackson's questions.

"What kind of name is 'Coclin'?" Jackson continued.

"It's Greek."

"Greek? I never heard a Greek name like that before!"

Around this time, Otelia and I arrived from another event. Once there, I saw my friend Maynard talking to a man I recognized from our short land look-see. "Jim Coclin!" I said, "What in the world are you doing here? Are you a politician? I thought you were a realtor!"

We talked more personally this time and got to know each other better in Orkin's yard, even as Otelia and Jim's wife, Georgia, introduced themselves and hit it off. It turned out that the Coclins were new in town, having moved to Atlanta from South Carolina a year earlier.

I needed a fresh white face to front for me because of the HUD money about to be released for affordable multifamily construction around the country. The timing of our reintroduction was perfect; I needed him.

"What are you doing Wednesday?" I asked him.

"I don't have any appointments Wednesday," Jim said.

"Good. Come down to the office; I want to see you. We've got a new Burger King across the street. We'll go over and have lunch."

We've been together ever since.

I proposed a business relationship to Jim in which he would represent me in the field without revealing my identity or the fact that I was black. "Before you answer, talk to your wife about the black/white situation; see if she's comfortable with it," I said. "If this works out the way I think it will, we'll be together professionally and socially and I don't want there to be any problems for you."

Jim didn't hesitate. "I know Georgia; there wouldn't be any problems," he said, and that was it.

"I was around black people almost all of my life in Waynesboro, Georgia," he said later.

> My daddy had the only restaurant in town for eighteen years. That's where I grew up and I worked with blacks in the front of the store and in the back. The front was the white entrance; the side street was a black entrance. Then we went to Buford, South Carolina, and built a new restaurant and a motel and we had a lot of black people with us. I always got along with them. We were always friendly.
>
> The Parris Island Marine Corps base and boot camp was right there. When young men graduated from recruit training, Mom and Pop and the entire family would come for the graduation. Every now and then we would get a black family looking for lodgings and we never turned them away as other motels did, despite the law. They were always good people, first-class people.

Georgia Coclin agreed with her husband. "Maybe because our parents had come from Greece, they were not mean or ugly to the black people or anything like that. My daddy had a little restaurant, and he had a lot of black employees, too," she said.

They were the ideal folks for me in business and as personal friends.

▪ □ ▪

Jim's job was to go in and represent me on the Q.T. He would go into a small Georgia town and ask around to learn the names of the leading realtors, representing himself as a broker and developer. He would need somebody to front for *him* with the locals when we inevitably bought land and went to city hall for approval to commence construction.

He and Georgia would make as many trips to that little town as necessary until we found the right site and could option it. The option was always subject to HUD approval for the loan so we were never on the hook. With that approval in hand, Jim would petition for rezoning if necessary, with the local realtor in the lead—a familiar face at city hall, someone they trusted and who spoke their language.

We formed the Georgia Southeastern Land Company and targeted small towns with average populations of no more than seven thousand. Jim and the realtor would get our land zoned for multifamily development, followed by utilities approvals. Next came a legal survey before we engaged an architect—usually Herman Murray or Al Landis—to design the apartment project. If Jim ever had a problem, he'd just go to Frank Rezek and Paul Lawson, attorneys specializing in HUD housing.

Almost all of this took place without me or anyone in my office knowing a thing about it. I never saw the site Jim acquired until—or often after—we broke ground. That was the level of trust between my Greek brother and myself. I would give him a signed check at the end of the process and Jim would pay for a building permit and bring me back a receipt.

"Jim," I'd say, "go find the next one!"

That system went on for twelve years with none of the white landowners ever catching on until it was too late to change course. Jim got to be really good at it because he did so many of them. We bought a number of properties that way, but we were never arrogant about it. It was business, not a contest to humiliate others. Those businessmen might not have liked what we did, but we made sure we did things in a way that they would have to respect—and that would hold up in court.

HUD advertised how many units it wanted built and Jim kept on top of that, knowing that RFP (requests for proposal) advertisements were assigned on a first come, first served basis. H.J. Russell & Company had a solid track record at HUD, so when government officials heard from Jim Coclin, they knew there were professionals on the job.

Jim told me that he and Georgia put one hundred thousand miles on two cars over a ten-year period going back and forth between Atlanta and whatever small town we targeted. We met in my office twice a week, usually at 7:00 AM, before anyone knew he had been there or could question why. It was also convenient because he could get on the road early.

Once in a while Jim would have to give up on a property, but not too often because he had an extraordinary eye for picking the right land in the right place at the right price.

His strategy was to be at or near the unmarked borderline between the white and black parts of town. Rezek and Lawson always had paperwork packages ready to submit to HUD the day the RFPs were requested, so nobody could get ahead of us. Out of thirty HUD developments on which we bid, we never lost——not a single project.

■ □ ■

I honestly believe that if anyone Jim bought properties from in all those years knew that he was fronting for a black man they would have run him out of town—or worse. But Jim never told anybody that he represented me.

Whenever they were curious, he said, "I work for a big developer who wants to remain anonymous. He doesn't want anybody to know who he is because he wants to come down here and get the project built without anybody knowing about it. He doesn't want all the competition to jump in right now."

If they wanted their big fat commission, that was usually enough to shut down the questions. You're supposed to split real estate commissions—which are typically 10 percent. But Jim gave the local real estate agent the *entire* 10 percent on a sale price of $50,000 to $100,000. It was double what they'd earn from somebody else, and the price was usually a lot for vacant land, so they'd go to work for us, no more questions asked. (Once in a while a bottle of Ancient Age bourbon wouldn't hurt.)

When the head real estate guy in a small southern town is on your side and he wants that commission, he will promote you to the nth degree. Never failed.

Jim would also tell them that this new development would enhance property all over their small town, which it always did. Once we identified a small town for opportunity, other developers always followed, whether to build supporting commercial, industrial, or retail.

When we built apartments in Fort Valley, Georga, Jim and Georgia chartered a bus and spent the night there with the Russells and the Hills—Jesse and Azira—after partying late with what seemed like every politician and official in the county. There was free food and the scotch and bourbon flowed freely.

"Man," they said to Jim, "when we going to have another one?" But I knew better than to go back once they realized they'd been had.

Jim made a trip to Americus, Georgia, late in our relationship, and it's possible that suspicions were aroused among the locals that there might be some smoke and mirrors around our proposed deal. Jim's brother-in-law, Al Lamas, and their wives had come along for the drive, too. Al turned to Jim at one point and whispered, "I think we better get the hell out of here because they will tar and feather us if we stay."

The couples quietly excused themselves, walked out the door, and didn't stop again until they were safely back in Atlanta. And no, Jim never went back to Americus.

That was the closest moment he ever had to being exposed—and endangered.

When Jim left a town with the signed paperwork in hand, they always thanked him for coming and spending money in their sleepy little village. It was a Section 8 government subsidy, but they didn't know it then. I further kept appearances up by always putting a white job superintendent on the site. The architects and attorneys were also white. Nobody cared if workers on the job were black—that didn't threaten anyone. No one knew until the thing was finished that I was the owner. Until then, they only knew Jim.

If the Internet had existed then, we couldn't have pulled this off because people could have looked up company names and connected the dots. Back then, Jim handed out a business card that put his office in my building, but the address didn't mean anything.

Believe it or not, being Greek was not much different than being Jewish or black in some of these backwoods Georgia towns. So if the local realtor or town officials got interested in Jim or the last name Coclin, Jim always had a story ready.

"I'd say my daddy was brought up right out of Belfast, Ireland," he recalled. "And you know why I thought of Belfast? Because during the war we had to take the landing barges over for the Normandy invasion and after we'd get them all in the English Channel, they'd give us a little three or four day R&R and we'd all go to Belfast because that's where all the pretty girls were."

For some, the difference between Greek and Irish wasn't obvious. And for some reason, Irish wasn't a threatening descent—especially coming from Jim, who after a lifetime in Georgia and South Carolina, could sound just like the next guy.

▪ ☐ ▪

When Otelia and I traveled to Canada with the Coclins, it was quite a different experience from the one my wife and I had had on our honeymoon. The Coclins' room was nice but it was small—unlike ours.

Otelia called Georgia and asked, "How are your accommodations?"

"Well . . ." Georgia said, hesitating. "They're all right, I guess. The room is clean, it's nice, but it's a little claustrophobic."

"You're kidding!" Otelia said, more than a little surprised. "Y'all come on down—we've got a suite."

"A *suite*?" Georgia said. "But *Jim* made the reservations! Y'all got a suite and I've got this little room?"

"Not only that," Otelia said, giggling. "We've got this big welcome basket filled with fruit, wines, and sweets." Until that moment, Otelia thought the Coclins had sent the basket.

The Coclins came to our room. We opened up the basket and shared the first bottle of wine. Just as we started to relax and unwind from the day's travel, we got a call from the front desk. They had made a *huge* mistake. *We* weren't in the right room. Not because of our color or anything like that; it was just an administrative mistake—right down to the fruit and wine basket!

▪ ☐ ▪

When Jim's mother died at 103, the funeral was in Augusta. Of course I was there to support one of my closest friends.

"HJ," Jim said, "you're riding in the limousine with us."*

---

*Many of my friends—and even my adult children—call me HJ.

"Jim, put the family in there," I said. "I'll be fine in my own car."

"You *are* family," Jim said. "Most of these other people, I don't see them except at a funeral or something. You're more family to me than anybody other than Georgia." So I rode with him.

When my youngest son, Michael, was a little boy, he loved riding around in Jim's 1978 Lincoln Town Car, which was silver. If Jim was going on a short trip, running errands, and would be gone for an hour or two, Michael would say, "Mr. Coclin, can I ride with you?"

Every time Jim came by the office, if Michael was around he'd ask Jim, "What time are you leaving today, Mr. Coclin?" because he was hoping for a ride home in that big fancy car. And if Jim didn't show up one day, Michael would call him.

"Mr. Coclin," he'd say, "this is Michael. You all right?"

■ □ ■

When tennis hit Atlanta in a big way back in the 1970s, I was very interested in developing skills and even built a court behind my home. Georgia Coclin was a member of the Atlanta Lawn Tennis Association, so Jim and I challenged her to a match.

"Get a partner," Jim said.

Otelia was not into tennis, so Georgia chose Michael, who was eleven.

I thought winning was going to be a piece of cake, but Georgia and Michael, who was just beginning to display his natural athleticism, wiped us out! Jim and I didn't win a single set!

■ □ ■

My business with Jim continued even after the wave of HUD deals wound down. We built a large assisted living facility in Jonesboro that Atria, a company focused on senior housing, bought as soon as construction was completed. When it opened, its clientele was all white, but over time more and more minorities entered the home and many of the white families relocated their loved ones elsewhere. Today it's a hospice.

Jim also put together the property for me to build and own a new ABC-TV affiliate, Channel 24, in Macon. TV wasn't a good fit for me, however, and I sold off the station and the building pretty quickly at a nice profit. It was a good investment.

Jim and I spent forty-two years in business together, putting together thirty different deals. Otelia and I were extremely close with Jim and Georgia. We flew to Greece with them to meet their families, and we also traveled together to Canada, Las Vegas, California, and Hawaii.

As the result of the active collaboration of Jim Coclin and me, I ended up being the largest developer and owner of HUD properties in the state of Georgia. In fact, HUD honored me for that with its Samuel J. Simmons Lifetime Achievement Award. Thanks in part to the HUD 236 program, by 1981 my total portfolio of properties had expanded to more than twenty-five hundred units. They were located in Atlanta and throughout south Georgia. I tried to stay on top of all of them, but I had so many projects going on that there were not enough hours in the regular workweek to visit them all, and so I started visiting some of the developments on weekends. The good news was that this helped me to better keep up with my construction projects. The bad news is that it took me away from family time.

Otelia knew this troubled me. She knew how much I loved to spend time with our children. She also knew how important it was for me to stay on top of things. She proposed a way I could do my weekend site visits and still enjoy time with my family: we would turn the site visits into family outings. One weekend a month I would take the whole family with me to visit the properties. The kids loved it. They had no idea they were going to work with Daddy. These were grand adventures as far as they were concerned. They got to visit new places and see buildings in various stages of construction.

It was great fun. I was able to get my business done and still enjoy my family. It also interested my children in my work so they never felt alienated or left out. I think that's one reason they all came back to work with me after college and I believe that's why *they* run H.J. Russell & Company now.

I would not have been quite the success I am today if Jim and Georgia Coclin had never entered my life. Not only that, we turned out to be the best of friends—it would have been only half as fun.

9

Desegregating the
Good Ol' Boys

The nature of my business began to change dramatically as the 1960s ended and a new decade began. I was still every bit the hands-on owner and manager of H.J. Russell & Company, but as we moved into the joint ventures described in the pages that follow, I made new friends and business acquaintances who opened doors to me that black men of the generation that preceded mine couldn't dare dream of.

In sharing the stories of H.J. Russell & Company's evolution over the years, I need to explain that as the company grew from plastering to general subcontracting to joint venture partner, we eventually became a general contractor ourselves. In fact we don't do any subcontracting anymore, having moved entirely to general contracting. This is actually common in our industry. We're not hiring individual electricians or people to put the drywall up; we hire subcontractors. The people on our staff are project managers and superintendents who oversee all the trades. The industry started moving that way in the late 1970s and '80s, and by the mid-'90s we were out of the business of doing any trade work ourselves.

Using H.J. Russell & Company as my base, I spread my profits from the previous four decades into a variety of active and passive investments as wide-ranging as massive sports facilities and ownership of sports franchises to construction of some of the tallest office towers in downtown Atlanta. I even became a beer distributor for a time and helped start an airport concessions business. And the company expanded beyond the Peachtree City, north to the Carolinas and Virginia and west to Texas and California.

There was no stopping us now.

▪ ☐ ▪

Believe it or not, I was elected president of the Atlanta Chamber of Commerce in December 1980. That's right—the same group that never wanted a black member before 1962 elected me to its top job eighteen years later. By then, the racial dynamic in the organization and the city had changed. I was actually the *second* African American to lead the group; my dear friend Jesse Hill Jr. had been the first.

I met Jesse in 1958. He had just moved to Atlanta from Saint Louis to take a job as an assistant actuary at the black-owned Atlanta Life Insurance Company. He was a likable and brilliant young man. Jesse had earned a degree in physics and an MBA from the University of Michigan and was only the second black actuary in the nation.

We hit it off the first time we met at the Butler Street Y. We were both serious about contributing to the civil rights struggle, shared clear and serious visions for our business careers, and were deeply devoted to our families.

For the next several decades, Jesse and I never went to sleep at night without talking to each other. There was not one civic or business decision that either of us made without consulting the other. I would take

Jesse on driving tours of towns when I was scouting development locations. He had such a good head for numbers that I always ran financing deals past him. We worked together on Maynard Jackson's mayoral campaigns and later Andy Young's mayoral and congressional races. People in Atlanta knew that if they made a convincing case for something to one of us, it was very likely they'd earn the support of us both.

On the civil rights front, Jesse and I worked together on voter registration drives and helped finance Atlanta's campaigns to desegregate schools, public facilities, and commercial establishments. Our relationship spilled across our families as well. Our wives were close and the Hills are godparents to my son Michael.

I'm sure that both Jesse and I would have had rewarding careers if we had never met. But I'm also sure that because of our friendship we are far more successful than we would have been alone. And I like to think that because of the friendship, strength, guidance, ideas, and inspiration we have given each other daily, we pushed each other to make the city we love better, too.

We were always there for each other. In the chamber of commerce, with his presidency and then mine, more black business owners gained membership; blacks and whites were now working together in business, civic, and social settings. We didn't always agree, but we shared a common commitment to make our city better. I'm proud of my role in it.

My years on the Atlanta chamber board of directors were full of challenges and satisfaction. We supported city infrastructure improvements to make Atlanta more attractive to relocating businesses and families. We paved the way for the new hotels and conference centers and gave financial support to our public education system. We saw it as our responsibility to make Atlanta the best it could be in every way for all its citizens.

But the most significant event of my tenure as president of the Atlanta Chamber of Commerce was not a happy one. It was a nightmare that descended upon the city—in fact, the nation at large—and filled our citizens with fear and dread for two terrible years.

▪ ☐ ▪

On July 21, 1979, fourteen-year-old Edward Hope Smith left his family's home to run an errand. He never returned. His body was found a week later, along with the remains of a friend, Alfred Evans, also fourteen. Both were black. Their killer or killers were never found.

On September 4 of that year, another black fourteen-year-old, Milton Harvey, disappeared while riding his bicycle. His bike was found a week later in a remote area of Atlanta. His body wasn't found until November.

On October 21, 1979, nine-year old Yusef Bell disappeared. His body was found in November as well.

The next two killings occurred in March 1980. There was another in May, and three more in June. Two child murders occurred during July 1980, those of Anthony Carter and Earl Terell. Between August and November, five more killings took place. Like the previous victims, all were black.

The police were alarmed by the increasing number of violent deaths. Yet, because the murders were not confined to any particular neighborhood and the cause of death was not clear in some cases, nothing suggested a pattern. So even as the number of killings grew, the police could discover no link between them. It was not until a year after the first murders that evidence emerged that suggested that the killings were related and possibly the work of a serial killer or killers.

In August 1980 the Atlanta commissioner of public safety, Lee A. Brown, formed the Metropolitan Atlanta Emergency Task Force to Investigate Missing and Murdered Children.

A week later the strangled body of thirteen-year-old Clifford Jones was found. He was the twelfth known victim of the figure they called the Atlanta child murderer.

By then the city was in a panic. It seemed that every day there was a new speculation about the killer's identity and his motives: Was it the work of the Klan? Rogue cops taking license with black children? Pornographers producing "snuff flicks"—films of actual murders—for a perverted underground market?

Everywhere I went I saw the fear in the people's faces. Adults accompanied their children to places that they previously had been allowed to go alone. Unaccompanied children were told to travel in pairs if not in groups. I shared their fear. I was frightened for my own loved ones.

Otelia and I made sure our own children took every precaution. They were young adults, but so were some of the killer's victims. As president of the Atlanta Chamber of Commerce, I was concerned about the effect this nightmare had not just on the Atlanta community but on my own family. No one was safe and everyone was scared.

Rumors and misinformation led to increased fear. Every week, a new type of person fell under suspicion: cab drivers, because of their mobility; Vietnam veterans and karate experts, because they knew how to administer chokeholds and killing blows (it didn't appear that any of the children had been killed with weapons); dog owners and owners of vans with carpeting, because the police had found carpet fibers and dog hairs on a number of the victims.

Because the murders were not confined to any particular area of Atlanta, parents in every neighborhood were frightened. No one knew whose child would be next.

Terrified community groups, frustrated that the police hadn't yet caught the killer, staged marches and protests. Their fears and charges were picked up by national news media. The "Atlanta Child Murders" became the defining face of Atlanta to much of America. Frightened tourists cancelled reservations and stayed away, several conventions moved to other cities, corporations thought twice about making Atlanta their home, out-of-state parents began to rethink decisions to send their children to Atlanta's fine university system.

As members of the Atlanta Chamber of Commerce we had a dual responsibility: to do everything we could to end the carnage of our precious young people and to assure tourists, conventioneers, and relocating businesses that Atlanta was still a safe and inviting city.

I used the clout that came with being among the most powerful and influential members of Atlanta's corporate community to encourage all the necessary governmental, law enforcement, investigative, and corporate players to come to the table to coordinate their efforts. The chamber offered a substantial reward for any information that could lead to the killer or killers. Finally, we continued to reach out to travel agencies and businesses across the country to give them a sense of how closely all the various sectors of Atlanta worked together for the betterment of our city.

The murders continued into 1981.

The community's desperation increased daily until it reached a fever pitch. Everywhere I went—the grocery store, the barbershop, business conferences, job sites with my workmen—it seemed to be all that anyone talked about. As spring turned to summer, the police made their first major break in the case of the Atlanta child murders.

On May 24, 1981, the naked body of Nathaniel Cater was discovered on the banks of the Chattahoochee River. He was the twenty-ninth victim of the Atlanta child murderer. When Cater's body was found, two policemen recalled having stopped a car on the James Jackson Parkway Bridge on the outskirts of Atlanta two days previously, after hearing a suspicious splash in the river below. They didn't see anything in the water, but they questioned the driver anyway, noted his identification information as a matter of procedure, then let him go.

The driver of that car was twenty-two-year-old Wayne Williams, an aspiring music promoter and disc jockey. Williams was arrested on June 21, 1981, after an exhaustive investigation.

Jury selection began on December 28, 1981, and lasted six days; the trial began on January 6, 1982. The most important evidence against Williams was similarity in the fibers found on some of the victims and fibers found in Williams's car.

On February 27, 1982, after nearly a two-month trial, Williams was found guilty of two felony murders and was sentenced to two consecutive life terms in the Georgia state prison at Reidsville.

Atlanta's long, deadly nightmare was over, and I was proud of my and the chamber's role in finally ending it.

As the president of the Atlanta Chamber of Commerce at the time, it was the most challenging period of my public life. I pray to God that never again will any city, at any time, anywhere in this world experience a nightmare like the one that racked my beloved Atlanta for two years and took some of our youngest and most innocent citizens from among us.

■ □ ■

Fortunately, there were much happier times in my many decades of public service.

Once I was accepted as a member of the Atlanta establishment thanks to my unexpected chamber acceptance, the years that followed resulted in many more invitations that a black man would not have dreamed possible a generation earlier. Eventually I had so many balls in the air that I had to be careful about the invitations I accepted.

For me to join a company or civic association's board of directors I had to feel that I had something to offer. On the one hand it had to be a situation in which my particular skills and experiences could benefit the organization. On the other, I wanted greater exposure to ideas, information, technology, or networking that could enhance my own company and me.

I appreciated each and every board I was invited to serve on, but I must say that Georgia Power was one of the most enjoyable. Professionally, it was a Georgia company; I liked the fact that our decisions made a direct difference in the lives of my neighbors. Personally, however, it was through the Georgia Power board of directors that I was introduced to a place that became a major source of pleasure and escape for my family and me.

It seemed that at every board meeting at least one of my fellow directors asked if others were going to "the lake." At first it meant nothing, but they talked about "the lake" so often that I finally asked, "What lake?"

They explained it was Lake Burton, a beautiful waterfront community nestled in the north Georgia mountains. The area was owned by Georgia Power; officers and directors leased land from the company to build vacation homes.

"Come see for yourself, Herman," they said. "It is one of the most beautiful places you've ever laid eyes on."

A couple of weeks later, one of the officers took me to see it. They were right—it was breathtaking. I was hooked. I immediately started looking for a lot to build on. I found a beautiful piece of land on a steep slope overlooking the lake. I engaged Claude Rickman, a highly recommended local contractor, to built us a gorgeous two-story, ten-thousand-square-foot, five-bedroom house with two master bedroom suites and a wraparound deck on each level. Otelia helped design it to her own tastes, knowing what we needed for family and entertainment purposes. That house is still a favorite gathering place for holidays and weekend getaways for my whole family, including my grandchildren.

One of my best experiences was hosting a high school class reunion at the lake for my entire graduating class on the occasion of our fiftieth anniversary. More than eighty of my classmates showed up from all over the country and we went up to the lake in two specially chartered buses for a full day of food, drinks, swimming, and fellowship.

It was a wonderful time. I have hosted many events, but I must say that sharing my home and my good fortune with my childhood friends was one of the most gratifying days I have ever had. That lake house has been a major source of joy for us. And I owe it to my affiliation with Georgia Power.

▪ ☐ ▪

I was elected as a trustee to the board of directors for the Commerce Club in 1984. The Atlanta Chamber of Commerce was where most all of the city's serious businesses were members; the Commerce Club was far more exclusive with fewer than twenty-five members at any given time.

The Commerce Club was founded by Mills B. Lane Jr., president of Citizens and Southern Bank (C&S) in 1960—at the behest of Mayor Ivan Allen—and led by old-school Atlanta money. Any Fortune 500 CEO who came to Atlanta during that era was elected to the board—including the leaders of Coca-Cola, Georgia Pacific, Georgia Power, and C&S—but there were only two African Americans on that board, Jesse Hill Jr. and myself. It was automatic for a past president of the Atlanta

Chamber of Commerce to become a member of the Commerce Board and both Jesse and I qualified in that way.

We met at the club's Broad Street location—on the sixteenth floor—and that was where all the big decisions in the city were made. Mayor Allen told my friend—and future mayor—Andrew Young that by that time (he'd been elected in 1961) the city's white leaders didn't want Atlanta to be like Little Rock and New Orleans and the other places that were having racial riots. It was not good for business.

Coca-Cola chairman J. Paul Austin, who was from LaGrange, Georgia, had been the head of Coca-Cola in South Africa for fourteen years before he came back to take over the lead here. He had lived through the transition there from a fairly reasonable business climate run by a British economy to the takeover by the Afrikaners and the institution of apartheid. He came back to Atlanta convinced that South Africa was headed for a bloodbath but that Georgia didn't have to go that route.

Ivan Allen didn't discuss it with anybody, he just decided one day at the Commerce Club that the business community needed to take the lead in integration. The first time he said it out loud at a meeting, there was a deafening silence until Robert W. Woodruff took the cigar out of his mouth, leaned over, and in his raspy whispered voice said, "You're right, Ivan." And once the president and longtime leader of the Coca-Cola Company said it, everybody else fell in line.

■ □ ■

The Capital City Club was one of the oldest and most respected private clubs in Atlanta. Its membership had long included some of the most prominent names in Atlanta business and society. The names it did not include, however, were those of Atlanta's blacks and Jews, and most of its members were adamant that it would forever remain that way. That rankled the black community.

In the mid-1980s my joint venture partner on many projects, Bob Holder, came by to see me. "Herman," he said, "as a full member myself, I am inviting you to join the Capital City Club."

Bob was personally asked by the club's board to sponsor me for membership, and he got Roberto Goizueta at Coca-Cola and Ron Allen of Delta to further endorse me. The board also decided that instead of having some posting period of six to twelve months in which they would announce me as a new member and gather input, they were just going to announce that I was a new member—and if anybody didn't like it, that was just tough.

I was surprised, but by no means was I enthusiastic. I knew how prestigious and full of Atlanta's movers and shakers the club was, but I was doing just fine without it. And the city's exclusive, whites-only social club was the last aspect of the city yet to be integrated. As far as I was concerned, even if my membership was accepted, I didn't need the headache of spending time with a bunch of folks who didn't want me around—and paying good money for the "privilege."

I was still smarting from the years of the club's exclusion of blacks. I thanked Bob for his consideration, but declined. I knew he was trying to break the club's racist membership code and I certainly appreciated that, but I wasn't interested. And I certainly didn't want to be the only black member and for them to think that was enough to satisfy years of discrimination.

A few weeks later I received a call from Roberto Goizueta, the chairman, director, and CEO of the Coca-Cola Company, headquartered in Atlanta. Goizueta and I had a mutually respectful social relationship. H.J. Russell & Company, in joint venture with Holder Construction, had already completed a half-billion dollars' worth of construction projects for Coca-Cola.

I always thought Goizueta, being born in Cuba, knew what it was like to be poor, and he figured segregation was probably rougher on me than it was on him. I think he liked the hard work and dedication that he saw in me over the years. That probably made him take time and adopt me as a friend. The average person in our circles still didn't get the opportunity to dine with him as much as I did, many times in his private dining room at the Coca-Cola Company.

Goizueta's call took up where Holder's left off: "Herman, I know you turned Bob Holder down. But I want you to reconsider joining the Capital City Club."

Goizueta didn't ask me to join, by the way. He said, "Herman, I *want* you to join." It took me about two minutes to say yes. When you evaluate any request, it's important to recognize who is doing the asking. Holder asked me first; as a personal friend, I felt I could decline and he would accept my grounds.

What was different with Goizueta was that our relationship was rooted in business. I assumed he had overcome his own barriers based on racial discrimination. He had also been a strong business supporter of my company.

There was, however, one more hitch when I was informed of the cost of membership. I called Bob Holder. It was the only time he has heard me raise my voice in more than forty years of business and friendship.

"Bob," I said, "who the *hell* is going to pay this $75,000 bill I just got for my initiation fee into the Capital City Club?"

"Why, Herman," he said, "you are. Remember, we're making history and this is your part."

It never occurred to me that a club membership would cost anything like $75,000! And of course Bob and Roberto hadn't even thought of mentioning it to me. But in the years that followed, my joint venture with Holder did another $500 million in Coca-Cola business, which easily covered the membership fees.

With Goizueta, Holder, and Delta Air Line's Ron Allen as my sponsors, my membership was approved without any open controversy. I'm sure that some of the members—maybe a lot of the members—weren't happy about me integrating their club, but I never heard about it. That doesn't mean that I became one of the guys overnight, although everyone was civil to me. But with Goizueta and Holder making introductions, the other members got to know me and I got to know them. The chill eventually thawed. Since then, my time at the Capital City Club has been quite pleasant.

In 1995, I held my sixty-fifth birthday party there. Friends flew in from all over the country. It was an integrated group; my black friends and my white friends were all together. There were more black guests there that night than the Capital City Club had ever seen at one time. And it was probably one of the best parties they'd ever hosted.

Goizueta and his wife, Olga, joined Otelia and me at our table. Also sitting with us were Vernon and Ann Jordan and Johnny and Dale Cochran. It was a high-powered group, but Goizueta and his wife stole the show, dancing all night.

■ □ ■

Despite the success of black golfers such as John Shippen in the late 1890s and early twentieth century and Bill Spiller, Eural Clark, and even Joe Louis in the 1940s, the Professional Golfers' Association (PGA) formally excluded blacks as members until 1961. It finally admitted its first black member, Charlie Sifford, in 1964, almost fifty years after its founding.

In the late 1980s it came to public attention that a number of PGA member clubs still had not admitted black members. Among them was the Augusta National Golf Club. I suspect that had much to do with the call I received in 1989 from Carl Sanders, the former governor of Georgia. As a member for decades, he wanted to submit my name for membership at Augusta National. I was pretty surprised. I knew it had no black members. I would be the first, and thus another racial barrier would come down.

I wasn't interested.

"You've got the wrong guy, Carl," I said. "I'm not a golfer. I don't know a thing about golf. I've never been on a golf green. I've never even been a caddy. Thanks, but it's not for me."

In addition, I knew that membership dues were high. I wasn't a golfer. Who would want to pay that kind of money to watch *other* people play?

A month later I attended the regularly scheduled meeting of the Georgia Ports Authority. After making small talk, I mentioned Sanders's call to several of my colleagues. They looked at me in disbelief.

"Herman, that was a damn fool thing to do," one of them said. "No one turns down the Augusta National Golf Club! Do you have any idea how many people would give their right arm to be invited to join?"

"But I'm not a golfer," I said. "I'm not going to pay a lot of money just to sit around."

I gave the matter a great deal of thought. I knew there were certain social advantages to being a member of one of the most prestigious clubs in America. And because I am black I knew my membership would attract national attention, but that didn't mean much to me. I would gain some significant new business contacts, but I was doing well with the contacts I already had.

In the end, I decided I didn't want to join Augusta National. I could easily have afforded it, but whenever I thought about paying a big sum of money for a club membership, I thought of my father. There's no question what *his* answer would have been. It wasn't the cost that made me decide not to join. Being a member of a golf club just wasn't important to me. I wouldn't join any organization that I wasn't interested in, even if it was free. And all that talk about social prestige meant nothing to me. My idea of prestige is living honestly and with integrity. I made the right decision for Herman Russell.

■ □ ■

We used to say that Atlanta was a city too busy to hate. In fact, the chamber of commerce once put up $4 million for a campaign to convince people of that. We really weren't any different than any other southern city . . . except that the white leadership of ours decided that if we were going to get anywhere, we had to leave hate behind.

In most other cities desegregation began with integration of blacks and whites in the schools and conflicts resulted. Atlanta's integration process was more peaceful because it began with the desegregation of Atlanta's business community, resulting in integration from the top down.

In 1971, when so many other cities were still engulfed in racially charged rioting inspired years earlier by events in Watts, California, the Atlanta Action Forum, a group of twelve white and twelve black business leaders, was formed.* You had to be the CEO of a major institution based in the city to be a member. The original idea for the Forum belonged to black realtor W. L. Calloway, who approached Mills B. Lane Jr., president of C&S. Lane made it a reality almost instantly.

We met—not in secret, but in private—one Saturday morning a month and nobody could come but the CEOs. We spent the mornings together, talking about how to head off problems in the city. One of the most significant things we did was conclude that if we wanted to prevent racial violence from breaking out in Atlanta, we needed to create jobs. Within two weeks, we decided that we needed to create six thousand summer jobs for disadvantaged young people. Each of us started calling our suppliers.

By this time Jesse Hill and I were involved together not only in Atlanta Life Insurance Company but Citizens Trust Bank as well. We called the businesspeople for whom we wrote policies and to whom we loaned money and said, "I need you to create eight summer jobs and hire eight black interns."

In a matter of a few weeks, the business leadership of the city put together commitments for sixty-five hundred summer jobs. So instead of running in the streets or hanging around, getting in trouble, a whole generation of high school students put on a suit and went to work every morning during summer vacation. And that, in turn, created a city of teenagers who grew up thinking of themselves as young professionals.

Although its activities were rarely reported in the media, the Atlanta Action Forum and its powerful members were key players in protecting the South's leading city from experiencing the same racial riots that plagued other cities.

---

*Riots were triggered on August 11, 1965, by an altercation that ensued during the arrest of a black motorist for drunk driving. "The arrest became a flashpoint for anger against the police," according to the *Los Angeles Times* in a report forty years later. "After nearly a week of rioting, 34 people, 25 of them black, were dead and more than 1,000 were injured. More than 600 buildings were damaged or destroyed." Source: Valerie Reitman and Mitchell Landsberg, "Watts Riots, 40 Years Later," *Los Angeles Times*, August 11, 2005.

■ □ ■

Segregation in the South kept black people from enjoying the benefits of fair treatment in institutions such as insurance companies, funeral homes, educational institutions, and banks, so we started businesses of our own catering to our community. Many of these black institutions thrived because segregation all but guaranteed them a captive market. Banks were particularly important because it was difficult for the black business community to borrow needed capital from white banks.

Black banks became not only the financial centers of our communities but also a great source of pride and security, demonstrating that we were as well equipped to successfully function in the business world as anyone else. Most black folks had difficult times borrowing money from white banks. Not only were they held to different credit standards than whites and turned down at much higher rates even with comparable credit profiles, much too often they were humiliated in the process.

My first real experience with bank financing was several years after college. Prior to that I had financed my projects out of my savings. When I was stretching out to build my South Avenue duplexes, I asked around and tried to get financing from Home Savings and Loan.

I went to their main office early one morning with my business plan and my financial statements in hand. As I crossed the lobby to the loan officers' platform, a woman looked up and snapped, "Boy, what do you want?"

I told her I was there to apply for a construction loan. She stared at me for a moment, then called a loan officer. We went to his desk. I offered him my documents. He reluctantly took them in hand. It was clear that he thought I was wasting his time.

He glanced at my papers, probably just out of curiosity. He started leafing through them. Then he excused himself for a moment. When he returned, he said, "The bank president would like to meet you." I guess they were shocked that I had as much money as I did.

The bank president, Charlie Minor, told me he was impressed. Then he asked me a number of personal questions, starting with my church affiliation. He seemed really glad that I was an active churchgoer. He asked about my parents, my education, my hobbies, things that would be illegal for a banker to ask today. I didn't take offense, though, because I got the feeling that he was a sincerely religious and gracious man.

I left his office that day amazed at how respectfully I'd been treated. As I passed through the lobby on my way out, I noticed the woman who'd called me boy staring at me. I'm sure she was wondering who this "colored boy" was who was so important that the bank president wanted to see him.

I looked her way and smiled. She did not smile back.

The bank called a week later to inform me that I had been approved for a loan. In those days, I couldn't eat at a downtown lunch counter or stay in a hotel. But this bank saw the opportunity to help a young guy and make money with him, and they did just that.

When I returned to finalize the paperwork, the bank president had left instructions for me to come to his office. He showed the same level of interest in my personal life. I realized then that rather than just trying to satisfy his curiosity, the president was seeking to get a sense of my character, to see if it was as strong as my balance sheet. From that day on, he took a personal interest in me and pride in my every success. He was always offering advice, whether I asked for it or not.

A few years later, after H.J. Russell & Company had really taken off, Charlie Minor read in the newspaper that I was approved for a liquor license for Jet Liquor Store. He called me immediately.

"Herman, you are a God-fearing young man. Don't make money from selling liquor. It's not Christian."

I thanked him for his advice, but I pursued the liquor license anyway. I didn't always follow Mr. Minor's advice, but I always appreciated it. And because he respected me, I never again had to worry about financing for any of my projects. My experience with him was important in another way, too: it taught me that there were white people of good will who could be counted on to do the right thing.

■ □ ■

As my business interests grew larger and went beyond the construction business, I obtained my commercial financing from Mills B. Lane Jr.

and C&S. I'd had an account there since I was sixteen, thanks to John Hancock, a local black lawyer, who had been so impressed with my industriousness that he personally took me to C&S and showed me how to open an account. During that time I developed a good relationship with Mills Lane. I sought his counsel on business deals several times and his advice always panned out.

One afternoon I called on him to say that I was contemplating buying a large block of stock in Citizens Trust Bank and wanted his thoughts on it. We sat down together and Mills told me he thought it was a good idea and arranged for a $250,000, ten-year loan with a ceiling on the interest rate of 6 percent and a floor of 4 percent. It turned out to be a great deal because the prime rate exceeded 6 percent several times during the life of the loan—and I paid off the loan in just four years.

Unfortunately, the average black person never had the opportunity to prove his or her creditworthiness, as I did, with the white owned and operated banks. So Citizens Trust Bank filled a need as the first African American banking institution in Atlanta and one of the first in the nation that was owned and operated by black folks. Similarly, blacks needed to develop their own insurance companies in order to buy products to protect their families and businesses.

In 1909, Herman Edward Perry, a black Atlanta businessman, founded the Standard Life Insurance Company to serve the insurance needs of Atlanta's growing black community. By 1917, Standard Life had grown into one of the largest black insurance companies in America. That year, it established the Service Company, a holding company of Standard subsidiaries that included the Service Pharmacies, the Service Laundries, the Service Printing Company, and the Service Realty and Development Company.

Perry became one of Atlanta's most prominent businessmen, black or white. Yet when he requested that his feet be measured at a downtown department store so he could purchase a pair of socks, he was insulted and ushered out. It was then that it struck home to Perry that Atlanta must have a banking institution that would make capital available so black businesspersons could own and operate businesses that served the needs of black folks without having to depend on the whims and prejudices of white financial institutions.

Perry enlisted four other prominent black Atlantans into the venture: James A. Robinson, Thomas J. Ferguson, W. H. King, and H. C. Dugas. They became collectively known as the "Fervent Five" because of their passion for the mission. After raising capital, lining up potential clients, familiarizing themselves with stated federal banking laws and charters, and building a viable organizational structure, the Fervent Five secured a hard-won charter to open their bank.

On August 16, 1921 the Citizens Trust Company opened on Auburn Avenue in the heart of Atlanta's black business community. The goals of the bank were threefold: 1) to promote financial stability and business development; 2) to stress the principles of thrift; and 3) to make home ownership possible for a larger number of black people. The *Atlanta Journal* wrote, "Promoters of the Citizens Trust Company have been granted a charter for the immediate organization of the institution, a bank with $500,000 capital stock, all of which is said to have been already subscribed by Negro citizens."

Atlanta's black citizens, many with tears in their eyes, lined up to deposit their hard-earned dimes and dollars into a bank they could finally claim as their own.

Later, Citizens Trust became the first African American–owned bank to become a member of the Federal Deposit Insurance Corporation (FDIC). And in 1948, it also became the first African American–owned bank to join the Federal Reserve Bank.

In 1960, the directors of Citizens Trust were in search of capital to expand the bank's operations. They knew that I had a good business reputation. As directors, they also knew the size of my accounts at the bank.

It was much more of a surprise than it should have been when I received a call from L. D. Milton, the CEO and one of the directors of the bank, to discuss the possibility of my buying an interest in Citizens Trust to expand its capital base. Although I was only thirty-three years old, half the age of many of the directors, they invited me to join the board of directors. I accepted without hesitation. After due diligence was done by both sides, I became the youngest person ever to serve.

Once I got involved in the governance of CTB, I saw that it was an even better long-term investment and an even more important vehicle for serving our community than I'd realized from the outside. After talking it over with Otelia, I decided to do more than just invest; I decided to buy a majority stake.

In 1960, I applied to the Federal Reserve Bank of Atlanta for authorization to purchase 50 percent of its common stock. My fellow directors knew I was buying a larger interest but they had no idea I was going to be the major shareholder.

Because I was the bank's largest shareholder I was eventually elected vice chairman of the board in 1974. By then the board included many local African American icons including Benjamin E. Mays, then-president of Morehouse College, and Reverend Martin Luther "Daddy" King Sr. Four years later, I was elected chairman of the board. I took my oversight responsibility as chairman seriously. I watched trends in both the economy and the banking industry and perused all pertinent reports on the bank's loan portfolio and performance.

One day in 1983, Thomas Williams, chairman and CEO of First National Bank of Atlanta, invited me to stop by his office for a chat. I honestly had no idea what he wanted to discuss.

"Herman," he said, "we want you to join the board of directors of First National Bank of Atlanta."

I was surprised by the invitation because we both knew that Federal Reserve rules did not allow anyone to serve on two different bank boards at the same time and, of course, I was a director of CTB.

But before I could mention the Fed's rules, Thomas said, "Don't worry about the Fed. They've already given us special permission for you to sit on both boards."

He explained that there was a little-known provision in the Federal Reserve's rules that allowed a bank director to sit on the board of a separate bank if the arrangement would benefit that director's primary board of directors. In other words, you could sit on the board of a minority bank while also serving on a majority bank board if doing so would expose you to expertise that could be of benefit to the minority bank. Thomas had successfully argued that my presence on the First Atlanta board would constitute such a situation even before they invited me. It was a win-win: they got an African American business leader on their bank's board and our bank got a valuable inside view of how the big boys operated.

In the 1980s and '90s, a lot of new community banks started popping up in metropolitan Atlanta. Their competition forced us to seek greater efficiencies. After much negotiation we joined forces with First Southern Bank, a smaller African American bank. In addition to expanding our capital base, the merger gave us additional suburban branches.

In 1985, CTB was named "Bank of the Year" by *Black Enterprise* magazine. Three years later, CTB led a consortium of minority-owned banks to finance the high-profile construction of the new $5.5 million sanctuary of the historic Ebenezer Baptist Church in Atlanta. And in the spring of 1999, Citizens Trust Bank went public—another big step.

Citizens Trust Bank is still an African American bank, and my goal was and still is to make sure that blacks will always have an opportunity to walk in, apply for loans, and qualify. Having CTB made it easier for blacks to connect with other banks. I'm proud to say that's the case.

■ □ ■

I've always enjoyed playing sports—football and boxing in high school, for example—and watching them. That's why I was so excited to break another color barrier in 1981 when I was offered the opportunity to buy into a group of Georgians who owned several of Atlanta's professional sports teams, including the Atlanta Hawks (basketball), Atlanta Flames (hockey), and a soccer team. The group included Tom Cousins, Charlie Loudermilk, Robert Ledbetter, John Wilcox Jr., William Holstein, Dillard Munford, William Putnam, and Paul Duke.

Mills Lane, the president of C&S Bank who had signed off on the loan with which I purchased my original stake in Citizens Trust Bank, was not impressed about sports franchises as an investment. I wanted to borrow $1.5 million to purchase a 10 percent ownership stake in the three teams. The fact that I would be the first African American to ever own a professional team didn't move him, either.

He said, "What good is it to be the first at anything if you don't make any money?" He let that hang out there for me to think about it for a moment.

"This is a bad deal, Herman," Mills said. "You're going to lose your ass. I can't back you this time."

I appreciated his honesty, but I disagreed. I thought it would be a great opportunity for me as an investor and, especially, as an African American businessman, and I was going to go through with it. It was one of those rare times when my personal excitement overwhelmed my business sense.

When I confided in my potential partners that I was having a problem getting a loan at C&S, they suggested I go to First Atlanta Bank, which had already financed some of the other investors. I had no trouble getting the loan there.

Being a team owner—and passive investor—was fun. I enjoyed being able to invite family, friends, and clients to the owners' boxes. I learned about and really enjoyed hockey, which is not a popular sport in the black community. And during that time the basketball team had a number of exciting stars, including "Sweet Lou" Hudson, "Pistol" Pete Maravich, and Walt Bellamy.

One person who seemed to particularly enjoy my being a team owner was Daddy King, a fellow director at CTB. I invited him to his first Hawks basketball game and he fell in love with the team. He started calling me regularly for tickets for his grandchildren.

As much as I had fun as a team owner, Mills Lane's prediction turned out to be right: during the six years I was an owner, not only did I never make a dime, I ended up losing my entire investment just as he had said I would. My time as an owner predated the explosion of sports on cable and satellite television; basketball grew phenomenally in the decade that followed, but hockey and soccer still struggle to make money thirty-five years later.

The only thing that saved the deal from being a total bust was that I used the losses to offset taxes on my other sources of revenue. That, and I broke another barrier as an African American, opening doors for black men and women who followed me. In the end, we sold the teams off to

Ted Turner, who also owned the Atlanta Braves and who wanted their games to provide hundreds of hours of programming on his cable TV superstation, WTBS.

One other good thing that did come out of that experience was that some of the other owners became good friends.

10

A Leg Up and Over: Joint Ventures

Holder Construction is a general contracting firm started by my friend Bob Holder. In 1968, the biggest job he had to date came along, a big multiuse complex in midtown Atlanta. That was also to be one of the biggest opportunities in my company's history.

"We were in the process of bidding on the job," remembered Bob, "and my guys came in and said the low bidder on the plaster and drywall, which was a huge item in the contract, was H.J. Russell & Company. We all looked at each other, a bunch of Southern rednecks, and said, 'We can't possibly take a risk with a minority company.' But as we got into it a couple of things became clear. One was that Russell clearly had the most competitive price, and their reputation was really good. So we decided what the heck, let's do it."

The first time I met Bob was when I went up to his office and we made the deal. We laugh about it now; I told him over dinner in 2012 that I didn't even own a car back then. Bob said, "If I had known that, we wouldn't have given you the job!"

Bob Holder also recalled:

> I'm not sure we ever spent one minute wondering what our other contractors thought about it. It wasn't like Herman just came out of nowhere. He had a good reputation in his business. General contractors are very difficult on subcontractors, the way we drive them and manage them and expedite them. It was a whole new frame of reference to be dealing with a minority in a role like that.
>
> Herman turned out to be the best subcontractor of everybody on the project. He was a lot tougher about firing people that weren't productive than I was. I would be there overseeing and he'd come visit the site and check on his big crew on the job. I was so impressed at how hard he drove the crew and how relentless he was on everybody, black or white. I don't mean abusive, just really diligent about the whole thing.

We didn't become personal friends at that point, but Bob and I did get to know each other professionally. Several years later, Holder was doing work with Delta Air Lines and hoping to be hired for more. His contact at the company called one day and said Delta was going to build a big reservations call center in Atlanta. But he also said that Holder needed to know that Delta was making an equally big commitment to affirmative action hiring and he needed to take that into consideration when bidding on any new construction.

"I mentioned that we had some experience with H.J. Russell & Company," Holder recalled, "and they said, 'Wait a minute. *We've* already picked Russell. The issue is whether we're going to pick *you* or not.'" Times were definitely changing.

The first time that Holder Construction Company and H.J. Russell & Company officially did a joint venture, Holder was still a little nervous about exposing its estimating systems and procedures to an outside company, let alone a minority firm. Together, our lawyers wrote a joint venture (JV) agreement that was about three inches thick; most of the pages had to do with what would happen when there was trouble—how to settle disputes about every imaginable thing.

Over the years—and more than $1 billion in business later—not one cross word has ever passed between us. But we didn't know that would be true then, and of course the lawyers didn't know it.

Anyway, we worked everything out, including the split of profits and capital that was going to be needed. Holder was the bigger company, so it had the larger share of both. The day came to meet in Holder's conference room and sign the document.

Bob was on his side of the table with his guys, all of them white southerners, and I was sitting on my side of the table with my guys, all black southerners. It was a momentous joint venture agreement that the lawyers had given the name "Holder–Russell Construction Company, a Joint Venture of Holder Construction Company and H.J. Russell & Company." It was a huge moment—a life-changing moment—for our company.

Bob was sensitive to the fact that this was the first of its kind for both sides. "Herman," he said, "our lawyers drew this up and we didn't tell them what to call it. Are you happy with what we're calling it or would you like to do it differently?"

I paused for a minute and said, "I'll tell you what, Bob. If you'll give me 10 percent more of the profit, you can take my name out of it altogether!"

Bob told me later that was the day he knew we were going to be friends, not just business partners. Joint ventures through the years with Bob included the Jimmy Carter Library and Museum in Atlanta; Wachovia Bank headquarters in Winston-Salem, North Carolina; various buildings for Delta Air Lines including their Atlanta headquarters building; and the headquarters of the Coca-Cola Company, also in Atlanta. We have probably done more than $1 billion worth of construction together.

Bob and I had similar business philosophies and expectations. We believe in excellent and honest customer service and our workmanship must be of superior quality. Our management styles were also similar:

both were conservative when it came to costs and both believed in running a tight ship. We hired only the best staff and insisted that all of our managers and superintendents kept a close eye on the bottom line. Also like me, Bob is a straight shooter who does not like to waste time or money.

Over the years, our business and personal lives crossed over in multiple ways.

Bob Holder recalled:

We were doing a big job together at Hartsfield International Airport. His youngest son, Michael, was working out there in the concrete crew. He was fifteen years old. Hopefully, he was legal, but he was big enough and strong enough to work with the other laborers. Herman called me one day and he said, "I've just seen his paycheck. We're paying him twenty dollars an hour?"

I said, "That's right; that's the wage scale for common labor."

"Well," Herman said, "I want him paid *four dollars* an hour!"

I said, "Number one, we can't do that because he's working. He's a member of the crew. And number two, he's doing everything everybody else is doing, so I don't care whether you think it's too much or not. That's what he's got to be paid and should be paid."

And when my daughter announced her engagement, Bob Holder and his wife, Ann—along with Tom Williams, who at the time was the CEO of First National Bank of Atlanta, and his wife, Loraine—gave an engagement party for Donata at the Commerce Club. These two white guys and their wives were giving this party for my family and me, and in those days the Commerce Club was probably the only place in town they could have done that. The guest list was black and white, making it kind of a historic occasion in Atlanta society.

When the event wound down, I gathered my family alongside the Holders and the Williamses and talked to them about the importance of what had happened that night.

"This was not just another social get-together," I said. "This was a historic night in our community."

■ □ ■

When Maynard Jackson announced he would run for mayor of the city of Atlanta following a successful term as vice mayor under Mayor Sam Massell, he asked me to volunteer to be co-treasurer of his campaign against Massell. I was very fond of Sam and he had served the city well, but I thought it was time for a change. I backed Maynard that year for a number of reasons: he was qualified, he was a friend, and finally, it was the right thing to do.

Our primary responsibility was to fill Maynard's war chest, so my first stop was to see Charlie Loudermilk, the founder of the largest party rental and supply business in the country, Aaron Rents, Inc., and one of my partners in the Atlanta Flames and Atlanta Hawks.

I introduced Maynard to Charlie. Charlie was a friend, so I expected him to be gracious, but beyond that I wasn't sure what to expect. After all, Maynard was a political upstart, a black man running for an office that had always been held by white men, and a challenger to the very establishment of which Charlie was a charter member. But Charlie surprised me. He called his entire staff in to hear Maynard state his reasons for running and his vision for Atlanta. Maynard was so impressive, in fact, we left Charlie's office with a check for $10,000, which was a lot more money then than it is now. He supported Maynard primarily because he believed in me and *I* believed in Maynard.

Maynard's victory over incumbent Sam Massell—whom I had supported in his previous campaign—in November 1973 began a new era in Atlanta's politics. He served the city of Atlanta for eight years and turned the city's bidding process upside-down—changing my life and business in the process. Ever since Maynard Jackson broke through the city's color barrier, we have enjoyed a succession of extraordinarily talented black mayors: Andrew Young, Bill Campbell, Shirley Franklin, and Kasim Reed. Once the line was crossed, the voters of Atlanta have not gone back.

Even though H.J. Russell & Company had a successful track record and a reputation as a general contractor, some doors stayed closed to us in Atlanta until Maynard Jackson's affirmative action program pushed them open in the 1970s. Prior to 1974, the City of Atlanta awarded less than 1 percent of its contracts to minority-owned firms. Mayor Jackson's program required minority participation goals in all city contracts.

Suddenly black and minority contracting companies were in demand. White businesses that had previously enjoyed a near-monopoly on government contracts realized quickly that if they failed to reform their practices, they would get left out in the cold. They figured that the best way to be competitive in this new environment was to form win-win joint ventures with minority businesses.

The concept of joint venture was implemented in large measure to give minority contractors access to undertakings that could broaden their experience and expand competition and hiring. But I also viewed joint ventures (JVs) as one of the finest ways to learn new techniques and processes. JVs enabled H.J. Russell & Company to compete in the marketplace with some of the largest general contractors in the world.

We realized early on what makes a good—and not-so-good—joint venture. Real JVs require total participation. I learned early on that *people* are the most important aspect. Our company's long track record and relatively high bonding capacity made the firm a much sought after JV partner. However, I was careful about whom I chose to do joint ventures with. There was too much at stake to lose. Just because a white firm had been around did not particularly qualify them to joint venture with me.

H.J. Russell & Company received its first contract in the public sector in the early 1970s, when we became a JV partner with J.A. Jones and Batson & Cook, two of the country's largest construction companies. Together we built PeopleMovers—vertical escalators that connected all five terminals—at the Hartsfield International Airport. We also participated in the first big modern terminal construction project at Hartsfield.

That first partnership opened the door to decades of lucrative joint venture relationships with major companies on government construction contracts. But proving our worth in the marketplace also led to ever-larger *private* JVs as well, including one of the largest development projects ever in downtown Atlanta, the fifty-two-story Georgia-Pacific Building.

I had an existing relationship with Albert J. Bows, a member of the Georgia-Pacific board of directors and the head of the Arthur Andersen accounting office for Atlanta. He mentioned to me that Georgia-Pacific was going to relocate to Atlanta and construct a new headquarters building. I told him I would like to have an opportunity to bid on it and if he could put me in touch with the right person, I would appreciate it. He did and they, in turn, invited me to coordinate a team and submit a bid on the project.

I contacted a friend of mine, Gordon Mitchell, the Atlanta business representative of J.A. Jones, a well-regarded builder in the southeastern section of the country. He agreed to team up with H.J. Russell & Company to bid on the job, and together we won the contract to construct the new tower.

As a result of our experience on the Georgia-Pacific Building, our relationship with J.A. Jones blossomed and we pursued other projects together. The success of that job also brought our company to the attention of other white general contractors (GCs) and we received inquiries from other large potential construction partners. Beers Construction is another GC with whom H.J. Russell & Company joint ventured on several projects. Some of the more notable were the Centennial Olympic Park and Horizon Sanctuary for Ebenezer Baptist Church.

During this era we did a number of signature corporate construction jobs on our own, without relying on JV partners, including the Atlanta Gas Light Company, Georgia Power, BellSouth, and Procter & Gamble.

▪ □ ▪

At one time I was in a partnership with Jerry Blonder, Dr. Irwin Parnes, Dave Berkman, and Bruce R. Davis. The Securities Development and Investment Company was formed to develop, build, and manage apartments.

Once a week, my partners and I would meet and decide on purchasing land and other ventures to undertake. We built hundreds of apartments on the north side of Atlanta in residential areas of North Druid Hills Road and Buford Highway. North Atlanta was not yet populated with apartments, and these developments were considered to be out in the boondocks.

We also opened up a couple of specialty clothing shops for men. The stores lasted for about seven years and did well until our business interests drifted off on separate paths. Our personal friendship remained and we watched our kids come into the world, marry, and start their own families. There were times when it seemed as though I attended more bar mitzvahs than anyone else in Atlanta for their children and their grandchildren. We socialized publicly when it was unpopular to do so. What an education we all received from each other!

▪ ◻ ▪

I purchased several shotgun houses at the corner of Northside Drive and Fair Street to make room for a new H.J. Russell & Company headquarters in the early 1970s. The original site plan included an office building, a warehouse, and a fuel tank for company vehicles in the back.

The building has been renovated at least three times since its original construction and I have purchased more than fifty additional shotgun houses adjacent to the property. The location—home to H.J. Russell Plastering Company, H.J. Russell Construction Company, and Paradise Management Inc.—is fantastic because it is about two miles from the heart of downtown Atlanta known as Five Points.

▪ ◻ ▪

During the early 1990s our construction team expanded into Chicago. We provided management services on Chicago's McCormick Place renovation/expansion for the Metropolitan Pier and Exposition Authority. The $1.28 billion project resulted in more than 2.87 million square feet of convention center space.

Chicago is another city where H.J. Russell & Company left its mark, but our construction projects were not limited to Atlanta and Chicago. We experienced a significant national expansion beginning in the early 1990s that took us from New York to Washington, DC, to all southeastern states bordering our Georgia headquarters location. Additional high-profile projects were built in the major midwestern cities of Detroit and St. Louis. Our western reach extended to Dallas, Texas, and Phoenix, Arizona.

This growth was fueled by our reputation, financial strength, bonding capacity, relevant mega project experience, and relationships with several leading construction management/program management firms

Herman at twelve years old

Herman at sixteen years old working on his first building

Herman (in the front) in shop class at David T. Howard High School

Herman with the band he managed while in high school

Herman and Otelia on their wedding day with Herman's mother on the right

Herman with his parents on his wedding day

Herman and Otelia on their honeymoon trip

Herman with Martin Luther King Jr., Ralph David Abernathy, and
Ambassador Andrew Young

Verbena Hills, the first apartment complex Herman built in Atlanta

Georgia Pacific building under construction, a joint venture with
J. A. Jones Construction Company

Joint venture with Holder Construction to build the Coca-Cola headquarters

The Russell Brothers: Herman, Clifford, Lawrence, Rogers Jr., and Robert (Charles Russell is not pictured)

Family time spent after dinner, a time for the children to ask about whatever was on their minds

Herman with his college roommates (left to right) William Kimbrough, Herman, Felker Ward, Jimmy Hanes, and Warren Talley

Herman with President Jimmy Carter

Herman and Otelia with Azira and Jesse Hill

Herman with Vernon Jordan

Scott Hudgens, Herman's partner on many
deals and in particular Shenandoah

Herman and Otelia dining with Jim and Georgia Coclin

Herman with Governor and Mrs. Joe Frank Harris, Colonel Colin Powell and Alma Powell, Andrew Young and Jean Young, and Otelia Russell on the right end

Herman with Johnny Cochran

Herman and Otelia Russell in 2002

Herman with Hillary Clinton

Herman and Sylvia with President Obama

Herman and Sylvia on their wedding day

Jerome, Herman, Donata, and Michael (left to right)

across the United States. In addition, we provided mentoring relationships to each local community's disadvantaged, minority, and women-owned business enterprise contractors and subcontractors.

One of the questions I get asked often is this: If H.J. Russell & Company is hired as a minority or disadvantaged general contractor, will every worker on the job be a minority? The answer is no, which surprises some people.

Even going back to Georgia-Pacific, which was our first major joint venture, we brought an integrated team to the table. And when I say integrated, I don't mean racial; it's going to be a team integrated with other firms. Are we looking for diverse vendors at the sublevel? Yes, absolutely. But we don't go out and solely hire African American firms.

That said, an important part of our mission when we go into new cities is to bring African American firms to the table with us. We try to locate the best disadvantaged—a government term, not ours—subcontractors or vendors who we think could work with us. We're looking, too, for subcontractors in a protégé role who can partner with us now or later. That makes the most sense for H.J. Russell & Company and our mission. We want to make money first, just like everybody, but we've been in the position of being a smaller player trying to grow in a market, and we know that at some point you've got to give someone else that same opportunity.

I want the minority market to say, "H.J. Russell & Company is giving us a shot." That's a double-edged sword because people's expectations are raised sometimes and then the reality is they have to get the job done. But we clearly go to markets looking to be a positive contributor to the minority community, especially the African American community.

▪ □ ▪

Another golden opportunity came up with the Georgia Dome. Once more we formed a JV team of general contractors that included Beers and Holder and added C.D. Moody Construction, a black-owned firm. We won the rights to that project and built the Georgia Dome under budget. It opened in 1992 and stands today as one of Atlanta's signature buildings, and is within walking distance of my headquarters.

The partnership of Russell, Beers, Holder, and Moody scored again in the run-up to the 1996 Summer Olympics in Atlanta when we were chosen to build Olympic Stadium, home of the opening and closing ceremonies for the global event (and later known as Turner Field, home of the Atlanta Braves baseball team).

In the late 1990s, plans were revealed for the Sam Nunn Federal Center, one of the largest government structures ever built in the Southeast. H.J. Russell & Company, Beers Construction, and Holder Construction formed a joint venture that was the successful bidder. The finished structure—again within walking distance of Russell headquarters—added much to the south side of Atlanta.

■ □ ■

Construction of MARTA, Atlanta's rapid transit system, was a big opportunity for H.J. Russell & Company. We contributed work on our own and as part of a joint venture. We also were part of the teams that built Phase Three of the Georgia World Congress Center as well as Philips Arena, the home of the Atlanta Hawks NBA basketball team and the Atlanta Dream WNBA basketball team.

When I come to work every day and see these amazing buildings that H.J. Russell & Company built alone or in partnership with other companies, it gives me great satisfaction, because they will all be here long after the Lord calls me home. It's something that my unborn grandkids and my great-great-grandkids will see. It makes me feel like an artist who has created a living canvas.

What sometimes brings a tear to my eye is remembering how I looked at some downtown Atlanta buildings when I was only fourteen years old, never dreaming that one day *I* would be building those types of buildings myself.

■ □ ■

Today, H.J. Russell & Company is about management as well as execution of the work out in the field. Our superintendents and project managers have to know critical path management and construction technology, ideas that were in their infancy forty years ago. This new breed must know how to record situations out in the field and report back to the architects and owners using software packages. And with iPads, tablets, and smartphones, information from work sites flows between the parties much faster than ever before.

As a general contractor, we're responsible for the subcontractors executing the work on budget and on time, turning our job superintendents into a team of orchestra leaders. We are responsible for bringing seven hundred workers to a site and coordinating all the tradesmen so that they're not on top of each other, that X is coming before Y, and that the quality of their work remains high.

Not all private companies today reserve a percentage of work for minority companies. That said, we are proud to have worked with the Target retail chain for almost a decade. It was part of a conscious effort by them to look for diverse providers. Municipalities, on the other hand, still have diversity business goals that can be reached by hiring subcontractors or vendors such as H.J. Russell & Company. We still play in those areas where diversity matters, and those are usually big jobs. For instance, we were hired as part of the construction team at Dallas/Fort Worth International Airport to redo all of the airside terminals. We also built a new campus at Parkland Hospital in Dallas when the county wanted diversity. We're a solid solution in that situation because we have an excellent track record of over fifty years and because we have the financial capability to come to the table and stand shoulder-to-shoulder with non-minority firms.

■ □ ■

Of course, it was one thing to get into the big leagues; it was another to stay and thrive there. More than any other factor, I believe it was my relationship with a man named Scott Hudgens that laid the groundwork for the successes that were to come.

Scott was the real estate developer behind many of Atlanta's signature malls, including Greenbriar, Town Center, Gwinnett Place, and the Mall of Georgia. Not only was he the driver of these massive retail properties, he was also responsible for the development of apartment complexes, medical centers, nursing homes, and office parks around them. I met Scott through Cecil Day, the founder of the Days Inn hotel chain, when I bought a piece of land that Scott owned and Cecil sold to me as Scott's realtor.

Scott was born in Atlanta in the East Point/Fairburn area south of the airport. He was a World War II veteran who never went to college—after the war he went straight to work as an estimator for a lumber company. To his great delight he could estimate in his head how much lumber it would take to build a house and how much it was going to cost. Scott could calculate numbers in his head as well as anybody I've ever seen, even until the day he died. You could have your calculator, but Scott would have computed in his head a long time before any equipment would get there.

He advanced his career by building houses with his dad, followed by subdivisions and commercial real estate, particularly shopping centers and malls. He also formed two residential mortgage companies during his career.

Scott didn't change the way I did business, but he taught me a lot about how to buy land and how to consider *location, location, location*. But above all, he gave an African American the opportunity to partner with him and invest his money with him.

In the early days of my construction career, there were not many successful people in the business who took the time to coach those just entering the field, teaching them the fine points of Atlanta's construction industry. Scott was already quite successful by then, but he made the time to show me the ropes. Our relationship began with one specific piece of advice he gave me: "Some may buy land but I *select* land."

It didn't matter whether or not I had plans to develop the land; Scott insisted that I invest in or, as he would say, "select" property anyway. In particular, he was high on the development possibilities north of Atlanta. He bought all the property up that way that he could and advised me to do the same, specifically in Gwinnett County.

I usually accepted Scott's guidance, but this time I passed because I felt I should continue my development efforts in the South Atlanta area and I was proud of my work there—an area largely overlooked by other developers. In retrospect, rejecting that piece of advice is probably one of my biggest regrets and my greatest lost income opportunity, because that turned out to be a bonanza. If I had listened to my mentor, my wealth could have easily been one hundred times what it is today.

Don't get me wrong. I do not regret the development I did in South Atlanta; I did well there. But I also know that I missed out on what might well have been the most lucrative investments of my career.

Although I did not follow Scott's advice in that instance, he never wavered in his tutelage. And I never again went against his advice. He invited me to partner with him in the purchase of a commercial office building at 1600 Peachtree Street in Atlanta in 1993 that was at that time owned by the Equifax Corporation and served as its world headquarters. I agreed immediately. We then leased it back to them. They eventually built a new headquarters on another property we owned in Midtown together. (And we later leased the original property again, the second time to the Savannah College of Art and Design.)

When you find a knowledgeable mentor like Scott Hudgens who offers you solid guidance and ideas, it's OK to step out of the box, so to speak, and move into unfamiliar territory. That was what we did in 1984, when Scott and I decided to literally build a 7,400-acre new city—Shenandoah.

Up until that point I had only developed apartment complexes, but Scott had taught me to not think small, and building a whole new city was definitely *not* small. It was unfamiliar territory for me, but Scott was a visionary and unfamiliar territory is where visionaries operate.

Scott not only had vision, he also bore a keen sense of what some may call business savvy. He purchased several acres in Coweta County because he could tell from his research that the right development in this area would cause it to grow, thereby making it ripe for the picking. Scott's approach was to always buy the land even if he did not have immediate plans for it.

"Herman," he said, "we are going down to Coweta County and build us a city."

Honestly, I thought he was speaking *theoretically*.

But I knew Scott was up to something so I took the ride with him to see what this was all about. When we arrived, he pointed out several acres he had already purchased. Then he showed me the land he wanted us to buy together. Scott knew that we both wanted to create something bigger and better than our last individual projects. We were a perfect team; neither of us believed in wasting time when a project was ripe.

Scott always did his research so he already knew that both city and county leaders were looking for development and growth to create a tax base and jobs. We discussed this plan with Melvin Margolis, the deputy general manager of the US Department of Housing and Urban Development (HUD)'s Community Development Corp and explained our intention to build a city.

During this time, James Lynn was confirmed as the new HUD secretary and Shenandoah, a place intended to be home to approximately sixty-nine thousand people, was the first new city he authorized. It would sit on seventy-four hundred acres around the Newnan exit of I-85, about thirty miles south of Atlanta. Our city mapped out a wide range of housing, lakes, parks, playgrounds, schools, stores, and an industrial park for more than twenty-nine thousand jobs within fifteen minutes' drive of the most distant house.

Scott and I formed H & H Acquisitions and set out to acquire more land. This time we went to the city of Canton in Cherokee County, Georgia. Scott loved the beauty of the mountains. He knew that people would want to live there because of the breathtaking views and picturesque scenery. The fact that it was close enough to Atlanta to commute would make it attractive to those who needed to work in the city but would enjoy coming home to an area with a north Georgia view. Scott compared Cherokee County to Gwinnett County in its early days. It had good access, good leaders, and an airport, but lacked any real upscale development.

We assembled two large tracts—one in the city and one in the county, along with several other parcels. Eventually, all the land was annexed into the city of Canton. Jones Textile Mills, which once owned significant parts of Canton and caused the city to be nicknamed "Mill Town" because it employed most of Canton's citizens, sat on eighteen hundred acres of the land we purchased. This parcel, although large, did not have enough frontage on a main road needed for commercial development, so we also assembled several small tracts to provide the access we needed to Georgia Highway 5.

During this time, a defunct tract of residential land known as Summit Ridge was in bankruptcy court and eventually became available for purchase. It was located in Canton and had access on Highway 140, which sat across from the main access point of the Jones Textile property. This tract was approximately twelve hundred acres in size. It was already zoned appropriately so it was ready to go. We bought it as soon as the court system offered it for sale. All told, we assembled almost four thousand acres, enough for a significant mixed-use development.

A devastating flood in central Georgia that destroyed a lot of state roads provided an unexpected opportunity for us to move forward in 1994. The state made a decision at the time to relocate all state area roads out of flood-prone areas if possible. Prior to this time, we discovered a grade difference on the Jones tract elevation as well as on tracts adjacent to the existing Highway 5 elevation, all of which made the entire project questionable. We made a deal with the state in which we would donate the land necessary for relocating Highway 5 out of the Etowah River floodplain as well as provide and place the fill (a construction term for top soil, dirt, rocks, sands, and gravel brought to a development site) necessary for this job. The city/county would provide curbs and gutters and the state would pave the road. Scott and I already controlled 95 percent of the right-of-way needed to relocate the road out of the floodplain so we agreed to buy any additional land necessary and donate it to the state.

In 1996 we started development. Our initial retail tenants included Home Depot, Publix, JCPenney, and Belk. We named the development Riverstone and also changed Highway 5 to Riverstone Parkway.

Prior to Scott's death in 2000, we purchased one of the most prestigious plots of land in Atlanta—eighteen acres that included 1600 Peachtree Street, Rhodes Center, the Midtown Hotel, and the former Regency Hotel site. It was often referred to as the Triangle because it sits east of what is now Atlantic Station, west of Midtown, and south of Buckhead. I had an idea to build two condo towers with retail at the ground level, but neither Scott nor I were able to bring the project to fruition. Unfortunately, my friend and mentor passed away before we were able to start this project and the city developed differently than we expected. Still, the area was wildly successful and our investments paid off many times over.

Scott and I knew that if we shook hands on something, it didn't matter what attorneys wrote down or what happened after that, we knew what we said to each other and what we shook hands on. We trusted each other. Scott never made any decisions or commitments on any property we owned together without calling me, and most of the time he came to see me personally.

Scott always said of other people, "When it's time for me to go to the bank, I may have a partner, but it's only me in the car driving there." He appreciated that if he and I were going to do business together that we *both* would open our wallets and do what was necessary. That's the way it was between Scott and me.

Bruce Williams went to work for Scott in the early 1990s after Scott had open-heart surgery. As Scott slowed down a bit, Bruce handled much of our joint business.

"When Scott and I would talk about things," Bruce remembered, "he'd say, 'Have you talked to Herman?' I'd say, "No, sir,' and he'd say, 'Well, better get in the car and go talk to Herman and tell him I need his input before I'll form an opinion.'"

Scott was also a great philanthropist who accomplished a lot of things around Atlanta without letting anyone know about it. He was Mr. Anonymous. Somebody would call him and he would give money, but he never wanted to see his name attached to it. He hated being in the newspaper for anything. Like me, he liked to fly under the radar and do our thing, helping other people out and making money along the way. Scott always said that God gave him vision to be a developer and the burden to create jobs.

On June 30, 1992, Scott wrote me one of the greatest letters I ever received. It read, in part:

Herman, you are the greatest of the greats that I have known in my lifetime; a person I know I can call without any doubt, day or night, and you will get out of bed, if necessary, to help me, as well as others. You are a person I have seen and known throughout the years to never flinch or back away from an obligation or anything you have started to do or said you would do. I guess I have told a million people that I haven't had many partners in my life but the greatest partner I ever had was Herman Russell. You are one I never even thought to doubt about or wonder about, but one I could very much enjoy working for, with and learning from. I guess I could go on forever saying good things because there are no bad things that I know about you, and that goes for your family, also.

No person I know deserves and should enjoy this success that has come your way more than you. I know the reason it came your way is because of your honesty, your persistence, and your ability to always do the job well and better than someone else. It also came about because of your never forgetting the involvement of the community. You are like myself in that you believe in putting something back into what you have been able to take from.

In a strange twist, I received the Scott Hudgens Award in May 2012 from Peachtree Christian Hospice. The award was named for Scott because he donated the money to build the hospice. The award was given to me at the Atlanta Athletic Club, for which Scott donated the land on which it was built.

Sitting with me that day was Bruce Williams. "It is kind of funny," Bruce said. "Scott's up in heaven just laughing that you're getting an award named after him. *You* don't want awards and *he* never wanted anything named after him—so I guess it's only fair!"

Although he is not physically here with me in our partnership, his words and enthusiasm remain with me today. They guide me and remind me that I must always think outside the box. Scott and I always laughed and said that we were friends before it was the "in" thing to be friends between black and white. We really enjoyed one another and trusted one another with each other's money. And I really loved that man.

▪ ☐ ▪

In recent years, H.J. Russell & Company took on the challenge of managing properties many other managers didn't want to tackle. In order for these properties to remain desirable places to live, we incorporated three primary objectives: timely rent collection, routine and preventive maintenance, and effective resident programs.

Our public housing experience began in December 1994 when we were awarded a contract to manage the 754-unit James E. Scott Homes development in Miami, Florida. Based on successful affordable housing management, ours was one of the first private management agencies to be selected by the Dade County Department of Housing and Urban Development (DCHUD). We soon had similar contracts in Chicago and Atlanta based on our experience. Some may ask why I spent so much of my career developing and managing affordable housing. After all, there is more money in developing and managing apartment complexes that are not deemed affordable housing.

My answer is simple: Deverra Beverly.

Deverra Beverly was a resident of an affordable housing unit we managed in Chicago. She lived there for more than twenty-five years. Known simply as Ms. Beverly, her ability to make peace and work collaboratively is known throughout the public housing community, making her one of the most powerful leaders among residents. She served as president of the local advisory council of her development.

Ms. Beverly was not only an active part of her residential community. She showed that affordable housing allows its residents an opportunity to focus on education, leadership development, and success. Parented by her single father, Ms. Beverly grew up in affordable housing and raised six children there. She never allowed her challenges to distract her from being a productive citizen and an involved mother.

When one of her daughters died, Ms. Beverly immediately assumed responsibility for her granddaughter. She instilled in her granddaughter all the things she taught her own children. She made sure that her children and her granddaughter understood that affordable housing gives you an opportunity to do greater things. Her granddaughter heard that message and today she is a graduate of Notre Dame University.

I am committed to affordable housing because I believe that these developments can and will produce success stories like Ms. Beverly's that may not have happened if they were not available. This is why I do what I do.

IV

It's a Living

11

Before Takeoff and After Landing, Visit Us at Concessions International

When my old high school and college buddy Felker Ward returned in 1967 from his military service in Vietnam, he enrolled at the Emory University School of Law, having long ago become convinced that construction and architecture were not his destiny. He graduated in '71 and practiced law for a few years in a small firm that he and another lawyer started, but gave that up to join a large firm as a partner a few years later.

One of that firm's clients was Host International, a large company engaged in airport concessions including food and beverages, newsstands, and duty-free gift shops. Host wanted to make a bid for the concessions contract at Atlanta's Hartsfield International Airport. But there was a new Federal Aviation Authority (FAA) requirement for minority business enterprise participation in the bidding and contract process. When Howard Vernon, the CEO of Host, asked in the mid-1970s for a recommendation of a local minority businessperson with whom the company could partner, Felker recommended me.

While I was not in the food business, Felker knew I was a good businessman and that I would be a good partner. Host also needed someone who was known and respected around Atlanta. The day Howard came to my office to pitch a joint venture with Host was a game changer.

The opportunity was concessions management at Hartsfield International in Atlanta. Dobbs Paschal was the company currently under contract at the airport. Dobbs Paschal was a partnership between the majority firm Dobbs House, Inc., the airport feeding subsidiary of the Greyhound Dial Corporation, and Paschal Midfield Corp., an Atlanta-based African American firm owned by two well-known and highly respected brothers, James and Robert Paschal. The Paschal brothers owned the historic Paschals Motor Hotel and Restaurant.

I was flattered, but I knew nothing about the food business. My only experience was as a short-order cook at Roy's, my brother-in-law's hamburger shop on Auburn Avenue where I worked some weekends in high school. Howard said he would be happy to teach me the ins and outs of his business. Host offered to put up my share of the initial investment in the form of a loan that would be paid back out of my share of the income stream. In other words, I could buy into the partnership without a dime out of pocket.

"This could be such a profitable partnership," he said, "that I think it would be well worth it."

I said I needed some time to think it over and he agreed. A few weeks passed and we met for a second time. "Howard," I said, "the only way that I would get involved would be for me to put up my prorated share of the money. My people would have to be involved. You would have to teach and train us—a true joint venture. I don't want to sell my color to be a part of picking up a check without earning my keep."

To my surprise, he said, "It's a deal." We shook hands and bid on the contract.

We lost.

■ □ ■

Two years later, I received another call from Howard.

"Herman, the international terminal in Los Angeles has a set aside requirement for minority business enterprises and we would like you to come out and qualify for it," he said. In the years since our Atlanta bid, I had paid more attention to the airport concessions business and felt better prepared to attempt it. And the H.J. Russell & Company construction business was booming, so diversifying seemed like a good idea.

I sent my vice president, John Lawrence, to a required pre-bid conference. Because it was in Los Angeles, a city with a historically large Hispanic population, we expected to encounter a great deal of competition. But when John returned he said there was only one other African American firm among the bidders.

One of the catches in the Los Angeles bid was that the city required that the minority partner have restaurant experience. That left me out on the face of it, but not Felker, who had owned three Burger Kings during the late 1960s and early '70s. It became abundantly clear that he could bring the third dimension to the partnership that was needed, so we became true partners in that venture.

Howard took me at my word when I told him that I wanted to be fully involved—that I would put up my own capital and take the loss subject to him giving my people the chance to learn the business. Howard lived up to his word, ultimately creating a company that frequently competed for—and sometimes won—business against his own company. I will always be grateful to him for that.

Host won the contract and brought Felker, our friend Jesse Hill Jr., and me into the deal. Concessions International was born. I retained a 70 percent interest with Jesse and Felker sharing the other 30 percent.

I had met Jesse and Azira Hill through the Butler Street YMCA at a time when the Y was the center of everything in the black community. Jesse and I were both heavily involved in the membership campaign one year—we were both on the board of directors—and there were dinners and membership reports and it was all very social. We had children very close in age, and Otelia and I asked the Hills to be godparents for Michael and Jerome.

We did all the usual school and sports activities that parents do together, and that led to the four of us frequently traveling together as well. We cruised all over the world together and the Hills usually spent the days after Christmas with us in southwest Florida. In addition, Jesse and I often took the boys to Super Bowl games together; while we did that, Otelia and Azira would take simultaneous trips—*elsewhere*.

Jesse and I were *inseparable*. For years, he usually stopped by my office in the morning before going to his own at Atlanta Life Insurance Company, where he was president for twenty years. As partners, sometimes we talked Concessions International business, other times it was just two friends passing the time.

It was often said that you could not do business in Atlanta without coming through Jesse Hill. Jesse wanted to be a partner, and Felker and I knew Jesse would be a real asset. He knew his way around the country as well as anybody I've ever known and was experienced in going to other cities and forming partnerships. Ironically, because we had been close friends so long, it was strange we had never been in business before this. Jesse was instrumental in helping CI grow, so he was a real asset to us.

Our responsibilities at CI were split according to our individual strengths. Felker had operational and military training that made him the best at organizing and operating the business. He handled the day-to-day relationships with vendors, employees, and airport management. Whenever we prepared a proposal for a new concession, it was Felker's responsibility to put it together and vet it.

Jesse would go out on the road and use his contacts and his relationships to identify good local partners for us in all the new cities where we went. He was extremely good at the politics, so he would also be the one to reach out to decision makers and tell our story in a meaningful way. He was at church; he was at civic events; he was at business events; and he was at sporting events. In a restaurant, he would come the long way through the room, shaking hands with people he knew, saying hello to those he didn't. He shook hands with everybody; it was a natural part of him. In Atlanta, a city that had a growing number of successful black families, he was a tremendous asset. You'd never see Jesse obviously working a room; it was just his natural charm and personality in play.

It was never on paper that X was Jesse's responsibility, Y was Felker's, and Z was mine. It evolved daily, and we used our best combined strengths to make the enterprise work. Over time, we were together less often socially, although it was a tradition among the partners that every year we took our wives out as a group for Valentine's Day, which was always a ball.

Felker pursued a legal career. Jesse became CEO of Atlanta Life Insurance. I moved from subcontractor to general contractor in ever-larger joint ventures. Although over time our friendships endured, our other responsibilities pulled each of us in different directions.

We eventually operated at Los Angeles International Airport (LAX) for fourteen years, moving from the old international terminal to the new Tom Bradley International Airport. Concessions became a major profit center as our success at LAX eventually led to more contracts at other airports including Cleveland, New Orleans, Seattle, Louisville, and Hartford.

It seemed odd to many in our company that we achieved great acclaim operating airport concessions across the United States but had yet to get a chance in our hometown of Atlanta. That changed in 1994 as the city prepared for the 1996 Summer Olympics.

A request for proposals (RFP) was issued for the management of the concessionaires at Atlanta's Hartsfield Airport. Jesse, Felker, and I worked long hours to ensure that we would win the Atlanta contract because it meant so much to Concessions International. We knew that we were going up against some of the largest competitors in the industry, including Host. To bolster our bid, we asked James Paschal, formerly of Dobbs Paschal, to be part of our joint venture team to cover the Minority Business Enterprise (MBE) portion of the bid. (Anyone who has been coming to Atlanta for the past sixty years knew about the legendary

Paschal Brothers fried chicken.) Concessions was no longer classified as an MBE, having graduated from the program and into the big leagues nationwide.

The RFP required bidders to submit two bids, each for roughly one half of the concessions at the airport. Splitting the concessions in this way would allow for more MBE involvement at the airport. Concessions International submitted the best offer on both bids. However, under the terms of the RFP, we could only be (and were) awarded a contract to manage half of the concessions at the airport.

H.J. Russell & Company joint ventured with Holder Construction and Batson-Cook Construction on the construction of the People Mover at Hartsfield. However, CI provided construction management to the build-out of the concessions areas. The airport was completed on time for the start of the 1996 Olympics.

∎ □ ∎

The Russell family's primary nonconstruction or real estate business, Concessions International, operates restaurants and food-and-beverage outlets in airports throughout the United States. The easiest way to explain what we do is to say that, in part, we're a restaurant franchisee in airports. If you understand that every Wendy's is not run by Wendy's and every McDonald's is not run by McDonald's, then that's what we do. We're a licensed franchisee of these brands and our specialty is that we do it in airports.

And in each of these airport operations, we usually have joint venture partners although there are some that we wholly own. Within each airport we typically operate different national brands. And then we have some in-house CI brands that we name ourselves, such as Coach's Corner or Last Call.

In Atlanta today, we operate a Paschal's Restaurant across from our corporate headquarters, as well as a Paschal's and other concessions at Hartsfield International Airport. And we have the restaurant concessions at the World of Coca-Cola Museum, where we run the *Pemberton Café*.

A major way that CI succeeded through the years has been in the hundreds of young men and women it trained to do great things. I'd like to tell you about a few of them.

Daniel Meachum

Daniel Meachum was corporate counsel for Concessions for several years. But he was hired as our vice president of general counsel without the knowledge of Jesse, Felker, or myself. A fellow who once worked for us knew Danny through mutual friends. He called Danny up and said, "I have a job for you. I think you'd be great for this job as general counsel of this new food and beverage company in Atlanta."

Danny flew down for a job interview with a CI executive and— without being introduced to any of the CI principals—Danny received an offer letter a few days later. Being the typical lawyer that he is, Danny responded by sending back a tight employment contract. The CI executive signed the contract and *then* told Danny he needed to come down and meet with Jesse, Felker, and me. Someone picked Danny up at the airport and brought him to my office. We got in my car and I drove us both over to the 191 Building downtown where Felker's office was.

Once together with Danny and the man who hired him, we fired the latter.

Now it was just us and Danny, who we didn't hire, didn't know, and didn't quite know what to do with. He had a four-year employment contract that he had written himself and that a now ex-executive had signed while still employed by us. Jesse, Felker, and I started asking Danny all kinds of questions, not knowing whether he and the other man had colluded on Danny's hiring or if it was all the result of someone who hadn't made a decision that was in the best interests of Concessions International.

"This is a company that I love," I told Danny. "We worked hard to build this company. I can't believe that you would write a contract like this against my company."

"Mr. Russell," he said, "no disrespect to you, Mr. Hill, or Mr. Ward, but I would think that the three of you would *want* to have a lawyer smart enough to write an airtight contract like this."

Felker looked up at me and said, "Herman, I think he's got a point, doesn't he?"

Jesse later on told me that it was obvious that Danny was a smart lawyer and that we should try to apply his competence to what we were doing. (Only later did we learn that Atlanta mayor Maynard Jackson had known Danny since Danny was a college freshman at Maynard's alma mater, North Carolina Central University in Durham.)

Danny stayed with us for the duration of his original contract. One day he repeated my own words back to me about controlling his own destiny and announced he would be leaving CI. In 2000, he put out a shingle in Atlanta as a sole practitioner specializing in complex litigation, although he may be best known for the athletes and entertainers he has represented over the years, including actors Denzel Washington and Wesley Snipes, and five Atlanta Falcons football players including Michael Vick.

Danny made a big difference in our journey and I am mighty proud of what he achieved as a private lawyer after he left CI.

■ ☐ ■

I first met Johnnie when Concessions International was negotiating with the board of the Los Angeles International Airport for its food and beverage contract. Johnnie was a member of the board. We hit it right off and always got together for dinner or a drink when we saw each other at airport conventions. At one in particular, he saw me having a drink with a beautiful young lady and business associate named Dale Mason. Johnnie made it his business to join us and I introduced him to Dale. Pretty soon I noticed that he wasn't as interested in what I was saying as usual.

A couple of years later he called to tell Otelia and me that he and Dale were getting married! Over the years, the four of us vacationed at their beach house in Malibu and they visited with us at our lake house and our Florida home.

Johnnie was fun and funny, but he was also warm and deeply compassionate. He was brilliant and had the kind of inviting, captivating personality that could light up the room. After the O. J. Simpson murder trial in 1995, he was one of the most famous people in America, but that never changed him. He remained down-to-earth and totally dedicated to helping the underdog.

Two of my favorite memories of him stand out because they were vintage Johnnie Cochran.

When I called to chat with Johnnie one evening, Dale told me that he had been working day and night preparing for the O. J. Simpson trial. I suggested she bring him to our lake house for a long weekend and a little quiet and relaxation. I told her that if he needed to work while he was there he could use my office, a lovely sunroom off the top deck that overlooked the lake. The lake view and the quiet, majestic beauty of the mountains would do him good.

Dale started making arrangements to come the minute we got off the phone. Also joining us were US representative Julius Dixon and his wife, Betty.

We drove to the mountains together to settle in for a relaxed and good time. The lake house has a great kitchen—Otelia made sure of that. She was such a great cook that we usually ate at home looking out over the lake and the surrounding mountains. I pride myself on the sense of hospitality I inherited from my mother, so the day before they were to catch their flight home I announced that I was taking everyone out that evening to dine at my favorite restaurant in the area.

"We have reservations for seven," I said, "so be ready to go at six thirty."

Ever the dapper dresser, Johnnie asked, "Do we need to change our clothes?" He had on shorts and sandals.

"Yeah, I think so. Nothing fancy, though. The folks up here don't stand on as much formality as we do in the city," I said.

At 6:25, Otelia and I were waiting at the front door. Dale emerged from the guest suite looking lovely in comfortable slacks.

"Where's Johnnie?" I asked.

"He's still in the bathroom, Herman." She then stuck her head in the bedroom door and said, "We're waiting on you, honey."

A minute later Johnnie walked out. To my surprise—actually to the surprise of all of us—Johnnie had on blue jeans. I don't mean stylish jeans. These were stiff, shiny, new cowboy-looking jeans with yellow-orange stitching around the seams and pockets. Imagine the suave, urbane, well-tailored Johnnie Cochran, a man whose good taste was the stuff of legend, standing before you in cowboy jeans. And dress shoes. We all just stood there with our mouths open.

Finally, Dale said, "Johnnie, you look like you're going out on the range."

We burst into laughter.

"Herman told me to change my clothes," he protested. "I'm just trying to dress like they do up here in the country."

I said, "It's the mountains, Johnnie, not the Wild West!" We laughed until we cried. Johnnie laughed the loudest. He had a great sense of humor. He was still laughing when he went into the bedroom to change. I don't know what he did with those blue jeans, but I do know that we never saw them again.

The other story is vintage Johnnie Cochran, the celebrity lawyer.

One of my holdings is a high-rise office building in downtown Atlanta. The building was leased to a Fortune 500 company. We'd had a good working relationship with the firm, but for some reason they hadn't paid their rent in months. My people had called repeatedly to discuss the situation, but the company did not respond to any of our inquiries. After months of calls, they offered to pay us a small fraction of the amount they owed us. We tried to negotiate, but they would not budge. Finally it became clear that we had no choice but engage to legal counsel.

I don't believe in doing anything halfway. If I had to go the legal route, I might as well have the best representing me. And who was the best negotiator and legal mind I knew? Johnnie Cochran, of course. Johnnie informed the company by mail that unless they were willing to negotiate in good faith, we were headed to court. They didn't find the prospect of facing Johnnie Cochran in court particularly inviting, so they agreed to meet.

I picked up Johnnie from his hotel. We went straight to the meeting. As we entered the lobby I said, "You know that they're going to throw their entire legal department at us, don't you?"

Johnnie just smiled and said, "Don't worry. I think we'll handle it."

I trusted Johnnie's judgment and of course I knew he was one of the best lawyers in the country, but I still was a bit concerned. I mean, there was only him against what would surely be a conference room full of opposing lawyers. Little did I know that Johnnie had a secret weapon: his celebrity.

The receptionist invited us to be seated while she announced us. Then she started excitedly whispering into her telephone. I had no idea what was going on. Johnnie just smiled. All of a sudden the waiting room was full of the firm's employees. They milled around him, grinning and asking for his autograph. Someone had found a camera and everyone in the room wanted to take a picture with Johnnie Cochran. I've never seen anything like it. Johnnie just took it in stride. He was used to it.

Then a group of well-dressed fellows emerged from an office and approached Johnnie. They handed him journals, datebooks, even stray pieces of paper for him to autograph. This went on for about fifteen minutes.

After the hoopla died down we were ushered toward a conference room where the firm's attorneys awaited. Yes, the conference room was filled with lawyers just as I'd feared. But *these* lawyers were the same group of fellows who'd earlier held out their datebooks and journals for Johnnie's autograph. Even now, at the negotiating table, they still seemed a bit starstruck.

I chuckled to myself. I knew we had the negotiation in the bag.

We went back and forth. Each time they made an offer, Johnnie upped the ante. They hemmed and hawed, but before long they found themselves offering much more than when we started. By now all of them looked shell-shocked and a bit green about the gills. Apparently Johnnie had maneuvered them into offering much more than they had planned. And he still wasn't finished. He just kept chipping away. Finally, the lead attorney asked if I would leave the room. I looked at Johnnie. He just smiled that cool smile.

"It means that they're going to ask me to accept their offer," he whispered. "They have no more money to offer and they don't want to admit it in front of you."

Johnnie had gotten those lawyers to agree to pay almost all they owed us without us making any meaningful concessions. The truth is, though, that Johnnie had won that case before we even sat at the bargaining table, just by being Johnnie Cochran.

■ □ ■

In the winter of 1999 Dale called me. "Herman, I have bad news."

My blood ran cold. "Is it Johnnie?"

"Yes, Herman." She paused. "He has brain cancer."

I felt like someone had kicked me in the stomach. "How bad is it, Dale?"

"It's bad, Herman."

It was very bad. Johnnie had terminal brain cancer. I visited him a few times in early spring and we talked on the telephone several times. Each time, his voice was weaker. Johnnie was mostly bedridden by then, but he still had that upbeat spirit, though it was a bit muted. Still, not once did I hear a hint of self-pity from him. Nor did he lose his sense of humor. His laughter wasn't as hearty, but it was still there.

In December 2004, Dale called again. She sounded calm, but tired.

"Herman," she said, "I think this would be a good time to come see Johnnie."

My heart dropped because I knew what that meant. I took the first available flight to Los Angeles. Dale met me at the door with a big hug then immediately led me to Johnnie's bedside. In her telephone call and when she met me at the door she had told me how sick Johnnie was, but I wasn't prepared to see the toll the illness had taken on him. He was very, very thin. He seemed too weak to move and that wonderful voice was barely a whisper. I couldn't help it. I just broke down and cried. I turned my back and stepped into the bathroom to compose myself. When I returned he was crying, too. In a matter of weeks my dear friend Johnnie Cochran was dead.

His funeral testified to the love and joy he brought wherever he went. People came from all over the world to celebrate his life. I was honored to speak at Dale's request and to tell the world of the love Otelia and I had for him. Johnnie was much more than a friend—he was my brother. He touched the lives of my family in such a way that my children thought of him as almost a second father. We traveled together and spent many wonderful summer weeks together.

Finally, I shared that Johnnie was a people person with a huge heart and magnanimous personality that lit up any room he entered. Johnnie never met a stranger, and if you were fortunate enough to spend time with him you were guaranteed to have an evening of uncontrollable laughter.

▪ ☐ ▪

When my daughter, Donata, asked me about working for H.J. Russell & Company a few years after college graduation, her idea was to spend six months working in each division to better understand our businesses and see where she might make the best fit.

That was a good idea, so she started in property management. But I kept telling her about this other company that Jesse, Felker, and I had started called Concessions International. It didn't yet have the high profile that our construction business did, so she was unaware of it. But I was convinced that she would like it, and six months later she was up to her neck in it, starting out in an administrative management role.

She eventually went out to Los Angeles to see the food and beverage operation up close. Once Donata understood what the airport concessions business was about, she fell in love with it. The operations and marketing side appealed to her, but, even more so, it was a lot more fun than property management and development.

Donata eventually took charge of CI, but that was still several years in the future. Returning from Los Angeles, she became a general administrative assistant to Jesse, Felker, and me. It was a great way to learn the business from the inside out and she mastered it quickly.

▪ ☐ ▪

Concessions International reached a tipping point in 1999 when CI received unsolicited buyout offers from other companies. My partners and I vacillated for more than a year over whether to sell. Jesse and Felker were more interested in taking the money on the table, but I wasn't. We needed to either invest more money to get bigger or sell out. I wasn't ready to leave the business; in fact, I wanted to grow CI as a business and I believed Donata was the ideal person to lead. After a year of debate, I stood up at a CI board meeting with my friends and partners and said I wanted to buy out their shares.

"I put so much time in this company that I'm just going to buy it," I said. "I want to control my own destiny." With that, I bought out the interests of Jesse Hill Jr. and Felker Ward in May of that year.

I had so much confidence in Donata that when I bought out Jesse's and Felker's interest in CI, I officially put her in charge as president of Concessions International.

■ □ ■

Airport concessions is a fascinating business. Seeing people from all walks of life coming and going through the terminals simply fascinates me, and I enjoy providing a good and valuable service to the traveling public. Today, Concessions International is one of the sixth largest concessionaires in food and beverage in the country. We operate in seven major airports throughout the country, and it gives me great personal satisfaction that Donata has earned the position of CEO of Concessions International.

12

The Beer Years

I was the first African American to be issued a liquor license in the city of Atlanta.

It was not easy for a black man to obtain a liquor license during that era, so when Schlitz announced that it was seeking a minority business for a new Atlanta distribution territory, I immediately expressed interest. As it turned out, five of Atlanta's top businessmen were also under consideration for it, including my friend Hank Aaron, the Atlanta Braves baseball legend. (When Hank realized it would require him to be a hands-on owner—especially during baseball season—he begged off.)

After weeks of combing through our proposals and financial statements, Schlitz selected me to be its beer distributor in Atlanta. I was attracted by the very profitable nature of the opportunity—especially having seen the money that could be made on beer at airports via Concessions International—and the chance to establish another first in my community. We purchased part of a territory from a company called Premium Beverage, established our own company, City Beverage, and acquired rights to distribute domestic beers such as Schlitz Malt Liquor, Stroh's, and foreign beverages such as Molson and Beck's. Later we added a small line of wines.

Every business we serviced was in the inner city and our number one selling product was Schlitz Malt Liquor. We did, however, have a thriving on-premise business downtown with hotels, bars, and restaurants with Stroh's, Beck's, and Molson. And we sold bottled, canned, and keg beer products at the old Omni arena.

In running a business as complicated as liquor distribution, it gave me great confidence to have a manager in whom I had the utmost personal and professional confidence: Bill Kimbrough. My high school and college buddy stayed in the army for five years as a second lieutenant after graduating from Tuskegee Institute. Bill was commissioned and, when he came out, went to work for the post office for twelve years. As he prepared to retire from the government, I asked Bill to come and work with me and that's what he did, for the next thirty-five years.

Most of those years were spent in property management, but when I acquired the Schlitz beer distribution business in Atlanta, I made Bill the assistant general manager at City Beverage. Bill and I have always been truthful and honest with each other. Our relationship never changed through the years; money never got in the way. I always knew I had a friend in Bill and I always knew I could confide in him. As far as friends go, I felt if I needed him, he was there and I've known he felt the same way about me. That trust made him the ideal person for me to have overseeing our beer business.

To be honest, though, Bill thought that was one of the toughest jobs he ever had. Selling beer at the wholesale level was fraught with laws and regulations that drove him crazy at times. For example, we were not supposed to offer any freebies, but there were stores that wanted two more cases for free if they bought ten. Bill dealt with stuff like that for three years—three years too many, I think he'd tell you!

In 1973 I built Jet Liquors on the corner of Simpson and Burbank Streets. I hired my brother, Robert Russell, to manage it for me. Robert was the only brother who was not a plasterer. He was a baker by trade, making him the only one of us in the family with some form of retail experience.

Sales of beer and liquor in this country alone run into billions of dollars every year. There are always retail stores cropping up to sell alcoholic beverages, and the same with the restaurants, bars, and taverns that serve it. The distributorship was quite profitable. Things went so well that in 1979 we were granted a Coors franchise in Chicago, the largest Coors distributorship in the nation. Our territory included the downtown Chicago area they call the Loop, but also DuPage County, a large suburban county adjacent to the city.

I sent my accountant, Courtney Pollard, and my oldest son, Jerome, to run the Chicago operation. Jerome had worked his way up through the family businesses, first in construction, then in the Schlitz distributorship in Atlanta. When he was twenty-three I decided to let him get a little more hands-on, independent managerial experience in establishing the new business. They set up an office and a warehouse downtown and got to work.

When we first considered establishing the Chicago franchise we conducted a market analysis that took into account every significant economic, financial, and demographic factor. There was one we overlooked, however: race.

Chicago, like Atlanta, had a long history of racial strife and violence, but by the late 1970s things had changed greatly. Sure, there was still some racial dislike and distrust on the part of both blacks and whites, but we learned to work together to some degree and we got the Chicago franchise running smoothly for a while. There were, however, certain taverns in DuPage County that one of our white supervisors advised Jerome not to go into because of race issues.

After several years of operations in Chicago, we found racism isn't unique to the South when it came to blacks. It was an extreme wake-up call to discover so much racism in a northern city in the United States. I expected better of Chicago, but perhaps I was naive.

Back in Atlanta, we were forced to get out of the wholesale beverage business altogether because, under Georgia state law, you could not have both an on-premise business selling beer and wine—such as Concessions International at Hartsfield International Airport—and a wholesale business such as City Beverage. For that reason, we sold off the rest of the City Beverage distributorship business in Atlanta in 1995.

Some long-term good did come from our brief time in the beverage business, including the development of new marketing talent in my son Jerome Russell and my niece, Fanitra Russell. And it taught me that you have to know when it's time to move on.

13

The H.J. Russell Institute
of Good Common Sense

There is no greater point of pride in my life than seeing a young person whose career I've touched succeed and, even better, exceed.

And with more than sixty years in business and thousands of employees having passed through the doors of our many entities at H.J. Russell & Company, I have been given the opportunity to launch or influence a number of successful careers. In our business, what comes first is know-how: there's no substitute for it. If you don't have it and if you don't master what you engage in, you're heading for disaster. To give your best, you've got to be married to what you're engaged in. That's the only way, in my opinion, success is going to happen for you.

To be a successful entrepreneur, it's also very, very important to have the capital that's going to be required to finish what you start. If you don't bring something to the table because you think you're going to borrow everything, it's not going to happen. You may be lucky enough one out of a million times, but without capital, you're sunk.

My philosophy, as a chief executive, is work hard . . . and always stay focused. Also look for people much sharper than you.

It begins with being honest. That's important. If you're not honest, your potential will never be realized. You've got to be honest with yourself because when you're honest with yourself, you'll be the first one to look yourself in the mirror and say, "I didn't do that right. I didn't do the job that I was capable of doing." And honesty allows you to regroup and come up with a better approach to solve whatever the problem may be.

I have no patience with people who are not willing to give 100 percent or more of themselves for the greater good. I have patience to teach, and to give people opportunities, but when you live like there should be a free meal and all you're going to bring to the table is an appetite and give nothing back, I don't have patience for that.

I look for the best people I can find; I don't care about their race or sex. I don't care how they look. You don't have to be traditionally handsome or a beauty queen. I like a United Nations atmosphere in my office. I don't bear any prejudice in my heart or in my mind.

The most difficult and disappointing part of being in business, the thing that probably gets to me more than anything, is when I see people with a lot of potential, but they're so lazy that they won't let that potential develop. Those moments are the most hurtful of my career. Is it hard for me to fire someone? No. If I give you an opportunity and you're not living up to your part of the bargain, after I warn you, after I remind you of my expectations, after I give you an evaluation, I will not hesitate to fire you at the drop of a hat.

Some call this the H.J. Russell Institute of Good Common Sense. What follows are some of my favorite stories from over the years of men and women who exemplify our company's basic philosophies, told in part by me, in part in their own words.

Egbert Perry

I've always hired promising young men and women, but I insist that they must be fully qualified and willing to work hard to succeed. And they have to be smarter than me in ways that will make a contribution to H.J. Russell and at the same time further their own careers, whether or not they stay with our enterprise. Egbert Perry was one such young man.

I received a call one day from my daughter, Donata, while she was a student at the University of Pennsylvania. "Daddy," she said, "there's a young man here who is in the job market. I think you ought to talk to him. His name is Egbert Perry. It would be worth you investing in an airline ticket to bring him down and talk with you."

I met Egbert the next week. He had completed his studies at Penn with a masters in civil engineering and an MBA. When Donata met him, he was tutoring Penn students in engineering and math. After a half-hour of conversation, I was so impressed that I offered him a job on the spot as my special assistant; he joined our company in January 1980 and stayed for the next thirteen years.

Egbert was your classic workaholic. He was also focused on the tasks at hand, quick and eager to learn everything I knew about the business. He was a fast learner who was not only well educated but also possessed good old common sense.

I took him through H.J. Russell & Company's diversification, which included, among others, project management, program management, project development, and, of course, construction. Egbert studied hard and worked long hours. I opened my entire portfolio to him and taught him everything I knew. I withheld nothing, not even the boardroom. He mastered every aspect of the business so well and so quickly that in 1982 he became president of H.J. Russell & Company.

Egbert Perry said:

> I tell people there's nowhere else that a wet-behind-the-ears twenty-four-year-old—even though I thought I knew everything—would have gotten that opportunity. *I* would have fired me if I were him, many times along the way. I'm appreciative of the opportunity he

gave me, and it's an opportunity he gave to a lot of other people. If you ask me what his biggest legacy will be, all you have to do is look at all of the Herman Russell alum that are out there and that, to me, is a testimony to what he actually did and what his contribution was.

A decade later, Egbert struck out on his own and formed the Integral Group LLC, where he is the chairman and CEO. The company has been involved in more than fifty public-private partnerships with a total development cost exceeding $1 billion. Through subsidiaries, the firm also provides property management, program management, and construction services to public, private, and institutional clients.

Egbert Perry continued:

The Herman J. Russell "Institute" was by accident, not by design, which I think is what's best about it. I don't care how sophisticated or thoughtful you thought your presentation for him was, he had a simple way of distilling it down to two or three questions for making a deal:

- How much money am I going to have to put in?
- What is my risk going to be?
- What else are you asking me to do beyond the money that may be reflective of some kind of commitment?

All of the other sophisticated mathematical analyses and sensitivity analyses could be on paper, but you had to be prepared to answer the core and most fundamental questions as well.

H.J. Russell & Company and Egbert's company have partnered in joint ventures both here in Atlanta and in Alabama, keeping us in business together for many years. Egbert always had his own opinion about stuff, but he was a good, hard worker. What I like about him is he doesn't let up. He works, works, works. There's no end to it.

Noel Khalil

Noel Khalil spent more than six years with H.J. Russell & Company running the development division. In his own words:

The words I want to use to describe HJ are "absolute gentleman." In business there are times that you're going to have friction. It's natural. He had a way of communicating his concerns in a respectful way, and I don't know how to do that. He was always incredibly patient and extremely supportive of you when you had success and he was supportive even when you failed. It was the most incredible experience. I get emotional thinking about it.

When we met, Noel was a corporate executive with U.S. Home Corporation and had just been transferred to Atlanta. The way development happened in Atlanta was that the north side was predominantly white and the south side was heavily black. Noel's job was buying land for U.S. Home on the north side.

The white businesspeople he dealt with there were unaccustomed to seeing an African American representing a major corporation with huge sums of money behind him. A few who knew me thought I'd be interested in meeting such a young man and they were right. "There's a black guy up here," they said. "You need to meet him. He's doing multimillion-dollar deals and he seems to know what he's doing."

I called and from that very first conversation, I asked him to help me create a real estate company focused on market rate development. Prior to that, of course, Jim Coclin and I did a lot of subsidized HUD housing for the federal government.

I asked Noel, "What do you make at U.S. Home?"

"Sixty thousand," he said.

I thought about it and said, "I'll pay you thirty thousand. I'll pay you just enough so you won't starve, but if you're half as good as you say you are, then you'll be making a lot more than thirty thousand pretty quickly."

A lot of people would have stuck with their guaranteed $60,000 and laughed at my offer of a guarantee that was just half that. But Noel saw the entrepreneurial opportunity that it was because I also offered him a 20 percent ownership stake in the new company.

I hit the ground running the day I joined Mr. Russell because I *was* starving. And he wanted me to be starving because then he knew I'd be hungry and make something happen.

The second negotiation between us was over what to call the company. Noel wanted to name it "Khalil, Russell and Associates." I said, "Don't call it Khalil, Russell and Associates. Call it Khalil and Associates. You keep the ego. Give me the money."

After thinking it over, Noel suggested calling the company Gibraltar Land. If I didn't care if my name was on it, Noel decided it didn't matter to him, either.

> We were going to some type of event. Mr. Russell drove and when we got out of the car, I saw him bend down to pick up a penny. He held it up for me to see and said, "Look, Noel. Look how much richer I am today! See how good God has been to me?"
>
> We did a corporate brochure for the development company and we put the penny story on the back of it.

Today, Noel is the chairman and CEO of Columbia Residential in Atlanta, responsible for strategic planning, overseeing corporate operations, and the formation of strategic alliances with communities, nonprofit CDCs, financial institutions, and governmental and public housing authorities. He has developed more than five thousand housing units in metropolitan Atlanta and over ten thousand units throughout the United States.

John Jackson

John Jackson was born and raised in Atlanta. After graduating from the University of Georgia, he took a job with my external CPA, the late Anthony Halligan, who liked John and suggested we meet. Tony, unfortunately, died at a young age. John and I served as pallbearers at his funeral, which was the true beginning of our long friendship.

John spent the next fifteen years with Bank South and another fifteen at SouthTrust before cofounding Bank of Atlanta in 2005. I've been both a mentor and a customer of his for many years.

When SouthTrust recruited John, he came to me for advice about whether to accept their offer. "If you have weighed all of the facts, and if this is what you want to do, then go for it and we'll see what happens,"

I said. By the time he left SouthTrust a decade and a half later, John was CEO of the bank's Jacksonville, Florida, operation. When Wachovia bought the bank, however, John got passed over for a promotion in favor of someone who had already been with Wachovia. He came back to Atlanta and was offered another opportunity. He asked me, once again, what I thought. It was just before Christmas 2004.

"Mr. Russell," he said, "I'm thinking about starting a new bank. We'd need to raise about fifteen million dollars in capital to do it. I think I can be successful. What do you think?"

"John," I said, "you know how I feel about you; I look at you like a son. But if you're going to start a bank with fifteen million dollars— *don't do it*."

He was shocked.

"Really?" he said.

"It's not that you *can't* do it, but let me tell you something. Times are good right now, but John, it can change fast. In the bank business, you've got to have the capital to withstand the bad times."

"But Mr. Russell," he said, "the airport, residential construction— they're all going great!"

"That's true, but I'm telling you it doesn't matter. I'm telling you don't do it."

"Yes, sir, Mr. Russell."

But I wasn't done.

"If you decide to go forward anyway," I said, "I'll still help you."

John went right back to the people he had gathered to start the bank and told them, "Guys, we can't do it. Mr. Russell, whom I have the utmost respect for, has given me some advice and if we can't make it work, let's not do it. He said that we need to raise thirty to forty million dollars, at least. So now *I* think we need to raise fifty million."

In the end, John and his partners raised $60 million, one of the largest stock subscriptions in Georgia history for a new bank. And because of that, the Bank of Atlanta survived the Great Recession of 2008–10, a time when far more experienced financial institutions went out of business.

By the way, by 2012 the Bank of Atlanta's capitalization stood at $200 million.

Joia Johnson

Attorney Joia Johnson's rise through H.J. Russell & Company and beyond is all the more remarkable when you learn that I've known her since she was a little girl.

Joia and Donata were the best of friends and went to high school together. Donata went to the University of Pennsylvania, while Joia headed to Duke University, but they stayed in contact and frequently visited each other on campus. Upon graduation, Donata elected to stay in Philadelphia, working for IBM. Joia wanted to pursue a law degree and MBA and chose to attend the University of Pennsylvania Law School so she'd be close to a friend so far from home.

Both girls eventually came back to Atlanta. Donata came to work for me at Concessions International; Joia joined the law firm of Long & Aldridge. At some point, Donata told Joia that H.J. Russell & Company had grown a lot since they were kids and that I was looking to hire in-house counsel for the first time. Joia gave Donata her resume and I hired her.

> I was a young lawyer; I'd been out and practicing about three years at the time. What's most unusual, more than going to your friend's dad's company, is being somewhere as general counsel as a twenty-nine-year-old, third-year associate. And I was the only woman on HJ's senior team. Those things were probably more significant challenges to deal with than the fact that I was Donata's friend and everyone knew it.

It was a lot cheaper for me to hire Joia on staff than to keep sending all of our legal work out. It was much more efficient because every time we did hire outside counsel, someone had to supervise that lawyer. And we had grown so much that the legal complications of our business—construction and real estate development, HUD property management, litigation, joint venture agreements, contracts, benefit plans, workers' comp, ERISA issues—were piling up.

Joia proved her competency pretty quickly and we put her over Human Resources and Risk Management as well. By the time she left ten years later, she was also responsible for Real Estate Development.

I could not have survived in that role if he hadn't supported me the way he did. That was absolutely crucial. He took me under his wing. He took me around to all kinds of meetings. He challenged me when I would tell him things, but at the same time he would support me in front of other executives. He also deferred to me around other executives. Those are the kinds of things in any environment that contribute to someone A) having the confidence to do their job and B) having the *power* to do their job.

He was confident in me from day one. He knew me as a child and back then he would periodically sit down when I came over after school with Donata and ask me how I was doing. He had said, even when I was growing up, "You're going to work for me one day." He may not remember that, but I do.

I went from a pressure-cooker, all-white environment where I was one of very few African Americans and one of very few women—not the most relaxed and comfortable or confidence-building environment—to a mostly black company where I felt, for the first time, I would exclusively be judged on the quality of my work.

One of the downsides of developing great executive talent is that word gets around. One day, Joia got a call out of the blue from Atlanta-based Rare Hospitality International Inc., which was a public company that owned chains of Longhorn Steakhouse and Capital Grille restaurants nationwide. It was looking for its first general counsel, someone who could create an in-house legal staff.

It was a job opportunity to which she couldn't say no. And that one only led to an even better one. Today, Joia Johnson is chief legal officer, general counsel, and corporate secretary for Hanes Brands, which includes Hanes, Champion, Playtex, Bali, L'eggs, and WonderBra.

But I still have the benefit of her advice and years of experience: she's now on the H.J. Russell & Company board of directors.

Dallas Smith

In 1989, Dallas Smith was the first black commercial real estate broker hired by Cushman Wakefield in Georgia. At that time, Cushman was owned by the Rockefeller Group. It was a really big deal in the South that they had hired this young black broker.

And once hired, Dallas's first cold call was to me. "I'd been following the Herman Russell story my entire life," he said. "And to me, he was bigger than life. If you asked me who'd had the most influence on me, it would have been Herman Russell."

He called my office and introduced himself to my secretary, Barbara Murphy, and asked to speak with me. Dallas had written a basic script with the key points he wanted to make in conversation with me and others, including what Cushman Wakefield offered that no one else could.

"Please tell Mr. Russell that I'm also the first black broker that Cushman hired in the state of Georgia," he said, "and I know that if I am going to be anything in this city, I need to have the blessing of Herman Russell."

Barbara said, "I will give him that message."

Smith relaxed after the call, figuring it could be days or weeks before I'd call back. What he didn't know was that Barbara gave me precisely the message he left—fifteen minutes later—and conveyed the young man's excitement and urgency. I called him right back.

He was a young guy who had been recognized by one of the top real estate firms in the city. They thought enough to hire him as an agent. Of course I would give him the benefit of the doubt and listen to him and open up a door for him to come in.

Dallas was having a snack in the company's break room when his secretary found him and told him he had a call. She didn't say my name, apparently, and he figured it was his wife asking him to bring some bread or milk home after work.

"Just send the call to the break room," he asked.

When he picked up, I said, "Dallas? This is Herman Russell."

He was completely surprised. All the great things he prepared to say just went out of his head. "Mr. Russell," he said, "I'm really thrown off; I didn't expect you to call me back. My script's at my desk, but I'm just going to tell you that I'm the first black broker Cushman Wakefield's ever hired in the state of Georgia. And I'm not really calling you for anything specific. I just wanted to meet you because I knew that, moving forward in this town, in some form or fashion, our paths would cross and I would need your blessing to move forward."

I couldn't help but laugh. "Dallas, I'm glad you called. I'm very proud of you. That's very admirable." I told him to talk to Noel Khalil, who was in charge of development at the time. "Tell him that I told you to call."

"Um, sure," he said. "Thank you."

Noel invited Dallas to our office to identify some possible properties for acquisition. While there, he literally bumped into my son Jerome. Jerome was a property manager at the time, and when Jerome found out that Dallas worked at Cushman Wakefield he said, "We need to get together."

The opportunity in front of Dallas at Cushman Wakefield was as important for him as it was to us; as his status as the first black broker in their Atlanta operation indicated, his was a special situation. Jerome and Dallas had breakfast or lunch every month for the next several years. We were quite interested in tracking the progress of Dallas Smith. At one of those meetings, Jerome said, "Dallas, when I become president of the company, I want you to come over and start a brokerage division."

Dallas wasn't sure how serious he was, but when I named Jerome president of the company, Jerome called Dallas that very same day and made a formal pitch to him. Not long after, we hired Dallas and he pioneered the brokerage division for H.J. Russell & Company.

Using the contacts and experience Dallas had developed in Atlanta since we first met him, we signed deals with Bell South, AT&T, and General Motors, among others. Name the Fortune 500 company, and if they were in Atlanta, we were working with them. In addition, we used Dallas's skills to assemble the land that became the Castleberry Inn & Suites and Paschal's Restaurant.

Dallas recalled:

I learned so much from him. Quite honestly, I didn't really realize the lessons I learned until after I had actually left. It's like drinking from a fire hose when you learn from him, you don't realize what you've got until you leave and you go "Wow." I thought he was the cheapest guy alive and now I'm the guy writing the checks for my company and I understand exactly. I watch every penny and I thank him for that lesson of being frugal.

My favorite days were his Monday meetings with the vice presidents and the executive team. He would say some of the most profound things. I kept a notebook where I'd write down the things he'd actually say.

I'll give you a perfect example. This was classic Herman Russell. HJ asked, "Has anybody talked to the mayor?"

He looked around the table. I'd just come back from Dallas for the week, and somebody else was coming back from Chicago, somebody else came back from Tennessee. The entire executive team had been out of town all week.

HJ started pounding on the table.

"No more travel! No more travel! All travel's coming through me! All travel's coming through me! You're running around here because you love to travel! You love it! You love to travel! But you've got to cut your own grass first. You want to run across the street and cut your neighbor's yard but your grass is up over the roof!"

It was such a great visual, but his point was that we were taking care of all this other stuff everywhere else, but here in our own backyard, we weren't taking care of home. I've been saying that ever since I heard it, that you've got to cut your own grass first.

Now that you know the story of Dallas Smith, much of it in his own words, I need to tell you that I have never actually called him Dallas. To me, he'll always be Darryl.

I moved into my office on a Friday and started work the following Monday by attending an executive meeting.

HJ started it off by saying, "Darryl, have you taken care of that problem?"

I was looking at the company CFO, Darryl Mims, while HJ was ranting and raving about this project in Birmingham that he needed to take care of. When I looked around, I realized that everybody else was looking at *me*.

HJ said, "Darryl, did you hear me? Did you hear what I said?"

Joia Johnson, who was general counsel at the time, said, "HJ, *his* name is Dallas."

"That's what I said!"

Needless to say, I was in Alabama the next day taking care of a real estate issue with one of the offices of H.J. Russell & Company.

I've been Darryl ever since.

On another occasion, I got a call from Herman and he said, "Darryl, I want you to go to this meeting with me," and I said OK. So it's the two of us in the car, and we go out to meet this guy for lunch.

"Hey," the guy said and he reached out to shake my hand and said, "Darryl."

And I said, "Dallas."

And he said, "Oh, OK. We talked about XYZ project." I didn't remember and I said so.

He said, "Didn't we talk? Aren't you Darryl Mims?"

And I said, "I'm Dallas Smith."

Mr. Russell looked at me and said, "Oh, shoot. I brought the wrong Darryl!"

Today, "Darryl" operates his own Atlanta business, T. Dallas Smith and Co. He also writes an occasional blog for the *Atlanta Business Chronicle* and once interviewed me for it.

"HJ, I've never asked you this question," he said, "but why did you call me back so soon the first day I called you?"

I said, "Darryl, I didn't know why you were calling me. You might've been calling me for some money or for a job. I wouldn't know till I called you back."

I told him that I got that kind of a common sense thinking from my father.

Zane Major

All three of my children have been through the Russell Institute, and while many of their children—my grandchildren—have worked summers in various parts of the Russell companies, Donata's son, Zane Major, is the first to reach the management level as I write this in 2012.

I'll let him tell you his experience without interruption from Granddad.

When I was eleven or twelve, my grandfather made it clear that I couldn't just hang out when I was off from school, or do whatever I wanted, that I was going to have to come in and work. When I was eleven, during summer vacation, my first job was shredding paper for about two weeks. As I got older, my assignments were on construction sites.

When I graduated from the University of Arizona I was kind of looking for a job, probably not as hard as I should have been, when he presented me with the opportunity to work at the Castleberry Inn & Suites, which is adjacent to Paschal's Restaurant. (My grandfather owns and oversees both.) To be honest, when it was initially offered, it was just kind of something that I was going to do until I found something else. The general manager who was here unfortunately got sick and had to leave. I took over her role temporarily, and when it was clear that she wasn't going to be able to come back, I jumped at the opportunity to do it permanently. It's more than challenging every day.

My grandfather's biggest thing is just to come in and work hard. He definitely asks a lot. He believes that if you're giving 100 percent, everything else will fall into place. I can tell he's proudest when he knows that I put max effort into something. And he's disappointed when he can tell I have not put the max effort into something.

I kind of view the hotel as my entry into the Russell businesses and it's an industry that nobody else in the family has conquered. I see it as my opportunity to bring a new industry under the Russell umbrella and grow it from there.

The hotel and restaurant are my grandfather's retirement project and this is what keeps him busy. He's not a golfer, he's not a fisher; he loves to work. It definitely makes me feel like I'm one of his . . . I'm somebody he speaks to every day, so it puts a lot of pressure and weight on me to do my best with this hotel.

He really *is* who he is. He doesn't sugarcoat it with anybody but he's very personable. If you're working with him or around him, he expects a lot of you. He's not going to let you slack off. What you see is what you get. It's not a charade. He really cares about everything and he's going to put his all in everything, every day of the week.

There are a lot of times when he'll call me on a Saturday and say, "We're slow. Why are two people working at the front desk?"

And I say, "Well, I can't really predict when we're going to be slow and when we're not. And it's better to have extra coverage than not enough coverage and that's why two people are here."

Or he'd say during renovations, "Why is there a housekeeper in room two hundred?"

And I'll say, "We don't have a break room right now, so I let them have their break in the room. They're just supposed to close the door."

I've learned I still have to pick my battles. Some of them, you're just not going to win with him. So I pick and choose which ones I want to win and which ones I just want to let *him* have.

My mom has said, "He's going to be demanding of you, it's going to be more stressful on you because you're his family, but you have to understand that he only does it because he loves you and he wants to see you succeed."

I kick my grandkids' butts like I did my own kids.

I may even be a little harder on them because their mamas and daddies are not as hard on them as I was on my kids. They're a little softer. The grandkids, like my own kids, know they have to walk the chalk line with me.

They all know I love them dearly, but they have to work. I even fired one grandchild who was working in the office. I gave her a part-time job in the rental office and she decided she wanted to take two and a half hours for lunch, and when she came back, she didn't have a job.

14

Mixing Business and Politics

In Atlanta, the bishops of many of the African Methodist Episcopal (AME) churches were close friends of mine and Jesse Hill's. (The church, by the way, was established in 1787 to combat racial discrimination against African Americans by white Methodists.)

Andrew Young, who wanted to be elected to Georgia's Fifth District seat in the US House of Representatives in 1972, said you needed to go through the bishops.

> I was trying to run for Congress and there was a fellow by the name of Fred Bennett, one of these typical political handymen who hang around and that know everything that's going on, and you think of them as kind of dumb, but it's a routine that they play.
>
> There are people with PhD minds that don't have a lot of formal education, but he said to me, "You are too smart to be so stupid. You've been to all the colleges and you don't understand how this city works."

I said, "What do you mean?"

"Nobody can get the preachers together but Mr. Hill and Mr. Russell."

"Why would they come together?"

He said, "Well, Herman built all those churches and Jesse financed them."

Herman also took me to see John Portman and Charles Loudermilk. He recommended me to them, and if he had not done that, I could not have gotten elected. They became my supporters in 1970 when I lost, and again in '72 when I won.

David Scott

In 1974, a young African American Wharton School of Business graduate named David Scott decided to run for the Georgia State House of Representatives. One of the first people he asked for support was me. He came by my office and told me his plans and I gave him his first campaign contribution, $200.

Then I said, "Who have you got supporting you?"

"Andy Young," he said, "and Maynard Jackson will support me. And . . ."

"That's great, son," I said. "But where are your white people, David? *Where are your white people?*"

"Herman," he said, "I ain't got no white people."

"You need to get yourself some white people," I told him.

David went out and did exactly that, starting with some white attorneys who eventually led him to then Georgia governor Carl Sanders. David literally told Sanders that I was supporting him but that "Herman Russell told me that I needed to find some white supporters."

David says that helped win him Sanders's support.

David—who is married to Hank Aaron's sister, Alfredia—also won his seat in Congress and has held public office ever since. He was a state representative for eight years, a state senator for twenty years, became the first African American to be chairman of the state senate's Rules Committee, and then won election to Congress. He became the first

African American in the South to win a congressional district with less than 40 percent African Americans of eligible voting age—37 percent, to be exact.

In all those years, I've only asked him for one favor and it had nothing to do with business. But in 2008, I called and asked him to do something personal for me.

"David, you know I never did think I'd live to see the first black president, and I want to get to the inauguration," I said. "Can you help me?"

> I said, "Can *I* help *you?*" One of the proudest moments of my life was to be able to get Herman Russell tickets and seating—best seats, sitting, not standing—right there in the front when the president of the United States, Barack Obama, was sworn in. Herman Russell was there. I was able to do that for him. I was so proud.

Georgia Governor Jimmy Carter

In 1973 I was elected chairman of the Butler Street YMCA. It was a position of great influence and respect in Atlanta's black community, and I was quite honored to follow in the footsteps of some of Atlanta's most prominent African American citizens; my immediate predecessor was Dr. Benjamin Mays, the legendary president of Morehouse College.

The keynote speaker at my installation ceremony was the little-known first-term governor of Georgia, a fellow named Jimmy Carter. His remarks were inspirational. After the ceremony we talked for a while and have been friends ever since.

I liked Jimmy's politics and I liked him as a person. We got to know each other well and developed a good rapport and a strong mutual respect. He appointed me to serve on several important boards in Georgia when he worked to reorganize the state government. I worked hard to support my friend. In his last year in office as governor, Jimmy called me and about five others to the governor's mansion. We met upstairs in his private den. I didn't know why he called us.

"I've invited you fellows here to ask you to raise a couple of million dollars to set up my campaign to run for president," Governor Carter said.

"Wait, Jimmy," I said, "you mean *vice* president don't you?"

He smiled.

"No, Herman. I mean *president.*"

And he proceeded to lay out his plan for us.

Ted Kennedy had already announced that he was running, and he was widely expected to walk away with the Democratic nomination. The question on all of our minds was, how could a former Georgia peanut farmer possibly beat the Kennedy machine? It was a question for which Carter was prepared. He showed us various analyses of historical voting patterns from recent elections and identified other major fund-raisers and politicians upon whom he could count.

It took about three hours, but Jimmy convinced us that he had a real chance to win. Everyone in that room knew that this was a historic moment. We were really energized. How many people get the opportunity to launch a national presidential campaign, victorious or not?

"So what do you need us to do?" I asked.

He said, "I need you to raise a quarter of a million dollars to get us started."

We raised that initial $250,000; ultimately we would raise much, much more. Jimmy Carter's campaign for the presidency of the United States was on its way. And I was proudly there at the beginning.

As an initial fund-raiser and advisor, I was part of Carter's informal "kitchen cabinet." But our relationship went deeper than that. Several times I visited his home in Plains, a little town in southern Georgia. His mother, Miss Lillian, lived there, as did his wife, Rosalynn, and their daughter, Amy. Miss Lillian was a real card. She wasn't shy about sharing her opinions—about most anything. She was a kind woman and boy, could she cook! She would fix us great meals while she regaled us with down-home stories of her life experiences. On one visit she fed me a slice of her homemade sweet potato pie. With my first bite I thought I'd died and gone to heaven. I raved over her sweet potato pie so much that she gave me a whole pie to take home.

Once during Jimmy's campaign I was with Rosalynn when she spotted former world heavyweight boxing champion Joe Louis seated across the room. She was as excited as a bobbysoxer at a 1940s Frank Sinatra concert.

"*Oooh*, Herman," she whispered, "there's Joe Louis! Would you take me over to meet him?" I didn't personally know Louis, but I'd heard that he was always gracious to fans, so I took her over to meet him and she gushed over him.

After he was in the White House, President Carter appointed me to the National Housing Board. In that position—and as a member of his kitchen cabinet—he wanted me and my friend Jesse Hill Jr.—who had also worked on the campaign—to meet the new members of his official cabinet. The cabinet secretaries briefed us about their range of duties and the plans they hoped to implement during their tenure.

One cabinet member stood out from the rest: Patricia Roberts Harris, the secretary of Housing and Urban Development (HUD). She and I just clicked. And when it came time for government business she was no-nonsense.

Pat enlisted me to represent her department on a number of occasions. One of the most memorable was when she sent me to Russia for two weeks to advise the Russian government on modern building construction technology. One of my official duties was to attend a formal dinner in a well-to-do Russian businessman's lovely country home. The dining room accommodated twenty-five guests. When Russians got together they loved to drink vodka and sing, and that was certainly true of our host and his guests. Everybody was drinking and laughing and singing at the top of their lungs without being the least bit self-conscious, with each person taking a turn as soloist and song leader. I drank, laughed, and sang along—at least I called it singing—as loudly as anyone. I was a government envoy in Russia on official business, but that didn't mean I couldn't enjoy myself!

Then someone turned to me and said, "It's your turn now, Mr. Herman."

I tried to tell them that I couldn't sing a decent note if my life depended on it, but they kept calling on me. The more I shook my head no, the more they demanded it. Soon they were chanting, *"Mr. Herman! Mr. Herman!"*

I didn't want to insult their hospitality, but between my speech impediment and my inability to hold a tune, I have always been reluctant to try to sing in public. My guide must have realized that, because it was at that moment that she did something that to this day brings tears to my eyes.

She leaned over and whispered, "I will sing with you, my friend. We will sing 'We Shall Overcome' together."

Think of that: a middle-aged African American man and a young Russian woman together singing a protest song of the 1960s civil rights movement. And she knew the words, too. It just brought tears to my eyes. By the time our song was finished everyone in the house was singing with us.

When it was time for me to return to the United States, I asked my guide what kind of gift I could give her to show my appreciation for her many kindnesses. She smiled and said, "Mr. Russell, just send me some American blue jeans." That's what she wanted. As soon as I got home Otelia and I sent her half a dozen pairs.

President Jimmy Carter

In 1979, President Carter came to Ebenezer Church in Atlanta to give an address on Dr. King's birthday. When I mentioned to one of President Carter's aides before the service that I was going to Washington that evening to attend a meeting of the National Housing Board, President Carter invited me to fly to DC on *Air Force One* with him. I couldn't say yes fast enough.

Flying on *Air Force One* was an amazing experience. But the experience started before we got anywhere near the airport. As the president was leaving the church for the airport he beckoned toward the presidential limousine and said, "Come on, Herman, ride with me."

We arrived at the airport, lights flashing and sirens blaring, and immediately boarded *Air Force One*. We lingered for a moment while the president spoke to aides and reporters, then we retired to the president's private suite. It was like stepping into the finest suite at the world's finest luxury hotel. It was absolutely gorgeous and had every imaginable comfort. It's something I wish every American could see.

Mayor Andrew Young

When Andy Young became mayor of Atlanta in 1982 (following three years as President Carter's ambassador to the United Nations), it put a strain on our relationship for many years. H.J. Russell & Company was routinely a bidder on many city construction contracts before, during, and after the Andrew Young administration.

Don't believe me; listen to Andy:

> I couldn't see them. I couldn't go to Herman's beach house. Our wives had been good friends and my wife was invited several times to go down to their house in Florida and I said, "Baby, you can't go. Even if you pay your own way, we can't go." And every time Herman won a contract when I was mayor, I got sued. And so I stayed out of contracting.
>
> On the new city hall, we had $34 million budgeted for the city hall annex. Herman and Bob Holder brought in a bid for $30.5 million and they got the contract and everybody said, "Herman Russell got the contract because he is your friend." But that wasn't true. Herman got the contract because he and Holder made the best bid at the lowest price.

Andy ran unsuccessfully for governor in 1990. The following April, as a private citizen, he invited Otelia and me to accompany him and his wife, Jean, to Zimbabwe where Andy was speaking on an international relations panel. Also in our group was R. K. Sehgal, the CEO of a large engineering firm, and his wife and two young children. Years later RK would be the first CEO to succeed me as I technically retired and took an office off-property to oversee my other business interests.

The respect Andy inspired in Africa was quite astounding. When we arrived at the Victoria Falls airport in Zimbabwe, we received the red carpet treatment. I don't mean figuratively. I mean that there was an actual red carpet and an honor guard awaiting us. We were whisked through without a customs check to a car with a driver and police escort that the government provided us the entire time we were in country.

On our first evening in Zimbabwe, we had dinner with President Robert Mugabe. The meal was fabulous and the dinner conversation was quite interesting. His secretary of transportation was a woman. She was seated to my right. As the night wore on, Madame Secretary and I had a spirited conversation with a lot of laughter and playful flirting. I enjoyed the friendly back and forth until she made a remark that let me know that her flirting was less innocent than I assumed.

"Mr. Russell," she said, "you should move to Africa."

"Why?" I replied.

"Because here you can have more than one wife," she said with a twinkle in her eye.

Otelia, who was seated at my left, didn't hear the remark. But Jean Young, who was sitting opposite us, did. She leaned over the table and narrowed her eyes.

"Madame Secretary," she said, "I understand this is Africa, but we don't play that shit in America."

The entire table burst into laughter including Madame Secretary. And that was the end of the flirting.

After Andy's panel, we left Zimbabwe for a safari in Kenya. Because of Andy's stature in the international community we were again given the VIP treatment. The government put us up in the swank Victoria Falls Hotel. When we arrived, there was a group of white Americans standing in the lobby and we chatted with them briefly. They shared their frustration that they had been waiting for a week for a guide and driver to take them out on safari. We sympathized with their plight for a few minutes before hurrying to our rooms to change clothes so we could meet *our* safari guide and driver who by now were awaiting us in the lobby.

When we returned to the lobby the Americans were still grumbling. When they realized that *we* already had a driver and guide while *they* were still waiting, they pitched a fit. Our African hosts heard the grumbling and complaints, but they didn't care.

On the last night of our trip to Africa, Jean Young became sick. She was nauseated and unable to keep anything down. We were concerned for her comfort, but we thought it was just the flu or a stomach virus. About a month later we learned that it wasn't food or drink that had made her sick; she was suffering from cancer. She faced her illness with the same courage and spunk with which she'd approached every obstacle from her days in the civil rights movement until that moment. She fought the disease for all she was worth for five years, until her body gave out.

Jean was one of the sweetest people you could ever meet. She was Andy's backbone and inspiration, a major factor in his success. Andy took it hard and mourned her loss deeply.

In the years since, Andy was fortunate to find a new love to share his life. Carolyn is a wonderful woman. We couldn't be happier for him to have her.

■ □ ■

The only "favoritism" Andy ever showed me was when he was cochair of the Atlanta Committee for the 1996 Olympic Games. I was active with him in putting together Atlanta's bid. Andy came to me and said, "It doesn't pay for you to be on this executive committee for the Olympics because it means you won't be eligible to do any business with the Olympics; if we're going to do a billion dollars' worth of construction, you need to be eligible to do some of it."

Based on that advice I stepped down. It was some of the best political *and* business advice he ever gave me, as H.J. Russell & Company went on to help build Olympic Stadium (now Turner Field), the Georgia Dome, and the Georgia World Congress Center.

Arkansas Governor Bill Clinton and Hillary Clinton

I was hurrying across the lobby of the Renaissance hotel after a meeting there in May 1992 when I ran into Zell Miller, who was then Georgia's governor. After we had made small talk for a few minutes, Zell asked if I had a few minutes more. I told him yes, of course. Only a fool would turn down a request from the governor of their own state for a few minutes of their time.

"Good," he said. "I want you to come with me to meet the next First Lady of the United States."

We took the elevator to the presidential suite where several Secret Service agents greeted us. After clearing us, they ushered us into the spacious parlor of a large suite. An engaging woman with a warm smile stood to greet us.

"Mrs. Clinton," Zell said, "meet my friend Herman Russell." He went on to tell her a few things about me. Her handshake was firm; it was clear that she was confident. I liked Hillary right off. I thought to myself that a man with a wife like this must be pretty strong and capable. When we rose to leave she asked if I would support her husband for president. Without hesitating I told her yes.

I made good on that pledge, too. I helped organize my employees, friends, and community to ensure that voters had rides to the polls in November 1992. I also made sure that the tenants in my complexes had transportation to and from their respective polling places.

After he won the election, President-Elect Clinton invited me to his victory ball in Little Rock. When I got into town I ran into my dear friend Vernon Jordan, who had been appointed to chair Clinton's transition team. He invited me to a private dinner that evening for about twenty-five guests. I expected it to be purely a social gathering, but when I got there I saw that it was a *power* gathering. There were a number of Fortune 500 CEOs; seated next to me was a top executive of American Airlines. Also among the guests were four persons under serious consideration for the president's cabinet. Vice President-Elect Al Gore stopped by to say hello.

After the transition team completed its work, President Clinton invited me to a planning conference in Little Rock. The conference comprised the heads of some of the nation's largest companies and Clinton's nominees for the various cabinet posts. My good friend Ron Brown, Clinton's nominee for secretary of commerce, was there.

When we broke for lunch I ran into Dr. Johnnetta B. Cole, who was then president of Spelman College. She was having lunch with the First Lady. Johnnetta was about to introduce me to Mrs. Clinton when she stopped Johnnetta and said, "I know Herman Russell. He's one of the richest men in Georgia."

I said, "Mrs. Clinton, I probably don't have anywhere near the money you think I have!"

Jane Fonda

I was invited to the Clinton White House many times. My most special experiences there were at the jazz concerts that President Clinton sponsored. He was a real fan and a lot of fun to be around.

When the president and the First Lady redecorated the White House dining room, known as the Blue Room, she invited Otelia and me to the public unveiling.

I eventually got to know Hillary even better than the president. She and I would talk privately every time I attended a White House social event. I found her to be smart, courageous, and extremely sincere about helping the people in our nation who most needed a helping hand. I came to admire her very much. When she announced her candidacy for the US Senate in 2000, I didn't hesitate for a moment to support her.

Later I participated in a $1,000-a-plate fund-raising dinner for Hillary at the Four Seasons Hotel Atlanta. The room was packed and Hillary gave a dynamic speech that really moved us. I wasn't the least bit surprised when she won the New York election.

At the fund-raiser, I ran into actress Jane Fonda in the reception line. She was behind me and I invited her to stand ahead of me. We ended up greeting Hillary at the same time. When Hillary saw me next to Jane, she gave me a big hug and we chatted for a few moments.

Jane and I took seats together and laughed and talked for a good while. As the event neared its end, she told me she was going up to a suite to have drinks with Hillary and invited me to be her date for rest of the evening. There were about twenty people in the suite, including

Mayor Bill Campbell and his wife. Hillary was still quite charged up by the crowd's stirring response to her and she brought that energy upstairs with her. Being with Jane Fonda and Hillary Clinton, it was a fascinating evening.

As a result of that chance meeting, Jane invited me to serve on the board of directors of the Georgia Coalition for Pregnancy Prevention, which she founded. As rich and famous as Jane Fonda is, if she could find time to try to help young women avoid unwanted pregnancies and the pain, social stigma, and economic strain that so often accompany them, then so could I. I knew it would be a spiritually satisfying experience for me; I had no idea it would be socially satisfying as well.

At the time Jane was married to Ted Turner, the founder of CNN and then the vice chairman of TimeWarner. While I was on the board, Jane invited board members to the couple's Montana ranch for a retreat. I'd heard how beautiful the ranch was but it was beyond anyone's best description. It was tucked away in the Belt Mountains down a drive so long that it was invisible from the road. The ranch site itself was one of the most beautiful you could ever hope to see. Before the house was a gorgeous lake teeming with fish. In the background were sparkling, snow-capped mountains. There were so many buffalo that it looked like an old Western movie.

Jane was a genuine health buff, as any fan of her 1980s exercise videos knew, so there were yoga classes in the mornings and hiking and horseback riding in the afternoons. And healthy meals, of course, including our fair share of lean buffalo meat, which Ted raised on the ranch.

I only see Jane occasionally these days, but we stay in touch by phone, and every time we do run into each other it's just like we never left off.

Atlanta Mayor Kasim Reed

While receiving an award from the School of Business at Howard University in Washington, DC, I ran into a young Atlantan who I've known for some years, Kasim Reed. At the time, Kasim—currently in his second term as mayor of Atlanta—was a student representative on Howard's board of trustees.

Kasim, who grew up in Atlanta, subsequently returned home after college and practiced law with the firm of Paul, Hastings, Janofsky, and Walker, later moving on to the firm of Holland and Knight, where he eventually became a partner.

To the surprise of no one, Kasim decided to run for state representative, and in 1998 he came out to see me at my home and to ask for my support. Here's how he remembers it:

> I made the trip that all the young politicians make to Mr. Russell's home; it was an amazing experience. Folks who know HJ well know that he has a beautiful indoor pool where Dr. Martin Luther King Jr. used to come and swim. I was twenty-eight or twenty-nine years old. I remember HJ sitting quietly and hearing my case, as I'm sure he's done for so many politicians—not only in Atlanta, but around the country. You're sitting in his house, asking for his support, and you can be a bit overwhelmed by how long he has been an influence in the life of the city of Atlanta. His life literally runs through the life of the city of Atlanta, through almost every elected leader that we've had over a forty-year span of time. It's absolutely remarkable.
>
> I remember my first time there like it was yesterday. He said, "I think you're sharp. I think you're bright. I think you're a good lawyer with good training, but explain to me how you're going to *win*."
>
> The room was silent because, first of all, I'd never run for office. I was in a race with six people, including some who had more name recognition than I did. I believe that he decided to support me because in my presentation I said I was going to outwork everybody. Everybody who knows Mr. Russell knows that his own work ethic is legendary. When I talked about outworking everybody else in the race, I think that's the reason we connected. I didn't offer many other great reasons for him to support me over the other folks who were running. And then I won.

Kasim is correct in his assessment; he struck me as a fine young man with a good head on his shoulders who, just as important, impressed me with his commitment to outwork everyone else in the field. In the years that followed, I never waivered in my support of Kasim's political ambitions and we visited dozens of times on matters personal and professional.

When Kasim announced his intention to run for mayor of Atlanta in 2009, I must admit he put me in a tough spot. The city council president, Lisa Borders, was a lifelong friend of my daughter Donata and was someone I had known since she was a little girl. I had supported her previous political ambitions, and she had declared her candidacy for the mayor's office *first*. Over the years, I had introduced Kasim—socially—to all three of my children and Donata, Jerome, and Michael all had their own relationships with him.

I did the only thing I could think of: I supported both as equally as I could. I knew the city would be in great hands with whoever won, so why play favorites?

> HJ chastised me for not sharing my decision with him immediately, but it all turned out fine. We knew that HJ cared for both of us, and the fact of the matter is we were both in his life for a long time. And Lisa and his daughter Donata were very close. So that was fine with me.

Senator Barack Obama and Michelle Obama

The first time I met Barack Obama, we were both attending a fund-raiser in downtown Atlanta for my dear friend, Congressman John Lewis. Someone introduced me to then US senator Obama and took a picture of us. We chatted amiably for a moment or two until I spotted the late Robert F. Kennedy's wife across the room and, forgetting my conversation with the young senator, I ran over to hug her.

Fast-forward a year and Senator Obama announced his intention to run for president. I purchased tickets to one of his earliest Atlanta fund-raisers but when I found out his wife, Michelle, would not be in attendance I gave the tickets to my daughter, Donata, and friend and neighbor Earlene Harris.

Senator Obama returned to Atlanta for a second fund-raiser and, again, I purchased tickets. This time my wife and I attended. But I told

214 ■ BUILDING ATLANTA

the senator that I was disappointed that his wife had once more not accompanied him.

"Herman," he said, "if Michelle were here it would have cost you more than the five thousand dollars you paid!"

I laughed that he was so quick on his feet.

Television and film producer Tyler Perry threw a fund-raiser for Senator Obama at his beautiful Atlanta home and my wife and I bought tickets. We were about five feet from the candidate as he addressed his guests. After he concluded his remarks, I said to him, "This is the last time I am coming to any event with you and your wife is not present."

"Herman," he said, "I promise I will fix that!"

I continued to support the senator as he won his historic election in 2008 and his reelection to a second term in 2012. My wife and I were subsequently invited to the White House for a December 2012 holiday reception. I still had not met the First Lady, but I was hopeful that this would be the day.

A military official came up to me during the event and indicated that the president would be joining us shortly; she suggested that my wife and I move into the room where he would be greeting guests, which we did. About twenty minutes later the president and the First Lady came down from the living quarters of the White House. Each of them went to the podium and made a few welcoming remarks. They then went around the room greeting their guests and soon the president got to us.

"Mr. President," I said, "thank you for finally coming with the First Lady. I will now let you off the hook!"

The president laughed and we embraced. A moment later, the First Lady joined us and I told her that I had been on the president's back for years about meeting her.

She was so charming and before I realized what was happening, the First Lady rubbed my head and kissed both my cheeks. What an evening! I never expected that!

V

Family First

15

The Wonders of Otelia

One of my greatest blessings was Otelia. It's true we had a wonderful marriage, but what I'm talking about is more than that.

If Otelia had not misplaced her watch and then lamented to my sister-in-law Ruth about it, Ruth might never have thought to introduce us. And if Ruth hadn't really tried to keep Otelia from storming out the night we met, I might never have gotten the opportunity to let her see that I was more than the preening peacock she thought I was.

If she had left her watch on her dresser the day it was lost instead of wearing it; if it had fallen to the ground where she could have seen or heard it; if someone had found it and returned it to her; if any of a number of things had been different on her part or mine, we might not have ever met.

I've never been one to enjoy other people's losses, but I thank God that Otelia lost that watch.

From the first, Otelia and I were full partners. She began by helping me with my paperwork and payroll while we were still courting. She was totally supportive. She certainly had her own mind, and she was not shy about letting her opinions be known, but when it came to H.J. Russell & Company, she respected my judgment and supported my decisions.

She was good at managing money, so I never had to worry about her spending more than we should. Even in the beginning, when she fussed so much about having to ride in my truck, she went along with it because she knew that I was trying to build something for us both.

That's also how we raised our children: as partners. We weren't just a family because we lived in the same house. We had a real family life. Everything revolved around our family. We had dinner together every evening, with two special meals every week.

Friday was steak night. The children and I knew to expect mouthwatering T-bone steaks, baked potatoes, salad, and always a great dessert. Simple fare but delicious. We never did develop fancy tastes. Don't get me wrong—we enjoyed eating the fine foods and wines that were served in our social circles. I mean, at the White House you eat what they serve, and they can serve some very nice foods. But left to ourselves, a meal of chicken or beef stew was just as good.

Sunday dinners were special because they were leisurely and unrushed by the need to do homework and observe bedtimes. We allowed no TV watching at dinnertime. That was our time to talk as a family. Dinner was like a rap session. We talked about all kinds of things.

Otelia and I discussed our values, current events, and religion with a special emphasis on what it meant to be good people. We also encouraged our children to speak their minds. As long as they remained respectful, they could share any stories, thoughts, or complaints and ask any questions they liked. We really listened to our children. That empowered them to think and speak up for themselves and to feel confident that what they thought mattered. That's one reason they are such successful professionals and great human beings today. Discussions around the table could get very energetic. But we all found them enjoyable and gained much from them. More important, it kept us close in touch as a family.

Another thing that kept us tight was that we took all kinds of trips together, everywhere from the Grand Canyon to Niagara Falls and places in between. Once we flew to Chicago and took a leisurely train ride from there to San Francisco. I couldn't have asked for a better wife or a better family life.

You could not find a more loving mother than Otelia, but in spite of that—or because of that—she was a strict disciplinarian. She made our children toe the line; she didn't let them get away with a thing. We insisted on their being respectful and polite to everyone. She didn't allow harsh words or a lot of sibling squabbling. She gave all of them chores and made sure they got done. She made sure their homework was completed and done right and gave them whatever instructional help they needed. She was a real hands-on mother. I was always present in our children's lives, but I attribute 80 percent of their success to Otelia.

We had great fun together doing all kinds of things. Nothing fancy, but it didn't matter. We just loved being together. One of our favorite ways to spend an evening was to go to a good movie, then go to the Varsity, Atlanta's landmark fast-food restaurant (after it was desegregated).

When H.J. Russell & Company became a genuine success, we received invitations to high-class social events, black-tie dinner parties, and exclusive gatherings at country clubs, five-star hotels, and private homes.

And when our children got older, we developed a taste for more ambitious trips. Together we saw the world: mainland China, Hong Kong, Russia, India, several African countries, a number of European capitals, and more. We took our first cruise and discovered we enjoyed the slow pace, good food and accommodations, and disembarking at various ports for a day of shopping.

■ □ ■

Otelia enjoyed adding color to our life in a variety of ways.

She did the decorating in all of our homes, choosing different motifs in each. The kitchen at our vacation lake house had a chicken motif that was a lot of fun. It wouldn't have worked at our beach house or our penthouse, but it fit right in with the lake house's rural setting.

I don't know how she found them, but throughout the kitchen were practical and impractical objects all shaped like chickens: chicken salt and pepper shakers, chicken cookie jar, chicken calendar, chicken range cover, chicken napkin holder, paintings of chickens, and chickens gracing kitchen slogan signs. Then there were the chicken refrigerator magnets, chicken wallpaper, and yes, even a chicken teakettle. I bought her a spacious, state-of-the-art kitchen with granite counters, top-of-the-line stainless steel appliances, two separate ranges, a cathedral ceiling—and she filled it with chickens! But our grandchildren love it and it always gives guests a smile. But that was Otelia, always fun and always creative.

■ □ ■

Otelia's family was extremely close, too. Her sisters were her best friends and confidants for her entire life. Even after they were grown with their own families and living in other parts of the country, they still flocked together whenever they could. At every age, they were like young girls, laughing and fussing and just enjoying each other's company.

It was that love of family that she brought to our life together. She welcomed me into her family and from the beginning embraced my family as her own.

■ □ ■

There are so many wonderful things to tell you about what Otelia was. But there was one thing she most definitely was not.

Otelia was no diplomat. She allowed no filters on her opinions, or, in her words, she didn't believe in being a phony. If she didn't approve of someone's behavior or opinions, she wasn't afraid to say so.

One time I was in talks with a high-ranking member of Congress from our state about some projects we both thought would benefit Georgia. We were talking on the phone when he said, "Herman, why don't you and Mrs. Russell stop by my house this evening for dinner?"

I knew we had nothing planned that night, so I said, "Sure."

I called Otelia and told her not to worry about cooking because we were going out to dinner with a colleague. When I got home she was getting dressed.

"Who are we having dinner with?" she asked. When I told her, she had a fit.

"*What?* After the things that man is doing to this country and the way he treated his wife? You must be crazy if you think I'm going to his house for *anything*."

"But I already told him we're coming."

"Well, you should have known better than to tell that man that I would ever set foot in his house."

As hard as I tried, I couldn't convince her otherwise. Finally I just gave up. "All right, I'll call him and tell him you're not feeling well."

She didn't like that either. "Don't you tell him that! Tell him the real reason. Tell him that that I just don't want to be around him."

"I can't tell him that."

But Otelia refused to sugarcoat it. "Tell him, Herman! Tell him! Make sure you tell him exactly why we're not coming to his house."

She meant it. Most people would have just gone along with it. Not Otelia. She was blunt, but she was honest. She would give you the shirt off her back, but she refused to be a phony.

On another occasion were at a party, seated at a table with Peter Coors. Otelia knew I was in business with Coors but that didn't mean anything to her; when the waitress came around, she ordered a Budweiser.

I said, "What are you doing?"

She said, "I'm going to have what I want to have."

And one of her sisters, Ruth Hackney McMillan, recalls:

My sister lived life on her own terms.

Herman had thought that it would be a fun idea for them to repeat their vows. Otelia, in her funny way, she told him, "No, I don't think that's necessary. I'm not going to say 'I do' to the same man twice."

And this:

Otelia would always pick up something that she thought I could wear, and the dresses that she bought me I liked so much.

But one day my sister said, "I know you like this material, but I wouldn't buy it because I wouldn't be caught dead in it!"

■ □ ■

Egbert Perry has been a recurrent character in our lives, even after he left H.J. Russell & Company. For example, his roommate at the University of Pennsylvania was from Nigeria. His family was in the upper class and lived well; some of his cousins were in the Nigerian government. Egbert recommended this young man to me and I gave him a job.

He, in turn, thought that we needed to be working in his country because there were so many development opportunities. Curious, Otelia and I went to Nigeria and were guests in his mother's home. We were introduced to the country's movers and shakers and made many new friends. When our visit came to an end, they threw us a wonderful going-away party, inviting a Nigerian Who's Who as guests.

Grateful, I said, "Whenever you're in the United States, please get in touch."

One day, unannounced and unplanned, a large contingent of Nigerians showed up at our doorstep. It was quite charming, but Otelia was not amused. She said, "I don't know these people, and I'm not going to entertain and cook for them. They are welcome to stay, but I'm going." And she did, leaving me alone with them there for about a week while she went to her mama and daddy's home in Union Point. It wasn't because she didn't like the Nigerians; she just wasn't going to be inconvenienced by folks whom she didn't know.

They were good people, but African customs are a little different. They came to Donata's wedding, too, and after the wedding they didn't want to leave. They stayed on another ten days.

No matter how much our net worth grew, no matter how many famous and important people we called friends, no matter how many times we were invited to the White House, Otelia never changed. She was always down to earth. She was just as happy socializing with her old high school friends or sisters as she was with the high-class social set. She was always social, but she cared nothing about being a socialite.

■ □ ■

When our first grandchild was born, I think it's safe to say I was a little more excited than Otelia was.

I can tell you this story like it happened yesterday. Otelia and I were at our home in Sanibel, Florida. I got a very early call from my son Jerome, who said that at five o'clock that morning, my first grandchild, Herman Jerome Russell III, was born. He told me what size the boy was and that they were at Northside Hospital in Atlanta.

I was so happy!

I called the airport to get on the next flight back to Atlanta. I woke Otelia up and told her I was going. She said, "Go by yourself. I'm not going. That baby will be there when I get back to Atlanta."

So I left. I called a cab and was at the airport in about an hour and fifteen minutes. I caught a flight out at 6:45 A.M. By 9:00 I was at Northside Hospital holding the baby.

I called Otelia because I was so excited and she said, "Why did you call me and wake me back up?"

She was happy, but she wasn't as excited as *I* was!

■ □ ■

As dedicated as I am to earning and saving money, even after we became financially successful, Otelia never became extravagant.

A lot of people like to flaunt their wealth, especially if they come from humble beginnings like us, but Otelia didn't care about making a show or keeping up with the Joneses. She liked nice things, but she wasn't extravagant. If she liked something, it was because she liked it for herself, not because she thought it would impress others.

We still went to Kmart and other discount stores where we had always shopped.

■ □ ■

Otelia and Vernon Jordan's first wife, Shirley, were extremely close. So close that our daughters, who were the same age, also became close; they even went to the University of Pennsylvania together.

Otelia and Shirley did all kinds of things together. They shopped together, went on trips together, socialized with friends together. Even when Shirley and Vernon moved to New York City they still visited each other regularly and traveled together.

When Shirley was in her mid-twenties she started experiencing some health problems. After consulting several doctors, she was diagnosed with multiple sclerosis. MS is a debilitating disease, and little by little Shirley slowed down over the years.

But that didn't bother Otelia. Shirley was her friend and she wasn't about to treat her any differently. Shirley went from walking slowly unassisted, to walking with a cane, to using a wheelchair, but Otelia still planned trips and cruises with her the same as always. She acted as if she hadn't noticed that Shirley had changed. That meant the world to Shirley. As far as Otelia was concerned, Shirley was just Shirley. When Shirley moved slowly, Otelia moved slowly. If Shirley needed to stop and rest, Otelia stopped to rest. She stuck by Shirley Jordan until the end. That was the kind of friend that Otelia was.

■ □ ■

One of my dearest friends, Jerome Harris, came to Atlanta from New York City to be the second African American superintendent of schools in 1988. I wasn't looking for a new best friend but that's exactly what he—and his wonderful wife, Earlene—became.

When Jerome's employment situation changed, our friends moved back to New York for a few years. We remained in touch and they returned to Atlanta for my sixtieth birthday party. If we were in New York, we had dinner and went to the theater together.

In 1996, Earlene said she and Jerome were moving back to Atlanta— great news for us. In fact, they never had sold their condo downtown and we surprised them by moving into a building I owned, literally across the street. Living so close to one another, Otelia and Earlene saw each other at least four days a week, if not more. They joined the same health club and went to lunch together afterward.

At this point I was serving on the Georgia Ports Authority and we were planning a trade mission to South Africa. I told Jerome, "It would be nice if you all could go with us. You'll pay your own way, but I'll take care of the hotel. And, by the way, if you get a platinum American

Express card, you can buy one ticket business class and your second ticket flies free."*

A year later, Otelia invited Earlene and Jerome to take a Mediterranean cruise with her. I said, "I can't leave my job, honey. I've got work to do."

Pretty soon I realized that was a tactical mistake on my part and I joined them. It was the longest time I had ever been away from the office and I was surprised at how much I enjoyed it. After that, about every eighteen months, the four of us went flying and cruising somewhere.

Our friendship never did have anything to do with business. And Jerome, probably more than anyone else in the world, became the person in my life who could say anything to me. Although he does sometimes start a conversation by saying, "This may end our friendship, but I'm saying something you need to hear."

And I always tell him that there is nothing he could say that would cause that to happen.

■ □ ■

In 1982, Otelia discovered a lump in her right breast. A biopsy showed that it was cancerous and the breast was removed. The cancer was caught early enough that she did not need to undergo chemotherapy and she recovered fully.

For the next decade, her health was fine. But in the tenth year after her mastectomy, a routine checkup detected cancer in her right lung.

The operation to remove the tumor lasted almost four hours. The next day the doctor called me into the hallway to tell me that Otelia had a fifty-fifty chance of recovery. During the rehabilitation therapy that followed, I was told it was highly likely that she would be confined to a wheelchair for the rest of her life. But through physical therapy and much brave effort, Otelia fully recovered. She enjoyed another decade of good health.

But once more, in June 2006, a routine checkup found a cancerous tumor, this time in her stomach. We consulted several doctors, but all

---

*I'm always eager to share a bargain.

gave the same sad prognosis: there was nothing they could do. Her cancer was fast growing and terminal.

We maintained our regular life as long as we could, but our remaining time with her was limited. She was home for a week following the diagnosis, had complications, and went back to the hospital.

After two weeks in the hospital, Otelia was ready to be released to hospice care. My children and I thought the most loving thing to do was to let her spend her last moments at home. Donata and I outfitted the master bedroom with a hospital bed and hired three nurses so she could have the best possible around-the-clock home care. The day before we were scheduled to bring her home, Donata and I were finalizing the arrangements.

That day, Donata and her cousin Fanitra went to lunch and Earlene Harris and I separately went to get a bite to eat.

"All of y'all go," Otelia said. "I'm all right."

After lunch, Donata and I went to the hospital supply store to buy a chair for Otelia to use at home. While we were there, Donata's friend Julie Walker called her from Otelia's room.

"You better come back right now," Julie said. "Otelia collapsed moving from her chair to the bed."

When we arrived, the nurses would not let us into her hospital room and said they were "working on her." Shortly thereafter, a hospital administrator asked Donata a question that she knew wasn't good news. "Does Mrs. Russell have a living will?" Donata immediately requested that we be allowed to enter the room.

Inside, Donata found her mother quite different from the way she had left her. She could tell her mother was in a critical, near-death state. "Mom, I don't want you to leave," Donata said, holding her hands.

Just then, Donata heard the quiet voice of God say, "It's time." She realized it was time to let go of her mother. And this was just how her mother wanted to go—without much suffering.

"Mom," she said, "go to the light. It's going to be OK. Just follow the light."

And that was it. Donata and I were blessed to be there with her as she took her last breath. We were sad, but we were happy, too. Because we knew Otelia had lived a full, joyful life. She gave love and most of all she gave instructions. Along with the love came instructions. If anybody wanted to know what to do, ask her.

Some time later we received a letter from Dr. Harold Asher. He was the physician who cared for Otelia while she was in the hospital. Dr. Asher said that it was Otelia's wish to die in the hospital. It was not that she did not want to spend her last days at home with her family, the letter explained. She never discouraged all our arrangements to take her home, because she knew they came out of our love for her. But she had hoped to breathe her last before we took her home because she did not want to be a burden to us.

That was Otelia—always thinking of others. Always wanting to make sure her family was comfortable.

Otelia faced death like she faced life—bravely. She was at peace. She had lived a good life and had lived it with grace and love. She was ready.

■ □ ■

As I look back, our marriage wasn't perfect. No marriage is. But it was wonderful. And she was wonderful. There is no way I could be the successful businessman I am without her. She loved me, nurtured and supported me. She ran the household to give me the time and space to run our business. And yes, she could be tough. The world of construction is a rough-and-tumble world, and I learned long ago to be rough and to tumble with it. But believe me, Otelia could hold her own.

Like most long-term marriages, disagreements sometimes flared between us, but Otelia never kept the tensions going. She would chew me out one minute but share a laugh the next. We were held together by a deep mutual respect. In fifty years of marriage we never uttered a profane word to each other. And neither of us ever raised a hand at the other, not even in jest.

I miss her laughter and her loving ways; I always will. But I was blessed to have her by my side for fifty years. That is more of a blessing than most folks will ever know. So I won't complain.

16

Born Leaders

Otelia and I didn't raise our three children—Donata, Jerome, and Michael—to feel a sense of entitlement. We raised them to understand that they had to work for what they got. And what I gave them was not a kingdom but a chance to be *considered* for leadership positions within H.J. Russell & Company. They had to prove that they were qualified and motivated enough to run the business I have spent my life building. They run H.J. Russell & Company now only because they earned it the right way.

When they were coming up we made sure they got a glimpse of the hard side of life. We didn't give them a lot of free time to play and loaf around. Oh, we made certain they had great childhoods; none of my children would say otherwise. We also made sure that they knew how to work and its value.

Sadly, too often today we can read about pampered rich kids addicted to drugs, spending all their time partying and wasting their lives doing little that is constructive and accomplishing little of value. Usually the main reason for their aimless behavior is that they have been given everything; they are spoiled and don't know the value of hard work or a dollar.

Just like my father gave me independence, discipline, and a strong work ethic, we worked hard to do the same for our kids.

Donata Russell

My oldest child, Donata, is four years older than Jerome and six years older than Michael. Growing up, she was definitely daddy's girl; one of my fondest memories is that she and I would sit and have a bowl of ice cream together every night after dinner. We always had our special time.

Donata would come to the H.J. Russell & Company office with me when she was ten and would help the secretaries put files and supplies away. Many of our tenants came into the office to pay their rent, so as a teenager she collected checks and wrote receipts and entered the information on a ledger card.

After graduating from the University of Pennsylvania with a bachelor's degree in economics (management and marketing), Donata followed an IBM internship between her junior and senior years with a full-time job at the company. She stayed with IBM for three years and then wanted to return to Atlanta to work in our company.

"Of course I will give you a job!" I said. "I would love to have you come home. But I'm not going to pay you the kind of money that you are making at IBM!"

Donata initially shied away from a lead role in the business because she had kids and a husband at the time. She was really torn about being away from her young kids, because when you're a woman running a business, it often takes you away in the evening. She made it clear to me that, until her children were older, she didn't mind working days, but that was it.

When I bought out Jesse Hill and Felker Ward's interest in Concessions International in 1999, Donata's boys were twelve and nine. She felt they were old enough to handle a little more responsibility—and she thought she was, too.

But after three years of being vice chairman of Concessions, Donata said it wasn't working for her. The biggest demand of this business that is in airports all over the country was the constant travel. She wanted to spend more time with the boys, who were now in high school, and I understood. Donata stayed involved but backed off, handing much of the day-to-day responsibilities to CI president Anthony Joseph.

Today Donata is the chief executive officer of Concessions International and has been at its helm since 2013.

Jerome Russell

Jerome is president of H.J. Russell & Company and its real estate development arm, Russell New Urban. Just as his older sister did before him—and his younger brother after him—Jerome spent his summers working a variety of jobs for me, learning the trades and the responsibility of being a Russell. But, unlike Donata, he worked on actual job sites alongside grown men with wives and families.

> I found it pretty cool that I could get up and work with people and paint. I learned construction, although that was the hardest, particularly when we started a job during the summer. I even worked on the Georgia-Pacific building.
>
> I think my father told people not to treat us any different: "Make sure that you keep them busy." I'm pretty sure he told the people that, and they did. But we didn't know at the time. We were just working.

He attended the University of Tennessee for one year and then transferred to Georgia State University, where he earned an undergraduate degree in business administration and management. Before joining the construction company, Jerome ran City Beverage for us and lived for a time in Chicago, running the operation there.

After we sold off the beer distributorship, he returned to Atlanta and got his feet wet in the management end of Gibraltar Land's development business and got a bird's-eye view of how the business was managed. He worked well in all departments and, after eight years learning the company's ins and outs, I named him a vice president and put him in charge of development, real estate, and property management.

In 1995, Jerome was named president and chief operating officer of H.J. Russell & Company, focusing on the firm's strategic direction and new business development. This position cultivated his passion for community revitalization and urban renewal. He started Russell New Urban Development in 2003 to create in-town developments that excite people about urban living.

Jerome and his wife, Stephanie, have four children. He works hard and is supremely focused on whatever task is at hand. If I can convince him that golf is *not* a priority, he is going to be all right.

Michael Russell

Although he is my youngest, Michael Russell became the CEO of H.J. Russell & Company because one of his strengths is relating to people and seeing the big picture of an operation such as ours. He's an excellent problem solver for the greater organization.

Michael is a dynamic person who, like me, has never met a stranger. He is dedicated and likeable and extremely well equipped to be a leader in the company and our industry at large.

I started him at the bottom rungs of the company as soon as he could get around a job site without hurting himself or getting in the way. By the time he was seven years old, he was on the job wearing a hard hat with a shovel in his hand. And when I say he started at the bottom, I mean at the very *bottom*. I saw to it that the worst jobs fell to him. I didn't do it to hurt him or test him; I did it to build his character. One of those jobs was particularly, shall we say, character building.

We were refurbishing one of my apartment complexes. In one unit, the tenants had left behind a refrigerator full of food. The electricity had long been shut off and it was the height of summer. When we opened the refrigerator, the smell of rotten food almost knocked us off our feet. When we stopped gagging, I looked at Michael and he knew—without me having to say a word—that it was *his* job to clean out that refrigerator. He pulled on some plastic gloves and got to business. Don't get the impression that he was eager to do it. He looked more like a lamb going to slaughter than an eager beaver. But he did his job. He threw out all that nasty, stinking food and wiped down the entire refrigerator. The smell was so bad that I felt a little sorry for him, but I never showed it. As far as I was concerned, it was part of his education.

Michael attended the University of Virginia, graduating with a BS in civil engineering. He returned to Atlanta and completed his MBA at Georgia State University. He launched his professional career as a construction manager for Atlanta architect John Portman. He returned to the family business four years later with a broader understanding of the construction and development industry.

At H.J. Russell & Company, Michael served in various capacities including field engineer, project manager, and head of business development before taking the helm as CEO. In each of these roles, he executed with integrity and excellence and led the company to greater success.

I decided that I would "retire" again in 2003—or, as some have more realistically referred to it, *semi*-retire—and pass the reins of H.J. Russell & Company over to one of my kids, all of whom were very engaged in the business. However, I had not yet identified who that person would be.

I hired Beverly Smith of The HR Group to facilitate a dialogue that lasted seven hours. Except for a lunch break, Otelia, Donata, Jerome, Michael, and I worked tirelessly to determine the best course for H.J. Russell & Company and who would be the best person to lead us. We met and deliberated over the pros and cons of each sibling taking the reins.

Finally, after what seemed like a lifetime, we were unanimous in our decision that Michael would be the best fit for the position. My youngest son has an outgoing personality and enjoys engaging people around a variety of issues, so we felt that he would be the most comfortable in this role. With everyone's vote in (everyone, that is, except for Michael) the consensus was that Michael should be the CEO.

I believe that the best education for children is teaching them how to work and to save as early as possible. If Michael—who has two sons with his wife, Lovette—had balked at hard work or thought some jobs were beneath him or had showed himself disposed to laziness, he wouldn't be CEO today. In fact, he wouldn't have any executive position at my company.

■ □ ■

At 7:00 AM on September 13, 2005, my children showed as much character and familial love as anyone could ever ask for. It was a proud moment, but it was also one of my hardest moments.

Michael had struggled with kidney disease for some time. In early 2005 he was told he would need a kidney transplant. Otelia, Donata, Jerome, and I each gladly volunteered to donate a kidney to Michael. Jerome was the only one who was found to be compatible. When he heard the news he smiled and said, "Good. Let's do it," without one moment of hesitation.

Otelia and I arrived at the hospital at 5:45 AM the day of the operation. Both sons' ministers were already there—Reverend Walter Kimbrough and Reverend Artis Johnson. So were Donata, both of my daughters-in-law, and many of my grandchildren. And there lay both of my boys in their hospital beds waiting to go under the knife. Neither of them had ever undergone major surgery, yet they showed no fear.

Jerome, the donor, had to go to surgery half an hour earlier so his kidney could be transplanted into Michael immediately. When they wheeled Jerome out after his surgery, I had to leave the room to keep from upsetting my grandchildren with my freely flowing tears of love and pride.

Thank God, all went well. Michael's new kidney started functioning healthily right away. He and Jerome were up and about in just a few days. Neither has had a moment of complications since. I have thanked God for their good health every moment since. I also give thanks daily that I have been blessed to raise such extraordinary children.

■ □ ■

Georgia State University prepared a case study of my business success to be used in its MBA program. Because my children now run H.J. Russell & Company, each was interviewed about their respective roads to their executive positions.

This is what Michael told the researchers:

By example my father showed us the importance of hard work. How you could get up every morning and go out and be productive every day. Certainly he showed the aspect of having a commitment to your family and the value of earning and saving money. All these things he showed by example. He always made us appreciate a dollar. That is because he always kept us busy, he always had us working. It helped us to appreciate the value of a dollar and an education, too. As I got older and I worked on construction sites, one of the things that always struck me, and I am sure this was in his head, was I realized that if you get an education you give yourself options.

My son Jerome told that same interviewer:

When we were growing up my father never talked about money. I understand why my father has taken the position on money that he has taken. My family, Michael and Donata and myself, we are as a family paper rich, but relatively cash poor. What my father under-stood is if early on he had just laid it out there for us and allowed us to get into these trusts or just gave us money it would have just taken our drive away. And I am thankful, so thankful, that he didn't do that. Not having money keeps you hungry, it gives you urgency and drive. To this day, he still controls the safe. It really used to bother me though because I felt like I was old enough and I was working hard and I was creating value. But I have gone through some things when I did get [money] easy that if I hadn't gotten it that easy I wouldn't have done the things I did. So I understand it now. It is not about having a lot of money, it is about creating wealth for future generations. It is very important to my father that we sustain what he has built for future generations. I have accepted it and I realize that the slow and steady is going to win the race.

Many young parents today don't insist that their children have chores to do—washing dishes, cleaning up, making their beds every day. Even if you have live-in help, children should have to do chores to give them character.

One thing I can say about my children is that they have character. They stand on principle and always try to do what is right. They are also loving and caring people. Most of all, they know the value of family.

17

. . . And Hello to Sylvia

My niece, Valerie Calloway, asked me to attend a luncheon at which she was to be honored in June 2007. Hosted by *Business to Business* magazine, its purpose was to highlight the contributions of twelve outstanding female business executives in Atlanta's business community. Valerie was the senior vice president of the H.J. Russell Property Management Division, so I was happy to support her.

One of the other women honored at the luncheon was the newly appointed president of AT&T Georgia, Sylvia E. Anderson. I was pleased to see AT&T had an African American woman as its state president. Afterward, I went up to her, introduced myself, and congratulated her on the award and her new position. I added that I was a former president of the Atlanta chamber, and I would be happy to help her in any way I could, and that I would be delighted to talk to her some more about Atlanta's business community and the things she could expect to encounter, pro and con.

Sylvia remembered it this way:

> We exchanged cards and said maybe we can have lunch sometime, and I said, "Great, that would be wonderful."
> He said, "OK, I'll call you."
> And he didn't.

Unfortunately, as often happens, I became caught up in events that week and she's telling the truth, I forgot to call.

A few weeks later I ran into Sylvia again, this time at the Ritz-Carlton, Buckhead. I was there with Donata to attend the annual fund-raising gala for Big Brothers, Big Sisters.

When I saw Sylvia it hit me like a two-by-four that I had not called. I made my way to her table and apologized profusely. It was a little awkward because she was there with a date. And strangely, her date was trying to introduce *us*. We both cut him off and said we had already met.

Sylvia handed me her business card—again—and said, "I still look forward to your call." This time she added her cell phone number to it.

That weekend at the lake house in north Georgia, it dawned on me that I *still* hadn't contacted her, so I stopped what I was doing and made the call. We set a date for lunch but Sylvia called me back fifteen minutes later to say that she would actually be traveling during the time we agreed to meet, so she suggested an early dinner. I agreed.

A week later we met at the Capital City Club. We opened the club at 5:30 PM and ended up closing it, too. We talked and talked and talked, about business, of course, but also about much more: politics, our families, current events, our personal thoughts and feelings.

Sylvia told me that she was born in Germany to a black American career military man and a white German mother. She talked about her two sons, both of whom were in college.

We were so engrossed in our conversation that hours passed before either of us realized it.

"One of the perks of my position is that I am entitled to join a private club," Sylvia said.

"Do you know the different clubs in Atlanta?" I asked. She didn't, so I offered to take Sylvia to visit some of Atlanta's clubs—club hopping, if you will, to places to which a generation earlier neither of us could have gained admission. It was a very private environment, so we got to know each other without the eyes of Atlanta on us. I didn't plan it that way but it worked out beautifully.

The following week we had dinner at the Piedmont Driving Club. Sylvia, a wine connoisseur, ordered for both of us. Over good food and drink we had another great wide-ranging conversation—another three hours' worth.

We met again the next week, this time at the Brookhaven Country Club. The following week I invited Sylvia on a "real date" to a Sunday brunch at Canoe Restaurant—a romantic restaurant with beautiful gardens overlooking the Chattahoochee River. This get-together was something different. It wasn't a weekday dinner like the earlier times we got together, and our conversation didn't feel like business or light banter any more. I was sure something special had happened between us. I realized that I had begun to feel more, something much deeper.

After Otelia died I'd focused all my attention on my construction projects, being the workaholic that I am, and did not give much thought to finding love again. But now here was Sylvia, making my heart jump like a teenager with a high school crush.

When we were apart, I found myself wanting to be around her, counting the days before we would get together again.

It was at Canoe Restaurant that I shared my feelings with Sylvia.

"Honey, I want you to know, this is personal," I said. "I need to know if you feel the same."

"I'm not there yet," she said.

I was disappointed, but I said, "OK. I understand."

"But I'm not saying that I want to stop seeing you," Sylvia added quickly. "I think this has all been wonderful. I just don't know if I'm there yet."

We kept seeing each other on a regular basis, and, honestly, it was an old-fashioned courtship where we slowly got to know each other. Without any more being said, it became clear to both of us that our relationship *was* serious.

I decided that I should introduce Sylvia to Donata, but without telling Donata how Sylvia and I felt about each other. Sylvia remembered, "I was a little nervous because I know relationships between fathers and daughters. Donata was the apple of his eye. And I also knew that she lost her mother and here I come along . . ."

Donata is just like her mother so I knew she would not bite her tongue; she would say exactly what she felt.

I made dinner reservations for the three of us at the Capital City Club, where it all began. Sylvia met us there. It seemed like the ladies hit it off, but that could have just been wishful thinking. Both of them were too classy and cordial to let on if they weren't thrilled with each other's company. But when dinner lasted three hours just like the others had, I took it as a good sign.

During the ride home with Donata, I asked her how she felt about the evening and, more important, how she felt about Sylvia.

My daughter is shrewd.

Although Sylvia and I tried to keep things pretty casual between us, Donata could see that we had something special. It was obvious to her what I was asking—and why. Donata didn't beat around the bush. In her straightforward, no-nonsense way she said. "I like her."

Like me, she found Sylvia to be down-to-earth with a wonderful sense of humor. She spoke so warmly of Sylvia that it was clear that Donata had given her blessing for me to pursue a romantic relationship with Sylvia.

(And no, my sons didn't know for a while longer. I was in no hurry to tell them!)

▪ □ ▪

When Otelia was near the end, my children were around, of course, but so were our closest friends, former educators Jerome and Earlene Harris. They often went to dinner with me because I didn't want to eat alone. You couldn't have asked for better friends in such a trying time; in my book, Jerome and Earlene are honorary Russells.

After Otelia passed, I lived by myself across the street from Jerome and Earlene. I had a lady who would come over and clean the house from time to time, and she cooked sometimes. But I hated to eat alone so I'd call the Harrises. "Come on over," I'd say. "I've got the best food in the world!" But, truth be told, it didn't have any taste—not to me, anyway.

When this had gone on for several weeks, Jerome said, "Herman, look here. I'll cook for you next week and we'll bring the food over." That Tuesday, Jerome cooked for me and he and Earlene brought food over for the first time. And they've been doing it ever since—turkey wings, chicken wings, spareribs, spaghetti . . .

We did that for a couple of weeks. One week Jerome invited Donata to join us.

When Michael and Jerome heard about it, they became regulars, bringing their wives and all of the grandchildren, too, sometimes with dates. My brother Rogers Russell was a regular until his death in 2012, although his daughter—my niece Fanitra—is often there. Now Jerome literally cooks for roughly seventeen people every Tuesday. He plans the menu, and we eat whatever it is that he feels like cooking that particular week.

I start the evening by mixing a highball for Jerome. Jerome will complain bitterly that I didn't fix it right or something's wrong with it, and he'll go to the stove and start cooking. It is a good time for all of the Russells because it gives us an opportunity to talk—we always have a good conversation over Jerome's meal.

One of those Tuesday evenings I realized how much I wanted Sylvia to be there to share the love and laughter of my family. It was time for Sylvia to meet them and for them to meet her. I invited Sylvia to join us for our next Tuesday gathering. She came, all warmth and smiles, and fit right in. In fact she fit in so well that my family told her that she was expected to join us every Tuesday.

We could check the box with my family, so it was my turn to meet hers.

She invited me to dinner at her home with her grown sons, Eric and Kevin. After Sylvia prepared a delicious German meal—one of her mother's recipes—I had a candid talk with her sons. I was impressed with their maturity, manners, and character. The boys looked me right in the eye, even when I told them that I loved their mother. Meeting Sylvia's sons was just the beginning, however.

Next she invited me to accompany her to her sister Sheela's twenty-fifth wedding anniversary, held at a beachfront home in Kill Devil Hills, North Carolina. Sylvia's whole family was there: mom and dad, Sheela and her husband, Mark, plus Sylvia's three brothers, Alwin, Bernhard, and Tyrone, and their families.

> I'll never forget what I told Herman going into the parking lot. I said, "Herman, you're about to meet my family now and I'm going to tell you two things about my family. Number one, we're very loud. We talk over each other a lot, and number two, we're very direct. Herman Russell may be well known and respected in Atlanta, but they're going to want to know that you're a nice man. So good luck."
>
> Then we walked in and they all hooted, hollered, and applauded!

Everyone treated me like I had been a part of the family all along. *Whew!*

One way Sylvia's family was different from mine was that while we love to talk, hers likes to entertain. That night they put on a family talent show. Everyone moved into the media room and, one by one, each family member took center stage to share their various talents. Then it was Sylvia's turn, along with Sheela and her sister-in-law, Chrishelle. She stood, smiled, and sang the Supremes classic "Stop! In the Name of Love." Her voice was so beautiful it gave me chills. I knew then that I wanted to spend my whole life with the singer of that song.

At the conclusion of the weekend we said our good-byes and loaded our rental car for the drive back to the airport. We arrived about two hours before our flight and grabbed a bite to eat.

The success of the weekend had a real impact on me. We loved each other's families, we were magical together, and I adored and respected her greatly. It was time to take the final step.

"Sylvia," I said over lunch, "will you marry me?"

She barely took a breath.

"Yes, Herman," she said. "I will."

On the short flight from North Carolina back to Atlanta we worked out the wedding plans and a date. And we hugged and kissed.

When we got on the plane it was all about the business of working it out. By the time we landed, we had it all completely settled.

■ □ ■

One more story from Sylvia's point of view:

While Atlanta is a big city, it's also a relatively small community in many ways. And while some people knew me when we met, *everybody* knew Herman, so it was just nice the way we got to know each other, quietly, below the radar screen.

Now, here's a funny part. For Martin Luther King Day there is a wonderful celebration at Ebenezer Baptist Church every year, and Herman invited me to join him for that occasion before we announced our engagement. As it turned out, just about his entire family went that particular year. And it further turned out that the Russells had their own pew—in a very prominent place.

I was sitting next to Herman, who was on the aisle, and the rest of the family was next to me. I was sitting where a spouse or a significant other would sit, and that created a buzz. There had been other times when we had been in public places together, but it wasn't unusual because we're both in the business community.

Bill Clinton was there and came over and said hello to Herman and other people, which was very nice. Unbeknownst to me, the whole thing was broadcast live on television.

During the service, my Blackberry started going *ping . . . ping . . . ping . . .* "Is that you?" "What are you doing there?" "Why are you sitting with Herman Russell's family?"

So much for being under the radar.

■ □ ■

I have had the pleasure of meeting some wonderful folks over the years, but I must admit I have particularly soft spot in my heart for Jane Fonda, who was a fixture in Atlanta social and civic circles for many years during her marriage to Ted Turner.

The last time I saw Herman, he was with Sylvia. They weren't married yet, I don't think. And it was so sweet. He said, "I want you to meet her." We went out to dinner and he was just like a teenager. He was lit up! I asked him, "Should I mention sex? Meaning how clearly turned on you both are?" He just radiated around her.

■ □ ■

When Bob Holder learned that I was dating, he and his wife, Ann, really wanted to meet Sylvia. He invited us to his penthouse in Buckhead and then the four of us went to the Cherokee Country Club. At one point Ann, who could tell we were in love, looked me straight in the eye and said, "Herman, what are you going to do? You going to get married?"

"Well," I said, "we're thinking about it."

"Whatcha waitin' on?" she asked. "You know you love her, she loves you. None of us are getting any younger. Whatcha waitin' on?"

At some point, it was just Bob and me at the table. "You fool around, somebody else is going to get her," Bob said to me. "You keep waiting, she's going to find herself some other fellow."

They actually scolded us! Here's how Sylvia remembers it:

I had a ring three days later.

■ □ ■

When I told Vernon Jordan that I was dating, he said, "Wait, before you go any further, I have just two questions for you. One, is she over twenty-two years old? And two, does she have a damn job?"

I said, "Vernon, she meets both of those requirements." But I wouldn't tell him who she was on the phone; I said he'd have to come to Atlanta and meet her in person to get any more details.

Vernon is on the board of H.J. Russell & Company and has been for three decades, so the next time he came for a board meeting, the three of us went out to dinner.

He fell in love with Sylvia just as I had. But the next day he wanted to talk to her without me around. Waiting for his plane back to DC, he called her office.

"I'm Vernon Jordan," he said, "and I need to talk to Sylvia right now."

Her assistant walked into Sylvia's office, where a meeting was taking place, and handed her a note:

Vernon Jordan wants to talk to you. Right now.

He wanted Sylvia to know that he thought she was "the right one for Herman" and that he could tell we were truly in love. Later, he said the same thing in an e-mail to her. Sylvia was so touched by his e-mail message that she kept it over the years. Here's what it said:

Sylvia, it was a genuine pleasure to meet you and share a marvelous dinner with you and Herman. Herman has over the years taught me that "friendship is the medicine of life," and the longer you are friends, you will come to the same conclusion. It is clear that you bring him contentment, solace, companionship, partnership, love, respect, and admiration. And clearly, the feeling is mutual. Blessings be upon you both and "may your own dreams be your only boundaries." I look forward to seeing you soon again. Vernon

■ □ ■

A lot of people wondered about the age difference—twenty-four years—between us.

It wasn't an issue for me at all, though. I didn't know exactly how her parents would take it. And I knew that I would probably outlive her. I knew I had good genes. We work out together now because I realized eventually I'd have to take care of her if she didn't get into better shape.

I asked her father for his daughter's hand. He said it was perfectly all right with him. Sylvia often reminds me it's really not the age difference if God has blessed you with good health, with an open mind and an open heart, and you have a common thread that you enjoy each other.

We decided on a small, intimate wedding ceremony with just family and a few close friends in the chapel at Morehouse College. A reception followed at the Capital City Club, where our life together had begun. My good friend Andy Young performed the ceremony and our children stood on either side of us.

The irony was that Andy actually had met Sylvia years before I did. I'll let him tell the story:

Sylvia is *still* mad with me because I didn't remember her.

I was UN ambassador and the commencement speaker when she graduated from Rutgers University and she gave a speech to her fellow graduates.

When Herman introduced us years later, she quipped, "You don't remember me?"

"I don't even remember whether I have an honorary degree from Rutgers," I said, trying to be funny.

She later brought me the news clipping, which included a picture of her standing by my side.

■ □ ■

I was so fortunate to be at the right place at the right time to meet this lady. I never could have dreamed that we would complement each other as much as we do. We enjoy each other so much. She keeps me on the go and I keep her on the go, but we love what we do and we're so supportive of each other.

It has just been another wonderful blessing from the Lord that we got together and married.

VI

Sixty Years Later

18

All the Rest of My Days

Sylvia and I went to breakfast one morning at a local restaurant in Atlanta and a young man, an African American, waited on us. When it was time to pay the bill, he recognized my name on the credit card.

"Gosh," he said, "I didn't know you were *the* Herman Russell!"

He become flustered for a moment and then he said, "Could I ask you just one question? Would that be OK?"

"Sure," I said. "What's on your mind, son?"

"I've read about how successful you've been and how you built up so much of Atlanta and how you're now very successful and wealthy," the waiter said. "How can I do what you did, but it not take as much time?" He wanted to know the shortcuts he could take to avoid all that. That's the kind of kid I want to read this book to understand there are *no* shortcuts for *anybody*.

There were no shortcuts for me. It's true—you might get lucky. But that's why it's called luck. And I wouldn't want to depend on luck in planning my future.

The best way for young people to equip themselves for a good future is by working hard—doing quality work and staying focused. All of those subcontracts, joint ventures, and golden opportunities I received were because I worked hard and did quality work. I *performed*.

■ □ ■

I am eighty-two as I write this, enjoying my ninth decade of life on earth.

The conventional wisdom is that I should feel old, but I feel great. I had knee replacements, so I'm walking fine—in fact I feel better than ever. Still dancing, too. I start my day at 5:00 AM and exercise daily, including three times a week with a personal trainer. My weight is about the same as it was when I was in my forties. The truth is, most days I feel as good as I did forty years ago.

I'm semi-retired now, which everyone will tell you means that I'm working nine or ten hours instead of my usual sixteen.

My children, Donata, Jerome, and Michael, are responsible for running the bulk of H.J. Russell & Company, including Concessions International, and I don't spend much time looking over their shoulders. They consult me from time to time, but that's as far as my involvement goes on a day in, day out business.

Several years ago, I moved my personal business office off-premises and I have a staff of half a dozen good folks who help me run my pet projects in the Castleberry area such as the Castleberry Inn & Suites, Paschal's Restaurant, and my condos and rental properties.

Retirement, to me at least, does not mean that you completely stop working, especially if you spent your life doing something you enjoy. Entrepreneurship is in my blood and it will always be a part of my daily life.

■ □ ■

There were several reasons I chose to build my headquarters back in 1952 at its location on the corner of Fair Street and Northside Drive. It was conveniently located on a major traffic artery. The lot was affordable and large enough to accommodate our offices, warehouse, and garage.

And there was one more reason . . . or should I say *vision*? I've had a keen sense of discernment about real estate since I foresaw the potential of an abandoned lot for my childhood shoeshine business. Even then, I not only saw what the Castleberry area *was*; I saw what it *could be*.

It had escaped the notice of the major builders in Atlanta because with plenty of building room still available downtown and in the immediate surrounding neighborhoods, it was more profitable for them to concentrate their capital there. When they did venture outside of the downtown area they focused their efforts on the more fashionable areas of town. Working-class black neighborhoods such as Castleberry fit into neither of those categories, so at the time no one really paid attention to it.

But *I* did. I saw that it had two major things going for it. Not only was it on a major traffic artery, it was also only two and a half miles from Five Points, the very heart of downtown Atlanta.

I began buying land in Castleberry whenever I could. That was forty years ago. Little by little I acquired lots whenever they became available until I had accumulated two square blocks north of my offices and about eight square blocks to the south. One of my earliest investments into the area was the development and construction of an apartment complex we called the Villages at Castleberry.

Next I developed and constructed the Castleberry Inn & Suites, originally an extended-stay hotel. I've since converted it completely into a boutique hotel. Of course, a hotel is not complete without a restaurant. My old neighborhood cried out for a first-class restaurant.

One day while James Paschal and I were meeting in my conference room, he noticed the colorful renderings of my planned Castleberry. I told him of my dream to have a great place for dining.

"Why don't you have a Paschal's?" he said.

I could not believe my ears.

"Do you really mean that?"

"Of course I do," he said.

We already had three Paschal's at the Atlanta airport, but I imagined a really nice, upscale restaurant. He understood and we struck a deal to be fifty-fifty partners. The famous Paschal Brothers Motor Hotel and Lounge operated for nearly forty-five years before being sold to Clark Atlanta University in 1996. It thrilled me to no end to be part owner of a restaurant managed by a legend such as James Paschal.

A restaurant, however, is not easy to finance, as anybody who has opened his or her doors one day and been out of business the next will attest. To start with the name of an Atlanta legend, Paschal's, in front of my hotel and across the street from the H.J. Russell & Company office building was the ultimate win-win combination. I told Mr. Paschal that I would build the restaurant out of my pocket, just like I did the hotel.

We hired one of the area's best restaurant designers, Bill Johnson, and told him and his staff that we wanted something different and unique. I was particularly interested in the loft look that could be found in many of the old warehouses in our district that had been converted into lovely homes. It was important to me that the restaurant properly represent the community design.

A month later, the Johnson Studio delivered several concepts. We narrowed it down to the one that we liked best and signed off on it. George Rees was assigned to design the restaurant's shell. We presented our concept for the restaurant to the Castleberry Hill Neighborhood Association and they excitedly approved the entire package.

The hotel was completed in August 2001 and has performed very well.

Since its opening, Paschal's has served civic organizations, wedding receptions, family reunions, conferences, and regular patrons feasting on delectable dishes including Paschal's famous fried chicken. The main dining room accommodates about 150 patrons. The restaurant also has a banquet facility called the Maynard Jackson Room that seats 110, a private dining area called the RJ Room (after Robert and James Paschal) that seats 32, an upstairs loft dining area that can accommodate up to

40 people, and Le Carrousel Lounge, which has a lovely patio attached to it for guests who enjoy outdoor dining.

James Paschal was an incredible role model in training our staff in the days leading up to Paschal's grand opening, putting on his apron to teach our cooks and chefs the recipes that have thrilled and satisfied Atlanta for more than half a century.

To get started, I didn't waste valuable time looking for financing for either the Castleberry Inn or Paschal's. I knew getting financing in that part of town would be hard, so instead I paid for both of them out of my own pocket. Normally, I would have the common sense not to put up a lot of my own money, but I believed in the viability of the Castleberry projects that much. And my vision turned out to be correct. Both projects turned out to be successful and I later secured long-term outside financing without any problem.

Building this community out is my semi-retirement project and the completion of my forty-year dream. I'm having a great time seeing it all through. I am more excited about Castleberry Hill than about any project I've done in a long time. What is most exciting for me is that it will provide a long-neglected part of metro Atlanta with good, attractive homes and retail spaces. Today, in Castleberry Hills, you can choose from nice condos and apartments, shop at small boutique stores, visit art galleries, and eat at a variety of restaurants, including the best one of all . . . Paschal's, of course!

You just don't know how satisfying it is to me to see young professionals, families, the Sunday church crowd, and college students enjoying themselves in Castleberry Hill. I love it!

By the time the Castleberry project is completed I expect to have invested $300 million. But it will be worth it.

Through Michael, Jerome, and Donata, the Russell name continues to be synonymous with integrity and superior service. My children play major roles in the family business and in ensuring that my dreams for H.J. Russell & Company and Concessions International are achieved. Even some of the grandkids and one of my stepsons have been a part of it.

When it comes to family, no one could be prouder than me.

■ □ ■

Andy Young teases me by saying that I am the cheapest generous man he knows.

Just throwing money on the table and walking away was never the way for me. I always question where my giving can make the biggest difference in the things I care about. Over the years, I have given substantial amounts to the civil rights movement, to church and community groups, to education, and to other local causes. I wanted to make a lasting contribution to the social fabric of Atlanta's community that had given so much to me.

Entrepreneurship helped my dreams come true. I want the same for other young people looking to make good lives for themselves. That's why, in 1999, Otelia and I decided that we would donate $1 million each to four educational institutions to establish programs that would teach and encourage students to look at careers in entrepreneurship in a variety of fields. The four colleges included my alma mater, Tuskegee University, and Otelia's, Clark Atlanta University, as well as Morehouse College and Georgia State University.

There was a catch: each college was required to match our $1 million donation. I consulted with the dean and president of each college and discussed my intentions and the criteria for the gift before making a public announcement. I wanted the gift to be earmarked solely for entrepreneurial recruiting. Entrepreneurship is one of the most valuable courses that can be taught.

I'm a lifetime believer that for America to continue being great and provide enough jobs for its people, the only path is fostering a national entrepreneurial spirit. For black America, the best way to control our own destiny is to increase the entrepreneur class so we can create more jobs for our race and others. Once we, as a race, can control our own destiny, we will be better equipped to contribute back to the community.

On November 3, 1999, I publicly announced the gifts. My remarks on that occasion read in part:

Today we are announcing a gift of $4 million; $1 million to each college, to help realize their respective goals in entrepreneurship, endowed faculty positions, and scholarships. All four colleges have agreed to work together to launch an annual lecture series. They are exploring opportunities to develop a joint internship for the students enrolled in their courses. Many of these opportunities will be made available to minority students and to those whose dreams might not otherwise be achieved. Between my wife, our sons, and myself we have degrees from all of these colleges. I am proud to have my name associated with them. I look forward to sharing in the bright future of these institutions. If my family and I can help them grow and build on their already strong foundations, this may be the greatest building project we have ever undertaken.

It was satisfying to know that our gift would make a difference in young people's lives. Each school used our donation to establish some kind of entrepreneurial program. That was all that I asked or expected.

Georgia State University, however, used the money to establish the Herman J. Russell Sr. International Center for Entrepreneurship. I did not give the money to Georgia State to do that, but it was quite an honor that they bestowed upon me.

■ □ ■

Although I'd already given a great deal of money to worthy causes, I knew I had to do more. Why? Because I *could* do more. I'd been given much, so much more was required of me. When I looked at our community I realized that the need for all kinds of support programs for young people as well as our community is so great that my philanthropic efforts could make the biggest difference there.

In June 2006, Atlanta mayor Shirley Franklin heard that the late Dr. Martin Luther King Jr.'s papers were going to be auctioned by Sotheby's in New York; they were already on display at the world-famous auction house. Shirley thought this was a very bad idea; she wanted the papers to remain in Atlanta. Within days, she had $32 million in pledges—including a $1 million cash contribution from me and a bank note for a $3 million guarantee—to take our friend Martin's papers off the block and give them a permanent home in the Morehouse College archives.

■ □ ■

When Jane Fonda was living in Atlanta, she invited me to serve on the board of an organization she founded called the Georgia Campaign for Adolescent Pregnancy Prevention.

> I came to Atlanta from Hollywood and, prior to that, I had lived in Paris and in New York. I had never been exposed to entrepreneurial, upper-middle-class African Americans. I'd been exposed to successful black people in Hollywood because they were the actors, or sports figures.
>
> Coming to Atlanta, that was one of my big a-ha! moments. When I was looking for support for my organization, Herman was one of the first people I went to. He was willing to join the board and he gave us very good criticism and advice, but always with such sweetness. And he's very loving.
>
> Herman was great at bridging the racial gap. He got along with blacks; he got along with whites; and he was always very sweet.
>
> He had me come down to his corporate headquarters and speak to some of his employees about what we were doing; I just thought it was kind of amazing.
>
> We were in a stage, as an organization, of instability. It was early on; we were trying to do too much and we didn't have a proper business plan. Herman would point out certain problems, but he would do it in such a sweet way, with such a twinkle in his eye, and such a sweetness in his voice that you never felt that you were being put down.

■ □ ■

I cannot give enough credit to the men and women who every day give up a piece of themselves to make H.J. Russell & Company the remarkable enterprise it has been for more than fifty years.

I have been blessed with some of the finest employees in the world. I always took the position that I would not want any of my employees to do what I wasn't willing to do. Because whatever their role, it has been very important to the overall success of our company.

The only thing I miss today, with more than thirteen hundred employees, is that time when I knew all of my people, their spouses, birthdays, anniversaries, and their kids' names. Once you grow beyond a certain base, you lose that. But even if I can't recall all of the names of my employees at the time that I see them, I always want to know about the well-being of their family. It's important to me that they know that I am concerned about their families. They give up so much of themselves to make us great and that matters dearly to me.

Acknowledgments

This book has been a work in progress for many years. While the version you hold in your hands was ultimately coauthored by Bob Andelman, he was preceded by many fine collaborators over time, beginning with my longtime secretary, Iris Register, who was followed by Loretta Thompson. Obery M. Hendricks Jr. was responsible for a major early draft. I also appreciated the many contributions of David "Wes" Smith and Caroline Clark.

There are several people within the Russell organization who have helped me put this book together, none more so than my right-hand man, Antonio "Tony" Jones, who spent countless hours doing research and went above and beyond in keeping my story organized and on track.

I'm very appreciative of the fine direction of my editor and publisher, Cynthia Sherry of Chicago Review Press. And my agent, John Rudolph of Dystel & Goderich Literary Management, will forever have my gratitude for connecting me with both Cynthia and Bob and making this dream a reality.

A special thank you to the dozens of people who gave their time and shared their stories with my coauthor, Bob Andelman, including lifelong friends such as William Kimbrough, the late Bobby Jones, Felker Ward, and Vernon Jordan, all of whom I've known since attending Atlanta's David T. Howard High School.

I would also like to thank, alphabetically: Henry Aaron, Bishop John Hurst Adams, Judge Randolph Baxter, Arthur Blank, President Jimmy Carter, Arthur J. Clement, Georgia Coclin, Jim Coclin, Gordon Davis, Eugene Duffy, Jane Fonda, Marva Hackney, Earlene Harris, Jerome Harris, Sidney Harris, Azira Hill, Bob Holder, Dean Fenwick Huss, John W. Jackson, Charles "CJ" Johnson, Joia Johnson, Bobby Jones, Vernon Jordan, Anthony Joseph, Denise Kevil, Noel Khalil, William Kimbrough, Charlie Loudermilk, Zane Majors, Ruth Hackney McMillan, Daniel Meachum, Dougal Myer, Eugene Patterson, Egbert Perry, John Portman, Claude Rickman, Bermer Ridenhour, Michael Ross, Calvin Russell Sr., Donata Russell (Majors), Fanitra Russell, H. Jerome Russell, Michael Russell, Sylvia Russell, Congressman David Scott, Dallas Smith, John B. Smith, Don Stewart, Felker Ward, Bruce Williams, Philip Williams, and Ambassador Andrew Young.

Index

About the Author

Herman J. Russell, the founder and former chief executive officer of H.J. Russell & Company and Concessions International, is a nationally recognized entrepreneur, philanthropist, and Atlanta civic leader. A self-made man who grew up in a blue-collar family, he was recognized by *Forbes* magazine as one of the wealthiest African Americans in the United States.

Mr. Russell lost his first wife, Otelia, to cancer in 2006, just short of their fiftieth anniversary. In 2008, he married Sylvia Anderson, who is president of AT&T Georgia. They live in midtown Atlanta.

About the Coauthor

Bob Andelman is the author or coauthor of sixteen biographical, business, management, self-help, and sports books. These include: *Built from Scratch* with the cofounders of Home Depot, Bernie Marcus and Arthur Blank; *Fans Not Customers* with Vernon W. Hill, founder of Commerce Bank and Metro Bank UK; *Keep Your Eye on the Marsh-mallow* with Joachim de Posada; *Mind over Business* with Ken Baum; *The Consulate* with Thomas R. Stutler; *The Profiler* with Pat Brown; *The Profit Zone* with Adrian J. Slywotzky; *Mean Business* with Albert J. Dunlap; and a biography, *Will Eisner: A Spirited Life*.

He has also been a regular correspondent for *BusinessWeek*, *Newsweek*, and the *St. Petersburg Times* at different times in his career.

Since February 1, 2007, Andelman has also produced and hosted the extremely popular Mr. Media® online TV/radio interview show heard on his own site, www.mrmedia.com, and syndicated across the Internet to more than two dozen other distribution points including iTunes and the Stitcher Smart Radio mobile app.

You can reach him via e-mail: bobandelman@gmail.com.